the THIRD edition

New Headway

Elementary
Student's Book

Liz and John Soars

with Sylvia Wheeldon

OXFORD
UNIVERSITY PRESS

CONTENTS

LANGUAGE INPUT

UNIT	GRAMMAR	VOCABULARY	EVERYDAY ENGLISH
1 Hello everybody! p6	**Verb *to be*** *am/is/are* *I'm from London.* p6 *He's a student.* p9 **Possessive adjectives** *my, your, his, her* p6, p8	Countries *Mexico, Japan* p8 Using a bilingual dictionary p10 Everyday objects *a key, a newspaper* p10 Plural nouns *bags, apples* p10	Hello and goodbye *Telephone numbers* p11 *How are you? See you later!* p11
2 Meeting people p12	**Verb *to be*** *Questions and negatives* *What's her first name?* p12 *She isn't married.* p13 **Negatives and short answers** *No, she isn't.* p13 **Possessive *'s*** *Patrick's daughter* p14	The family *mother, uncle* p14 Opposite adjectives *old – young* p16 Food and drink *hamburger and chips tea, coffee* p18	In a café *Prices* p18 *Can I have … ? How much is … ?* p19
3 The world of work p20	**Present Simple 1** *he/she/it* p20 *She works 16 hours a day.* p21 **Questions and negatives** *Does he speak Spanish? He doesn't speak Spanish or French.* p22	Verbs *help, make, serve* p24 Jobs *A pilot flies planes.* p26	What time is it? *It's quarter past five. It's just after six o'clock.* p27
4 Take it easy! p28	**Present Simple 2** *I/you/we/they* *I go to the gym.* *We don't go out on Fridays. Why do you like your job?* p29	Verbs *relax, go out, play* p29 Leisure activities *dancing, skiing* p30	Social expressions *I'm sorry. Excuse me? Pardon?* p35

Stop and check 1   Teacher's Book p154

UNIT	GRAMMAR	VOCABULARY	EVERYDAY ENGLISH
5 Where do you live? p36	*There is/are* *There's a television.* p36 *How many … ?* *How many books are there?* p36 **Prepositions of place** *in front of the sofa* p37 *some* and *any* *There are some cups.* *There aren't any plates.* p38 *this, that, these, those* *This is the kitchen.* *What's in these cupboards?* p38	Rooms *living room, kitchen* p36 Things in the house *armchair, lamp, cupboard, washing machine* p36 What's in your bag? *bus ticket, mobile, keys* p39 Places *cinema, pub* p43	Directions 1 *Is there a post office near here? Yes, it's over there.* p43
6 Can you speak English? p44	*can/can't* *She can walk now.* *We can't write.* p44 *was/were* *Where were you yesterday?* p46 *could* *I could swim when I was five.* p46 *was born* *She was born in England.* p47	Countries and languages *France, French* p44 Verbs *translate, check, laugh* p45 Words that sound the same *I, eye; no, know* p50	On the phone Directory Enquiries p50 *Can I speak to Jo, please? I'll just get her.* p51
7 Then and now p52	**Past Simple 1** **Regular verbs** *She worked in over 50 films.* p52 **Irregular verbs** *His father got a job in London.* p54 **Time expressions** *last night yesterday morning* p55	Verbs *earn, act, study* p53 Verbs *get, leave, become* p54 Words that go together *drive a car, railway station* p58	What's the date? *the first of April* p59

SKILLS DEVELOPMENT

READING	SPEAKING	LISTENING	WRITING
Svetlana and Tiago p9	Introducing yourself p7	The alphabet song p10	**Introducing yourself** p9
An email from England p16	Talking about you p13 Your family p15	An email from England – Where is Danka? p16	**Write about your class** p16
Seumas McSporran – the man with thirteen jobs! p24	Asking about a friend or relative p23	Seumas's day p25	**Natural writing** Using pronouns p114
My favourite season p32	Leisure activities p30 What's your favourite season? p32 A questionnaire – Do you have a healthy lifestyle? p34	My favourite season – Where are they? p32	**Informal letters** To a penfriend p115
Living in a bubble p40	What's in your picture? p37 Talking about where you live p42	What's in Yoshi's briefcase? p39 Homes around the world p42	**Describing where you live** Linking words *and, so, but, because* p116
Talented teenagers p48	A questionnaire – What can you do? p45 What can computers do? p45 Roleplay – interview p48	Lucía can't cook p45	**Formal letters** Applying for a job p117
Two famous firsts – Amelia Earhart and Yuri Gagarin p56	The year I was born p54 When did it happen? p55	1984 – the year I was born p54 Where are the people? p58	**Describing a holiday** p118

3

LANGUAGE INPUT

UNIT	GRAMMAR	VOCABULARY	EVERYDAY ENGLISH
8 A date to remember p60	**Past Simple 2** **negatives – ago** *People didn't drive cars 100 years ago.* p60 **Time expressions** *at seven o'clock, on Saturday, in 2002* p61	Relationships *fall in love, get engaged* p63 Spelling and silent letters *answer, thought* p64 Phonetic symbols /wɛːk/ /ˈlisən/ p64	Special occasions *Thanksgiving Happy Birthday!* p64

Stop and check 2   Teacher's Book p156

UNIT	GRAMMAR	VOCABULARY	EVERYDAY ENGLISH
9 Food you like! p66	**Count and uncount nouns** *apples, apple juice* p66 **I like … ? I'd like … ?** *Do you like tea? Would you like some tea?* p67 **a and some** *a cake, some cake* p68 **much and many** *There isn't much milk. There aren't many eggs.* p68	Food and drink *chocolate, chips, beer, apple juice* p66 *chopsticks, noodles, sardines* p71	Polite offers and requests *Could you pass the salt, please? Could I have a glass of water, please? Can you give me the recipe? Can I see the menu?* p73
10 Bigger and better! p74	**Comparatives and superlatives** *The country is cheaper than the city.* p74 *Bati Island is the most expensive resort.* p76 **have got** *I've got a dog. They haven't got a flat.* p75	City and country adjectives *dirty, noisy exciting, safe* p74 City and country words *wood, museum* p80	Directions 2 *round the corner over the bridge* p81
11 Looking good! p82	**Present Continuous** *I'm wearing blue jeans. Who is smiling?* p82 **Whose is it?** *Whose is the baby?* p84 **Possessive pronouns** *mine, yours, hers* p84	Clothes *hat, coat, shirt* p82 Describing people *fair hair, blue eyes* p82 Words that rhyme *red, said; eyes, size* p88 Phonetic symbols *vowels and diphthongs* p88 Tongue twisters p88	In a clothes shop *What colour are you looking for? Can I try it on?* p89
12 Life's an adventure! p90	*going to* *I'm going to be a footballer.* p90 **Infinitive of purpose** *I'm going to Nepal to climb Mount Everest.* p92	Verbs *sneeze, jump, fall* p92 The weather *sunny, cloudy What's the weather like?* p96	Making suggestions *What shall we do? Let's go swimming!* p97

Stop and check 3   Teacher's Book p158

UNIT	GRAMMAR	VOCABULARY	EVERYDAY ENGLISH
13 Storytime p98	**Question forms** *Why … ? Which … ? How much … ? How many … ?* p98 **Adjectives and adverbs** *quick, quickly; good, well* p100	Describing feelings *bored, worried* p101 At the chemist's *suncream, shampoo, soap* p105	At the chemist's *I'm looking for some aspirin.* p105
14 Have you ever? p106	**Present Perfect** *ever and never* *Have you ever been to Barcelona? She's never been to Paris.* p106 *yet and just* *We haven't been there yet. They've just had a boat ride.* p108 **Present Perfect and Past Simple** *Maria's been to Berlin. She went there two years ago.* p107	Past participles *eaten, made, cooked* p107 At the airport *departure lounge, check in* p113	At the airport *check in your luggage go to gate 4* p113

Stop and check 4   Teacher's Book p160

Tapescripts p126   **Grammar Reference** p137   **Pairwork activities** Student A p148   Student B p150

SKILLS DEVELOPMENT

READING	SPEAKING	LISTENING	WRITING
Three inventions p62	Getting information – Famous inventions p60 Did you know that? p62 How did you two meet? p63	Three inventions p62 How did you two meet? p63	**Writing about a friend** Linking words *because, when, until* p119
Food around the world p70	Food you like p66 Roleplay – shopping p69 Meals in your country p70	My favourite national food p72	**Filling in forms** Booking a hotel p120
Viva la danza! – Havana / Buenos Aires / Seville p78	I've got more than you! p76 Talking about your town p78 A walk in the country/city p80	Comparing life in the city and country p74	**Describing a place** Linking words *which, where* p121
Flying without wings (Song lyrics) p86	Describing a person/scene p83 Getting information – Who's at the party? p84 My favourite things p87	Who's at the party? p84 A song – *Flying without wings* p86	**Describing people** Linking words *although, but* p122
Born free p94	Dangerous sports p94 Interviews p94 World weather p96	Future plans p90	**Writing a postcard** p123
A short story – *The Christmas Presents* p102	Childhood stories p99 Telling a story p100	Noises in the night p100 A short story – *The Christmas Presents* p102	**Writing a story** Using adjectives and adverbs p124
We've never learnt to drive! p110	Cities you have been to p107 Things you have done p108	What has Ryan done? p108 A honeyman in Venice p108 A song – *All around the world* p112	**Writing an email** Saying thank you p125

Word list p152 **Irregular verbs and Verb patterns** p158 **Phonetic symbols** p159

1 Hello everybody!

am/is/are · my/your/his/her · Countries · Everyday objects · Numbers · Hello and goodbye

STARTER

1 Say your names.

> I'm Ali.

> I'm Thomas.

2 Stand up in alphabetical order and say your names.

> I'm Ali.

> I'm Birgit.

> I'm Thomas.

> I'm Zak.

INTRODUCTIONS
am/is/are, my/your

1 **T 1.1** Read and listen.

A Hello. My name's Marco.
    What's your name?
B Emma.
A Where are you from, Emma?
B I'm from London.

T 1.1 Listen and repeat.

GRAMMAR SPOT

name's = name is
what's = what is
I'm = I am

4 Where are the people from? Write the countries from the box.

| the USA | England | Italy |

Buongiorno!

1 This is Marco.
  He's from _____.

Hello!

2 This is Emma.
  She's from _____.

Hi!

3 This is Lisa and Mike.
  They're from _____.

2 Write the conversation.

A Hello. My _____ Lisa. What's _____ name?
B Mike.
A _____ are you from, Mike?
B _____ from Boston. Where _____ you from?
A _____ _____ Boston, too!

T 1.2 Listen and check.

3 Stand up! Talk to the students in the class.

Hello! My name's _____.
What's your name?

Maria.

Where are you from, Maria?

I'm from _____.

T 1.3 Listen and repeat.

GRAMMAR SPOT

he's = he is
she's = she is
they're = they are

Unit 1 · Hello everybody! **7**

Countries, *his/her*

5 **T 1.4** Listen and repeat.

	● ●	● ●	● ● ●	● ● ● ●
the USA France Spain	England Poland Russia	Brazil Japan	Italy Hungary Mexico Germany	Australia

6 Where are they from? Write the countries from exercise 5.

Cześć!

This is Danka.
1 She's __from Poland.__

G'day!

This is Jason.
2 He's _____

Konnichiwa!

This is Akiko and Miho.
3 They're _____

¡Buenos días!

This is Rosa.
4 _____

Bom dia!

This is Tiago.
5 _____

Privyet!

This is Svetlana.
6 _____

Bonjour!

This is Luc and Dominique.
7 _____

Guten Tag!

This is Henning.
8 _____

Szia!

This is Zoli and Kristóf.
9 _____

7 Ask and answer questions about the people. Use *she/her* and *he/his*.

What's her name? Danka.

Where's she from? Poland.

What's his name? Jason.

Where's he from? Australia.

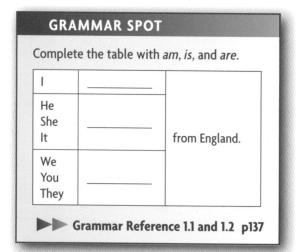

GRAMMAR SPOT

Complete the table with *am*, *is*, and *are*.

I	_____	
He She It	_____	from England.
We You They	_____	

▶▶ **Grammar Reference 1.1 and 1.2 p137**

PRACTICE

Talking about you

1 Ask and answer questions with a partner about the students in your class.

What's his name? | Where's he from?

2 Introduce your partner to the class.

This is Kurt. He's from Hamburg in Germany.

Listening and pronunciation

3 **T 1.5** Listen and tick (✓) the sentence you hear.

1. ☐ She's from Spain.
   ☐ He's from Spain.
2. ☐ What's her name?
   ☐ What's his name?
3. ☐ They're from Japan.
   ☐ They're in Japan.
4. ☐ Where's she from?
   ☐ Where's he from?
5. ☐ He's a teacher in Italy.
   ☐ His teacher's in Italy.

Check it

4 Complete the sentences with *am, is, are, his, her,* or *your.*

1. My name __is__ Emma.
2. Where _____ you from?
3. I _____ from Italy.
4. 'What's _____ name?' 'My name's Daniella.'
5. Lisa and Mike _____ from Boston.
6. This _____ my teacher. _____ name's Richard.
7. Where _____ he from?
8. This is my sister. _____ name's Miho.

Reading and writing

5 **T 1.6** Listen and read about Svetlana.

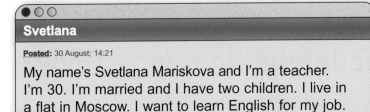

Svetlana

Posted: 30 August; 14:21

My name's Svetlana Mariskova and I'm a teacher. I'm 30. I'm married and I have two children. I live in a flat in Moscow. I want to learn English for my job.

6 Complete the text about Tiago.

Tiago

Posted: 2 October; 09:07

My name's Tiago Costa and I'm a student. I _____ 18. I'm not married. I have one _____ and two brothers. I _____ in a house in Fortaleza, Brazil. I _____ to learn English because it's an international _____ .

T 1.7 Listen and check.

7 Write about you. Then read it to the class.

VOCABULARY AND PRONUNCIATION
Everyday objects

1 **T 1.8** Listen to the alphabet song. Say the alphabet as a class.

abcdefghijklmnopqrstuvwxyz

2 Look at this extract from an English/Italian dictionary.

the pronunciation   the word in Italian

apple /'æpl/ *n.* *mela*

the word in English   the part of speech (n. = noun)

3 Match the words and pictures.

	● ●	● ● ●	● ● ●
a stamp	an apple	a dictionary	a magazine
a bag	an orange	a newspaper	
a key	a camera		
a watch	a ticket		
	a postcard		
	a mobile		

T 1.9 Listen and repeat.

4 Ask and answer questions with a partner.

What's a ?
It's an apple.
How do you spell that?
A, double P, ...

5 Look at the words. When is it *a*? When is it *an*?

a bag   a ticket   a mobile

an apple   an orange   an English newspaper

6 Look at the plural words.

two stamps   two apples   two dictionaries

Say the plurals of the other words in exercise 3.

▶▶▶ **Grammar Reference 1.4 and 1.5 p137**

EVERYDAY ENGLISH
Hello and goodbye

1 Say the numbers 1–20 round the class.

2 🔊 **.10** Read and listen to the telephone numbers. Read them aloud.

682 947	six eight two — nine four seven
07700 900318	'oh' double seven double 'oh' — nine double 'oh' three one eight
00 1 212 799 7050	double 'oh' — one — two one two — seven double nine — seven 'oh' five 'oh'

3 **.11** Listen and write the numbers you hear. Practise them.

4 Ask and answer the question with other students. Write a list.

> What's your phone number?

> My mobile's 07726 751180.

> My home number's 01632 77944.

> Thank you very much.

5 **.12** Listen to the conversations. Write them in the correct order.

1 ☐ I'm fine, thank you. And you?
☐ I'm OK, thanks.
☐ Hello, Lisa. It's Mike.
☐ Mike! How are you?
☑ Hello, Lisa Jefferson.

A _____
B _____
A _____
B _____
A _____

2 ☐ Thanks, and you. See you later!
☐ Bye, Marco! Have a nice day!
☐ Great! Bye, Emma!
☐ Yes, at 7.00 at the cinema.

A _____
B _____
A _____
B _____

3 ☐ Not bad, thanks. And you?
☐ Very well, thanks. How are the children?
☐ Hi, Alice! It's me, Charles. How are you?
☐ They're fine.
☐ Hello, 270899.

A _____
B _____
A _____
B _____
A _____

.12 Listen again and check.

Music *of* English

.13 In English we stress important words. Listen and repeat. Copy the stress.

How are you?

I'm OK, thanks.
Not bad, thanks. And you?
Very well, thanks.

Have a nice day.
See you later.

6 Practise the conversations with other students. Then practise again using your name and number.

2 Meeting people

am/is/are – questions and negatives · Possessive 's · Family · Opposites · In a café

STARTER

1 Count from 1–20 round the class.

2 Count in 10s from 10–100 round the class.

> Ten
>
> Twenty
>
> Thirty
>
> …
>
> One hundred.

3 How old are you? Ask and answer in groups.

> How old are you?
>
> I'm nineteen.

WHO IS SHE?
Questions and negatives

1 Read the information about Lisa Jefferson.

Surname	Jefferson
First name	Lisa
Country	the USA
Job	journalist
Address	89, Franklin Street, Cambridge, Boston
Phone number	(616) 326 1204
Age	26
Married	No

2 Complete the questions.

1 What's __her__ surname? Jefferson.

2 _____ her first name? Lisa.

3 _____ she from? The USA.

4 _____ _____ job? She's a journalist.

5 What's _____ _____? 89, Franklin Street, Cambridge, Boston.

6 _____ _____ phone number? (616) 326 1204.

7 How old _____ _____? Twenty-six.

8 Is she _____? No, she isn't.

T 2.1 Listen and check.
Practise the questions and answers.

3 Lisa has a brother. Write questions about him.

T 2.2 Listen and complete the information.

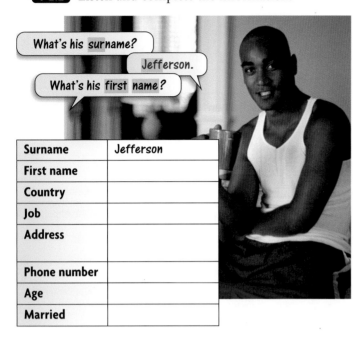

What's his surname?

Jefferson.

What's his first name?

Surname	Jefferson
First name	
Country	
Job	
Address	
Phone number	
Age	
Married	

Negatives and short answers

4 **T 2.3** Read and listen. Then listen and repeat.

Is she Spanish?

No, she isn't.

Is she English?

No, she isn't.

Is she American?

Yes, she is.

Ask and answer *Yes/No* questions about Lisa.

1 a student? a teacher? a journalist?
2 eighteen? twenty-one? twenty-six?

5 Ask and answer questions about Lisa's brother.

1 Peter? Daniel? Rudi?
2 a journalist? a student? an actor?
3 sixteen? thirty? twenty-eight?

GRAMMAR SPOT

1 Complete the answers to the *Yes/No* questions.

Is Lisa American?	Yes, she _____ .
Is her surname Smith?	No, it _____ .
Are you a journalist?	No, I'm _____ .

2 Look at the negatives.

She **isn't** married.   You **aren't** English.
But: I**'m not** a teacher.   ✗ I ~~amn't~~ a teacher.

▶▶ **Grammar Reference 2.1 p138**

PRACTICE

Who is he?

1 **Student A** Look at this information.
Student B Look at the information on p150.

Ask and answer questions to complete the information.

Surname	Binchey
First name	
Country	Ireland
Job	
Address	20, Model Farm Road, Cork City
Phone number	
Age	48
Married	

2 Ask and answer *Yes/No* questions about Patrick.

1 Smith? Jefferson? Binchey?
2 from England? from Italy? from Ireland?
3 an actor? a teacher? an accountant?

Talking about you

3 Ask your teacher some questions.

What's your first name?

Isabel.

Are you married?

No, I'm not.

What ...

4 Ask two students questions to complete the form.

	Student 1	Student 2
Name		
Country/town		
Job		
Address		
Phone number		
Age		
Married		

Tell the class about one of the students.

PATRICK'S FAMILY
Possessive 's

1 Write the words in the correct place.

brother	father	daughter	wife	aunt	grandmother	~~girlfriend~~

	boyfriend	husband		son		uncle	grandfather
	girlfriend		mother		sister		

2 **T 2.4** Read about Patrick Binchey and listen. Write the people's names in the correct place.

This is a photo of Patrick, his wife, and his children. His wife's name is Brenda. She's a teacher. His daughter's name is Lara. She's twenty-one and she's a nurse. His son's name is Benny. He's nineteen and he's a student. Lara's boyfriend is a nurse, too. His name is Mick.

3 Ask and answer questions about Patrick's family.

> Who's Brenda?

> She's Patrick's wife.

GRAMMAR SPOT

1 Look at *'s*.

She's a teacher: She's = She is.

His wife's name: His wife's name = her name

'*s* = possession.

2 Find other examples in the text of *'s* = possession and *'s* = is.

▶▶ **Grammar Reference 2.2 p138**

PRACTICE

You and your family

1 Ask your teacher questions about the people in his/her family.

> What's your mother's name?
>
> What's your sister's name?

2 Write the names of people in your family. Ask and answer questions with a partner.

> Pierre   Hélène   Marie   Jean-Claude   Alice

Ask a partner questions about his/her family.

> Who's Pierre?
>
> He's my brother.
>
> Who's Hélène?
>
> She's my aunt. She's my mother's sister.

3 Make true sentences with the verb *to be*.

1 I _'m not_ at home.
2 We _____ in class.
3 It _____ Monday today.
4 My teacher's name _____ John.
5 My mother and father _____ at work.
6 I _____ married.
7 My grandmother _____ seventy-five years old.
8 Marco and Carlo _____ my brothers.
9 We _____ in the café. We _____ in the classroom.

Check it

4 Tick (✓) the correct sentence.

1 ☐ I'm a doctor.
  ☐ I'm doctor.
2 ☐ I have twenty-nine years old.
  ☐ I am twenty-nine years old.
3 ☐ I no married.
  ☐ I'm not married.
4 ☐ My sister's name is Michelle.
  ☐ My sisters name is Michelle.
5 ☐ She married.
  ☐ She's married.
6 ☐ I'm an uncle.
  ☐ I'm a uncle.
7 ☐ I have two brother.
  ☐ I have two brothers.
8 ☐ Peter's the son of my sister.
  ☐ Peter's my sister's son.

VOCABULARY
Opposites

1 Match the adjectives with their opposites.

big	horrible
old	old
new	small
lovely	difficult
easy	cheap
hot	cold
expensive	slow
fast	young

2 Write about the pictures, using the adjectives.

1 a It's small.
  b It's big.

2 a It's _____
  b It's _____

3 a He's _____
  b She's _____

4 a They're _____
  b They're _____

5 a It's _____
  b It's _____

6 a It's _____
  b It's _____

7 a They're _____
  b They're _____

8 a It's _____
  b It's _____

T 2.5 Listen and check. Practise saying the sentences.

READING AND LISTENING
An email from England

1 **T 2.6** Danka is a student at an English language school in Brighton, England. Read and listen to her email to Jacek, her brother in Poland.

2 Match photographs 1–3 with a part of the email.

3 Correct the false (✗) sentences.
1 Danka is from Poland. ✓
2 She's on holiday. ✗ No, she isn't. She's at school.
3 She's in London.
4 The students in her class are all from Germany.
5 It's a very big class.
6 Becky and James are both students.
7 The student bars are cheap.
8 Danka's happy in Brighton.

4 Write the questions about Danka's email.
1 **Where's Danka from** ? Poland.
2 _____ ? Japan, Brazil, Switzerland, Germany, and Italy.
3 _____ ? Simon.
4 _____ ? They are brother and sister. They live with Danka.
5 _____ ? James is 25 and Becky's 19.
6 _____ Brighton _____? No, it isn't.

5 **T 2.7** Listen to three conversations. Where is Danka? Who is she with?

Writing

6 Write an email about *your* class.

From: Danka@brighton.ac.uk
To: Jacek.2006@star.com
Date: 12th July
Subject: Hi!

Dear Jacek,

How are you? I'm fine. Here's an email in English. It's good practice for you and me!

I have classes in English at The Embassy Language School. I'm in a class with seven students. They're all from different countries: Japan, Brazil, Switzerland, Germany, and Italy. Our teacher's name's Simon. He's very funny and a very good teacher.

I live with an English family in a small, old house near the centre of town. Robert and Valerie have a daughter and a son. Their daughter, Becky, is 19. She's a student at Brighton University. Their son, James, is a software designer for a computer company. He's 25. They're all very friendly, but it isn't easy to understand them. They speak very fast!

Brighton isn't very big, but it's very exciting! The restaurants and nightclubs are expensive, but the student bars and cafés are cheap. It's hot now, and it's lovely to be near the sea. I'm very happy here.

Email me soon!

Love, Danka

PALACE PIER

1 1 **T 2.8** Read and listen to the prices. Read them aloud.

£1.00	one pound	£7.50	seven pounds fifty
50p	fifty p /piː/	£10.75	ten pounds seventy-five
£5.00	five pounds		

2 **T 2.9** Write the prices you hear. Practise saying them.

2 Read the menu. Match the food and pictures.

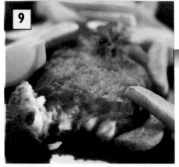

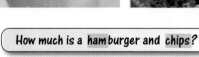
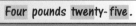

Brighton Pier Café

Menu

Chicken salad	£5.50
Tuna and egg salad	£5.25
Fish and chips	£4.95
Hamburger and chips	£4.25
Pizza	£3.75
Chocolate cake	£2.50
Apple pie	£2.25
Ice-cream	£2.00
Coffee	**£1.50**
Tea	**£1.20**
Mineral water	**£1.10**
Orange juice	**£1.00**

3 **T 2.10** Listen and repeat. Then ask and answer questions with a partner.

> How much is a hamburger and chips?
>
> Four pounds twenty-five.

> How much is a hamburger and chips and an orange juice?
>
> Five pounds twenty-five.

4 **T 2.11** Listen and complete the conversations in the cafés.

1 **A** Good morning.
   B Good _____ . Can I have a _____ , please?
   A Here you are. Anything else?
   B No, thanks.
   A _____ , please.
   B Thanks.
   A Thank you.

2 **A** Hi. Can I help?
   B Yes. Can I have a _____ salad, please?
   A Anything to drink?
   B Yeah. A _____ , please.
   A OK. Here you are.
   B _____ is that?
   A _____ pounds _____ , please.
   B Thanks.

Music of English 🎵

T 2.12 Words often link. Listen and practise the rhythm.

Can I help?

A cup of coffee, please.

a tuna and egg salad

Here you are. Anything else?

How much is that?

---

5 Practise the conversations with your partner. Make more conversations.

3 The world of work

Present Simple 1 – *he/she/it* · Questions and negatives · Jobs · What time is it?

STARTER

What are the jobs of the people in your family? Tell the class.

My father is a doctor.

My mother is a ...

My brother ...

THREE JOBS
Present Simple *he/she/it*

1 **T 3.1** Listen and read about István and Pamela.
What's his job? What's her job?

GRAMMAR SPOT

1 Underline all the verbs in the texts.
  is comes

2 What is the last letter of these verbs?

Pronunciation

3 Is *-s* pronounced /s/ or /z/?
  T 3.2 Listen and write the verbs.

/s/	/z/
works	is

Practise saying them.

---

2 Read the texts aloud.

István Kis

István <u>is</u> a music professor. He <u>comes</u> from Budapest in Hungary, but now he lives in the USA. He works four days a week at the University of Texas, Austin. He speaks three languages: Hungarian, English, and German. He's married to an American and has a daughter. He likes playing tennis in his free time.

20 Unit 3 · The world of work

3 Complete the sentences about István and Pamela.

1 István's a music professor. Pamela <u>'s</u> <u>a</u> doctor.

2 He comes from Hungary. She _____ _____ Canada.

3 He lives in a big city, but she _____ in a _____ town.

4 He _____ four days _____ week. She _____ 16 hours a day _____ .

5 He _____ three languages. She _____ to sick people on her radio.

6 He loves his job and she _____ _____ _____ , too.

7 He _____ _____ daughter. She _____ married.

8 He _____ playing tennis in his free time. She never _____ free time.

T 3.3 Listen and check. Read the sentences aloud.

Pamela Green

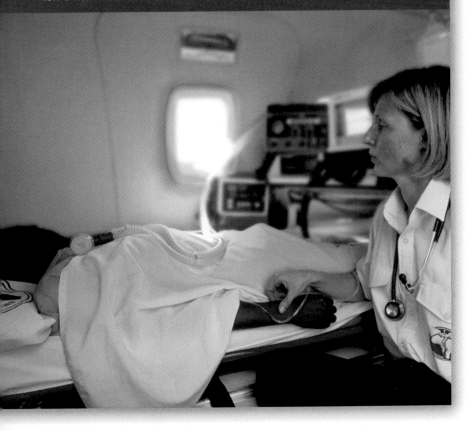

Pamela is a doctor. She's Canadian, but now she lives in a small town near Nairobi, Kenya, in East Africa. She isn't an ordinary doctor, she's a flying doctor. Every day from 8 a.m. to 10 a.m. she speaks to people on her radio, then she flies to help them. She works 16 hours a day non-stop, but she loves her job. She isn't married. She has no free time.

PRACTICE

Talking about people

1 Read the information about Fernando.

Fernando Diaz

Job	tourist guide
Country	Peru
Town	Lima
Place of work	in a tourist office
Languages	Spanish, English, and a little German
Married	no
Family	a dog (!)
Free time	walking his dog, playing football

2 Talk about Fernando.

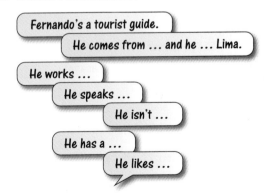

Fernando's a tourist guide.

He comes from ... and he ... Lima.

He works ...

He speaks ...

He isn't ...

He has a ...

He likes ...

3 Write about a friend or a relative. Talk to a partner about him/her.

My friend Anna is a student. She lives in ...

WHAT DOES HE DO?
Questions and negatives

1 **T 3.4** Read and listen. Complete the answers.
Practise the questions and answers.

> 1 Where **does** István **come** from?
> Budapest, _____ Hungary.
> 2 What **does** he **do**?
> He's _____ music professor.
> 3 **Does** he **speak** German?
> _____ , he does.
> 4 **Does** he **speak** Spanish?
> _____ , he doesn't. He doesn't speak
> Spanish or French.

GRAMMAR SPOT

1 What does he/she do? = What's his/her job?
2 Complete these sentences with the correct
form of *come*.

Positive   He _____ from Hungary.
Negative   He _____ _____ from Poland.
Question   Where _____ he _____ from?

Pronunciation

3 **T 3.5** Listen. Notice the pronunciation of
does and *doesn't*.

/dəz/
Does he speak German?

/dʌz/   /ˈdʌznt/
Yes, he does./ No, he doesn't.

Practise saying the question and short answers.

▶▶ **Grammar Reference 3.1 p138**

2 Complete the questions and answers.

> 1 Where _____ Pamela _____ from?
> Canada.
> 2 What _____ she _____ ?
> She's a doctor.
> 3 _____ she live in Canada?
> No, she _____ .
> 4 _____ she _____ her job?
> Yes, she _____ .

T 3.6 Listen, check and practise.

3 Write similar questions about Fernando the
tourist guide. Ask and answer with a partner.

Where does Fernando come from?
Peru.

PRACTICE

Asking about people

1 Read the information about Iman or Giorgio.

2 Talk to a partner.

Iman's a model and businesswoman.

She comes from Somalia.

She lives …

	Iman
Job	model and businesswoman
Country	Somalia
Town	New York
Place of work	in her office in New York
Languages	English, Somali, Italian, Arabic, and French
Family	married to the singer David Bowie, two daughters
Free time	likes cooking vegetarian food

IMAN™
Makeup

3 Write questions about Iman or Giorgio.

- What/do? **What does Iman do?**
- Where/come from?
- Where/live?
- Where/work?
- . . . speak French? **Does she/he . . .**
- How many children . . . ?
- . . . a dog?
- What . . . in her/his free time?
- . . . like cooking?

4 Ask and answer questions with your partner.

5 Now ask your partner the same questions about a friend or relative.

	Giorgio Locatelli
Job	chef
Country	Italy
Town	London
Place of work	in his restaurant in London
Languages	Italian, English, and French
Family	married to an Englishwoman, a son and a daughter
Free time	likes walking, riding, relaxing with his family

GIORGIO LOCATELLI

Listening and pronunciation

6 **T 3.7** Listen to the sentences about Iman and Giorgio. Correct the wrong sentences.

> Iman comes from Somalia.

> Yes, that's right.

> Iman lives and works in Somalia.

> No, she doesn't. She lives and works in New York.

7 **T 3.8** Tick (✓) the sentence you hear.
1 ☐ He likes his job.
  ☐ She likes her job.
2 ☐ She loves walking.
  ☐ She loves working.
3 ☐ He's married.
  ☐ He isn't married.
4 ☐ Does she have three children?
  ☐ Does he have three children?
5 ☐ What does he do?
  ☐ Where does he go?

Check it

8 Tick (✓) the correct sentence.
1 ☐ She comes from Somalia.
  ☐ She come from Somalia.
2 ☐ What he do in his free time?
  ☐ What does he do in his free time?
3 ☐ Where lives she?
  ☐ Where does she live?
4 ☐ He isn't married.
  ☐ He doesn't married.
5 ☐ Does she has two sons?
  ☐ Does she have two sons?
6 ☐ He doesn't play football.
  ☐ He no plays football.
7 ☐ She doesn't love Peter.
  ☐ She doesn't loves Peter.
8 ☐ What's he's address?
  ☐ What's his address?

▶▶ **WRITING** Natural writing *p114*

READING AND LISTENING
Seumas McSporran – the man with thirteen jobs!

1 **Seumas McSporran** /ˈʃeɪməs məkˈspɒrən/ comes from Scotland. (This *is* his real name!) Look at the photographs of some of the things he does every day.

2 Match a sentence with a photograph.

1. [h] He **helps** in the shop.
2. [ ] He **makes** breakfast for the hotel guests.
3. [ ] He **serves** petrol.
4. [ ] He **delivers** the beer to the pub.
5. [ ] He **collects** the post from the boat.
6. [ ] He **drives** the children to school.
7. [ ] He **delivers** the letters.
8. [ ] He **has** a glass of wine.
9. [ ] He **works** as an undertaker.

3 Read about Seumas. Answer the questions.

1. Where does Seumas live?
2. How old is he?
3. How many jobs does he have?
4. What's his wife's name?
5. What does she do?
6. How many people live on Gigha?
7. How many tourists visit Gigha in summer?
8. What does Seumas do in the morning?
9. What do he and Margaret do in the evening?

4 Look at the photos. Ask and answer questions with a partner about times in Seumas's day.

> What does he do at six o'clock?
>> He gets up and makes breakfast.

The man

a | 6.00 a.m.

b | 8.00 a.m.

c | 9.00 a.m.

d | 10.00 a.m.

e | 12.00 p.m.

f | 2.00 p.m.

with 13 jobs

SEUMAS McSPORRAN is a very busy man. He is 60 years old and he has thirteen jobs.

He is a postman, a policeman, a fireman, a taxi driver, a school-bus driver, a boatman, an ambulance man, an accountant, a petrol attendant, a barman, and an undertaker. Also, he and his wife, Margaret, have a shop and a small hotel.

Seumas lives and works on the island of Gigha /ˈɡijə/ in the west of Scotland. Only 120 people live on Gigha, but in summer 150 tourists come by boat every day.

Every weekday Seumas gets up at 6.00 and makes breakfast for the hotel guests. At 8.00 he drives the island's children to school. At 9.00 he collects the post from the boat and delivers it to all the houses on the island. He also delivers the beer to the island's only pub. Then he helps Margaret in the shop.

He says: 'Margaret likes being busy, too. We never have holidays and we don't like watching television. In the evenings Margaret makes supper and I do the accounts. At 10.00 we have a glass of wine and then we go to bed. Perhaps our life isn't very exciting, but we like it.'

5 **T 3.9** Listen to four conversations from Seumas's day. After each one answer these questions.

1 Is it morning, afternoon, or evening?
2 Who are the people? Where are they?
3 What is Seumas's job?

6 Complete the conversations.

1 A Good _____. Can I _____ two ice-creams, please?
  B Chocolate or vanilla?
  A One chocolate, one vanilla, please.
  B That's _____. Anything _____?
  A No, thank you.

2 A Only _____ letters for you this _____, Mrs Craig.
  B Thank you very much, Mr McSporran. And _____'s Mrs McSporran this _____?
  A Oh, she's very well, thank you. She's _____ in the shop.

3 A A glass of _____ before bed, my dear?
  B Oh, yes please.
  A _____ you are.
  B Thank you, my dear. I'm very _____ this _____.

4 A Hello, Mr McSporran!
  B Good _____, boys and girls. Hurry up, we're late.
  A Can I sit here, Mr McSporran?
  C No, no, I _____ to sit there.
  B Be quiet _____ of you, and SIT DOWN!

Practise the conversations with your partner.

g | 3.00 p.m.

h | 5.00 p.m.

i | 10.00 p.m.

VOCABULARY AND PRONUNCIATION
Jobs

1 Use your dictionary and match a picture with a job in column **A**.

A	B
a A pilot	designs buildings.
b A chef	wears beautiful clothes.
c A nurse	looks after people in hospital.
d A lawyer	makes films.
e An actor	writes for a newspaper.
f A journalist	cooks in a restaurant.
g A model	sells things.
h An architect	flies planes.
i A shop assistant	helps people in court.

2 Match a job in **A** with a line in **B**.

T 3.10 Listen and check.

3 Look at the phonetic spelling of some of the words. Practise saying them.

1 /nɜːs/   4 /ˈʃɒp əˈsɪstənt/
2 /ˈmɒdəl/   5 /ˈɑːkɪtekt/
3 /ˈæktə(r)/   6 /ʃef/

T 3.11 Listen and repeat.

4 Memorize the jobs. Close your books. Ask and answer questions with a partner.

> **What does a pilot do?**
>
> **He/She flies planes.**

▶▶ **Phonetic symbols p159**

1

2

3

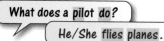

4

5

6

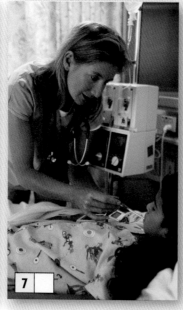

7

8

9

EVERYDAY ENGLISH
What time is it?

1 Look at the clocks. Write the times.

It's **five** o'clock.

It's **half** past **five**. 2 _____

It's **quarter** past **five**. 3 _____

It's **quarter** to **six**. 4 _____

It's **five** past **five**. 5 _____

It's **twenty** past **five**. 6 _____

It's **twenty-five** to **six**. 7 _____

It's **ten** to **six**. 8 _____

T 3.12 Listen and check. Practise saying the times.

2 Look at the times.

It's **just** before **three** o'clock.

It's **just** after **five** o'clock.

What time is it now? What time does the lesson end?

Music of English

T 3.13 In English the voice goes up and down. Copy the stress and intonation.

Conversation 1

Ex cuse me. Can you tell me the time, please?

Yes, of course. It's just after six o'clock.

Thanks.

Conversation 2

Ex cuse me. Can you tell me the time, please?

I'm sorry, I don't know. I don't have a watch.

Never mind.

3 With a partner, draw clocks on a piece of paper. Make more conversations.

4 Take it easy!

Present Simple 2 – *I/you/we/they* · Leisure activities · Social expressions

STARTER

1 What year is it? What month is it? What day is it today?

2 Say the days of the week. Which days are the weekend?

WEEKDAYS AND WEEKENDS
Present Simple *I/you/we/they*

1 **T 4.1** Listen and read about Ceri Bevan. What's her job? What does she do at weekends?

2 Complete the text with the verbs.

> trains   works   is   plays x2   lives   doesn't relax   has   loves

'I work hard and I play hard, too!'
says Ceri Bevan

Ceri _____ 28 years old and _____ in Cardiff, Wales. She _____ hard as a lawyer from Monday to Friday, but she _____ at weekends. She _____ rugby for the Women's Welsh Rugby team. On Saturdays she _____ with her team at the Rugby Club, and on Sundays she _____ in a match. She _____ no free time, but she _____ her job and playing rugby.

3 **T 4.2** Close your books and listen to Ceri. Does she have a busy life? Give examples.

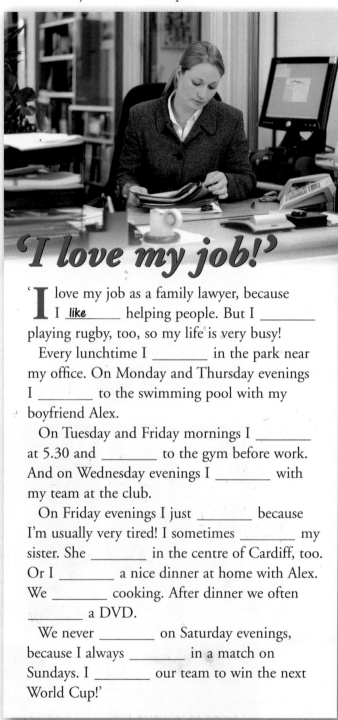

'I love my job!'

'I love my job as a family lawyer, because I __like__ helping people. But I _____ playing rugby, too, so my life is very busy!

Every lunchtime I _____ in the park near my office. On Monday and Thursday evenings I _____ to the swimming pool with my boyfriend Alex.

On Tuesday and Friday mornings I _____ at 5.30 and _____ to the gym before work. And on Wednesday evenings I _____ with my team at the club.

On Friday evenings I just _____ because I'm usually very tired! I sometimes _____ my sister. She _____ in the centre of Cardiff, too. Or I _____ a nice dinner at home with Alex. We _____ cooking. After dinner we often _____ a DVD.

We never _____ on Saturday evenings, because I always _____ in a match on Sundays. I _____ our team to win the next World Cup!'

4 Read and complete the text with the correct form of the verbs in the box. Look up new words in your dictionary.

| ~~like~~ love x2 get up go running go x2 train relax |
| visit cook go out play want live watch |

T 4.2 Listen again and check. Read the text aloud.

Questions and negatives

5 **T 4.3** Read and listen. Complete Ceri's answers. Practise the questions and answers.

Where do you work? _____ Cardiff.

Do you like your work? Yes, I _____.

Do you relax at weekends? No, I _____.

Why don't you relax at weekends? _____ I play rugby.

Roleplay

6 Work with a partner. One of you is Ceri. Ask and answer questions about your life.

- Where . . . you live/work?
- Are . . . married?
- What . . . job?
- . . . like your job?
- Why . . . like it? Because I . . .
- What time . . . get up on Tuesday mornings?
- Why . . . get up at . . . ? Because I . . .
- . . . like swimming/cooking?
- . . . your boyfriend like swimming/cooking?
- Who . . . you visit on Fridays?
- Where . . . your sister live?
- . . . go out on Saturday evenings? Why not?
- . . . have a busy life?

> **GRAMMAR SPOT**
>
> **1** Complete the table for the Present Simple.
>
> | | Positive | Negative |
> |---|---|---|
> | I | work | don't work |
> | You | | |
> | He/She | | |
> | It | | |
> | We | | |
> | They | | |
>
> **2** Complete the questions and answers.
>
> Where _____ you work?
>
> Where _____ she work?
>
> _____ you work in Cardiff? Yes, I _____.
>
> _____ he work in Edinburgh? No, he _____.
>
> **3** Find the words in the text:
> *always usually often sometimes never*
>
> ▶▶ **Grammar Reference 4.1 and 4.2 p139**

PRACTICE

Talking about you

1 Make questions. Then match the questions and answers.

Questions		Answers
1 What time	do you like your job?	a My mother and sisters.
2 Where	do you travel to school?	b To Spain or Portugal.
3 What	do you go on holiday?	c After dinner.
4 When	do you go to bed?	d I always relax.
5 Who	you go out on Friday evenings?	e At 11 o'clock.
6 Why	do you live with?	f Because it's interesting.
7 How	do you do on Sundays?	g By bus.
8 Do	do you do your homework?	h Yes, I do sometimes.

T 4.4 Listen and check.

2 Ask and answer the questions with a partner. Give true answers.

3 Tell the class about you and your partner.

> Kim goes to bed at 11.00. I go to bed at 10.00 on weekdays but at half past eleven at weekends.

> I live with my parents and my grandmother. Kim lives with her parents, too.

Listening and pronunciation

4 **T 4.5** Tick (✓) the sentence you hear.

1 ☐ What does he do on Sundays?
  ☐ What does she do on Sundays?
2 ☐ Do you stay at home on Tuesday evenings?
  ☐ Do you stay at home on Thursday evenings?
3 ☐ He lives here.
  ☐ He leaves here.
4 ☐ Where do you go on Saturday evenings?
  ☐ What do you do on Saturday evenings?
5 ☐ I read a lot.
  ☐ I eat a lot.
6 ☐ Why do you like your job?
  ☐ Why don't you like your job?

Positives and negatives

5 Make the sentences opposite.

1 She's French. **She isn't French.**
2 I don't like cooking. **I like cooking.**
3 She doesn't speak Spanish.
4 They want to learn English.
5 We're tired and want to go to bed.
6 Roberto likes watching football on TV, but he doesn't like playing it.
7 I work at home because I have a computer.
8 Amelia isn't happy because she doesn't have a new car.
9 I smoke, I drink, and I don't go to bed early.
10 He doesn't smoke, he doesn't drink, and he goes to bed early.

VOCABULARY AND SPEAKING
Leisure activities

1 Match the words and photos.

☐ playing football
☐ dancing
☐ skiing
☐ watching TV
☐ going to the gym
☐ taking photographs
☐ cooking
☐ playing computer games
☐ sailing
☐ listening to music
☐ swimming
☐ reading
☐ eating in restaurants
☐ going to the cinema
☐ going running
☐ sunbathing

2 Discuss in groups what you think your teacher likes doing. Choose *five* activities.

> I think he/she likes cooking.
>
> No, I think he/she likes eating in restaurants.

Ask your teacher questions to find out who is correct.

> Do you like cooking?
>
> Do you like eating in restaurants?

3 Tell the other students what you *like* doing and what you *don't like* doing from the list. Ask questions about the activities.

> I don't like watching TV, but I like reading very much.
>
> Oh, really? What do you read?
>
> Why don't you like watching TV?

4 Tell the other students things you like doing which are *not* on the list.

READING AND LISTENING
My favourite season

1 1 What season is it now? What are the seasons?
    2 What month is it now? Say the months of the year.
    3 When are the different seasons in your country?

2 Look at the photos. Which season is it? What colours do you see?

3 **T 4.6** Read and listen to three people from different countries.

4 Answer the questions.
    1 What sports do they play?
    2 Do Daniella and Axel like skiing?
    3 Where do Daniella and her family eat in summer?
    4 Where does Sumalee live?
    5 Which season does Sumalee like best?
    6 What do Sumalee and her friends do in February?
    7 Does Daniella like sunbathing?
    8 Why does Axel like spring?
    9 Where do Daniella's cousins live?
   10 Which months are winter months in the three countries?

5 There are six mistakes about Daniella, Sumalee, and Axel. Correct them.

> *Daniella* comes from England. In summer she goes surfing and sailing. She loves the beach and she likes sunbathing.

> *Sumalee* comes from the south of Thailand. Her favourite season is summer. She loves dancing.

> *Axel* comes from Norway. He likes winter best. He likes skiing, but he doesn't ski very fast.

6 **T 4.7** Listen to the conversations. Is it Daniella, Sumalee, or Axel? Where are they? How do you know? Discuss with a partner.

What do you think?

- What is *your* favourite season? Why?
- What do you do in the different seasons?

▶▶ **SONG** *Colours* Teacher's Book *p139*

▶▶ **WRITING** Informal letters *p115*

Daniella from Australia

I like summer best. We cook and eat in the garden, and we often go to the beach. I don't like sunbathing, but I love water sports. I go surfing and waterskiing, and I sometimes go sailing with my dad. Summer here is from December to February, so we always spend Christmas day on the beach. My cousins in England think this is very funny. They think it's always warm and sunny here in Australia, but in July and August it's sometimes cold and wet.

Sumalee from Thailand

I live in Chiang Mai in the north. We don't have four seasons, we have three – hot, rainy, and cool. I like the cool season from November to February. It's our 'winter'. It's quite hot in the daytime and it's cold at night. In February we have lots of tropical flowers – red, orange, and pink. So every year we have a beautiful Flower Festival. We sing and dance – I love it!

Axel from Norway

Here's a joke about my country: 'Winter is nine months long, and the other three months are good for skiing.' It isn't true! Here the winter months are December to February but it is often cold in spring and autumn too. Our summer is short but warm, with very long days. Spring is my favourite season. It's the best time to go skiing. I love going fast down a white mountain under a beautiful, blue sky. Sometimes you can still ski in June – isn't that amazing!

SPEAKING

Do you have a healthy lifestyle?

1 Read and complete the questionnaire about you.
Write ✓ or ✗, then look at the answer key. Are you healthy?

Do you have a healthy lifestyle?

Do you … ?	Me	T	S1	S2
A go to bed early on weekdays	☐	☐	☐	☐
B have breakfast every morning	☐	☐	☐	☐
C drink mineral water	☐	☐	☐	☐
D walk to school/work	☐	☐	☐	☐
E play a sport	☐	☐	☐	☐
F smoke	☐	☐	☐	☐
G drink alcohol	☐	☐	☐	☐
H like fast food	☐	☐	☐	☐
I watch TV a lot	☐	☐	☐	☐
J play computer games	☐	☐	☐	☐

KEY

A B C D E	✓ = 1 point		7-10 points	Very good!
	✗ = 0 point		4-6 points	OK
F G H I J	✗ = 1 point		0-3 points	Oh dear!
	✓ = 0 point			

2 Ask your teacher the questions, then ask two students.
Complete the questionnaire about them.

Do you smoke?
Yes, I do./Yes, sometimes.
No, I don't./No, never.

Do you like fast food?
No, I don't.
Yes, I like it a lot.

3 Compare with the class. Who is healthy in the class?

Writing

4 Use the information in the questionnaire. Write about you and a partner.
I don't go to bed early on weekdays, but Sofia does. We don't eat breakfast every morning …

EVERYDAY ENGLISH
Social expressions

1 Complete the conversations with the expressions.

1 A _____. The traffic is bad today.
  B _____. Come and sit down.
     We're on page 25.

> Don't worry.
> I'm sorry I'm late.

2 A _____.
  B Yes?
  A Do you have a dictionary?
  B _____ I don't. It's at home.
  A _____.

> I'm sorry,
> Excuse me.
> It doesn't matter.

3 A It's very hot in here. Can I open
     the window?
  B _____?
  A The window, can I open it?
  B _____.

> Pardon?
> Yes, of course.

4 A _____!
  B Oh, good morning Marco. Can I
     help you?
  A Yes, please. Can I have a ticket for
     the trip to York?
  B Yes, of course. It's £80. Do you want
     to pay £20 deposit now?
  A Sorry. _____?
  B It means you can pay £20 now and
     £60 later.
  A Ah. _____. Yes, please.

> I see.
> What does
> 'deposit' mean?
> Excuse me!

T 4.8 Listen and check.

Music of English ♪♫

T 4.9 Listen and practise the expressions in conversations 1–4. Pay attention to stress and intonation.

2 Practise the conversations with a partner.

5 Where do you live?

There is/are · Prepositions · some/any · this/that/these/those · Furniture · Directions 1

STARTER

1 Write the words in the correct column.

an armchair   a fridge   a television   a table
a shelf   a plant   a DVD player   a dishwasher
a sink   a lamp   a cooker   a washing machine
a telephone   a cupboard   a sofa

2 What's in your living room?
Tell a partner.

living room	kitchen	both

WHAT'S IN THE LIVING ROOM?
There is/are, prepositions

1 Suzie has a new flat. Describe her living room on p37.

> There's a television.

> There are two photos.

2 **T 5.1**   Read and listen. Complete the answers.
Practise the questions and answers.

Is there a television?	Yes, there _____.
Is there a computer?	No, there _____.
Are there any books?	Yes, there _____.
How many books are there?	There _____ a lot.
Are there any pictures?	No, there _____.

GRAMMAR SPOT

Complete the table.

Positive	There		a television.
			some books.
Negative	There		a computer.
			any pictures.
Question		there	a telephone?
			any plants?

▶▶ **Grammar Reference 5.1 and 5.2 p140**

3 Ask and answer questions about these things in Suzie's living room.

a cat	a dog	a DVD player	a fireplace
a mirror	a clock	a coffee table	a rug

plants	pictures	shelves	curtains
newspapers	photos	cushions	DVDs

Is there a cat?   Yes, there is.

4 Describe Suzie's living room. Complete the sentences with a preposition.

on	under	next to	in front of	behind

1 The cat is _____ the sofa _____ Suzie.
2 The DVD player is _____ the television.
3 There's a photo _____ the mirror.
4 There aren't any pictures _____ the walls.
5 There's a lamp _____ the sofa.
6 There are some magazines _____ the rug _____ the sofa.

What's in your picture?

1 Work with a partner. *Don't* look at your partner's picture.

Student A
Look at the picture of the living room on p148. Your picture is not complete. Ask Student B questions and find out where the things go. Draw them on your picture.

Student B
Look at the picture of the living room on p150. Your picture is complete. Answer Student A's questions and help him/her complete the picture.

Where's the lamp?   It's on the table.
Where exactly?   Next to the book.

2 **T 5.2** Look at the complete picture together on p150. Listen to someone describing it. There are *five* mistakes in the description. Say 'Stop!' when you hear a mistake.

Stop! There aren't three people! There are four people!

WHAT'S IN THE KITCHEN?

some/any, this/that/these/those

1 This is Suzie's kitchen. Work with a partner. Ask and answer questions about these things.

| apples | a cooker | a fridge | cupboards | cups | flowers |

Are there any apples? — **Yes, there are.**

Where are they? — **They're next to the cooker.**

2 **T 5.3** Listen and complete the conversation between Suzie and Matt.

Suzie And this is the kitchen.

Matt Mmm, it's very nice.

Suzie Well, it's not very big, but there _____ a _____ of cupboards.
And _____ 's a new fridge, and a cooker. That's new, too.

Matt But what's in all these cupboards?

Suzie Well, not a lot. There are some cups, but there aren't any plates.
And I have _____ knives and forks, but I don't have _____ spoons!

Matt Do you have _____ glasses?

Suzie No. Sorry.

Matt Never mind. We can drink this champagne from those cups! Cheers!

3 What is there in your kitchen? How is your kitchen different from Suzie's?

some and any

1 What's the difference between the sentences?
   There are **two** magazines.
   There are **some** magazines.

2 When do we say *some*? When do we say *any*?
   There are **some** cups.
   There aren't **any** glasses.
   Are there **any** spoons?

this, that, these, those

3 Complete the sentences with *this*, *that*, *these*, or *those*.

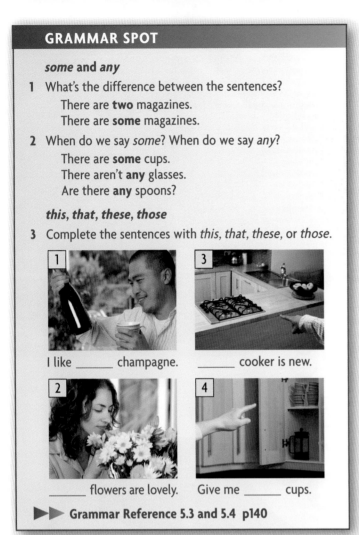

I like _____ champagne.

_____ cooker is new.

_____ flowers are lovely.

Give me _____ cups.

▶▶ **Grammar Reference 5.3 and 5.4 p140**

PRACTICE

In our classroom

1 Complete the sentences with *some* or *any*.

   1 In our classroom there are _____ books on the floor.
   2 There aren't _____ plants.
   3 Are there _____ Spanish students in your class?
   4 There aren't _____ Chinese students.
   5 We have _____ dictionaries in the cupboard.
   6 There aren't _____ pens in my bag.

2 What is there in your classroom? Describe it.

3 Talk about things in your classroom, using *this/that/these/those*. Point to or hold the things.

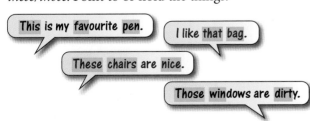

This is my favourite pen.

I like that bag.

These chairs are nice.

Those windows are dirty.

What's in Yoshi's briefcase?

4 **T 5.4** Yoshi Ishigawa is on business in New York. Listen to him describe what's in his briefcase. Tick (✓) the things in it.

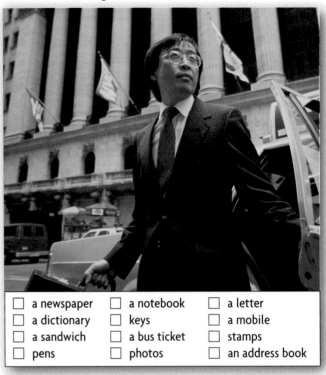

- ☐ a newspaper
- ☐ a dictionary
- ☐ a sandwich
- ☐ pens
- ☐ a notebook
- ☐ keys
- ☐ a bus ticket
- ☐ photos
- ☐ a letter
- ☐ a mobile
- ☐ stamps
- ☐ an address book

5 Look in your bag. Ask and answer questions about your bags with a partner.

Is there a dictionary in your bag?

Are there any stamps?

How many stamps are there?

Check it

6 Tick (✓) the correct sentence.

   1 ☐ There aren't some sandwiches.
     ☐ There aren't any sandwiches.
   2 ☐ Do you have some good dictionary?
     ☐ Do you have a good dictionary?
   3 ☐ I have some photos of my dog.
     ☐ I have any photos of my dog.
   4 ☐ I have lot of books.
     ☐ I have a lot of books.
   5 ☐ How many students are there in this class?
     ☐ How many of students are there in this class?
   6 ☐ Next my house there's a park.
     ☐ Next to my house there's a park.
   7 ☐ Look at this house over there!
     ☐ Look at that house over there!
   8 ☐ Henry, that is my mother. Mum, that is Henry.
     ☐ Henry, this is my mother. Mum, this is Henry.

READING AND SPEAKING
Living in a bubble

1 What are the names of the rooms in a house? What do we do in each room? Match the lines to make sentences.

We cook in	the living room.
We watch TV in	the kitchen.
We sleep in	the study.
We eat in	the bedroom.
We work in	the dining room.

2 Look at the photos. What rooms can you see?

3 Read about Cyril Jean and his house. Answer the questions.

1 Where is Cyril's house? How old is it?
2 Why is it called 'a bubble house'?
3 What does Cyril do?
4 What does Cyril collect?
5 How many rooms are there in his house?
6 Is there a garden?

4 Are the sentences true (✓) or false (✗)?

1 Cyril's house is modern.
2 There aren't any 'bubble houses' in the south of France.
3 There are a lot of clocks in the house.
4 The centre of the house is the kitchen.
5 Cyril doesn't like listening to music.
6 The windows don't have curtains.
7 There are three rooms upstairs.
8 Antti Lovag thinks the house is funny.

5 Work with a partner. Ask and answer questions about Cyril's home.

Is there a garden? Yes, there is.
Are there any bedrooms? Yes, there's one.

Ask about these things:

- a study
- pictures
- curtains
- clocks
- a TV
- plants
- a lot of kitchen cupboards

What do you think?

- What do you like about Cyril's home? What don't you like?
- Describe your perfect home.

Living in a bubble

Is this a modern house? Is this a house of the future? Well, no, it isn't.

Cyril Jean's house in the south of France is 40 years old. There are more houses like this in the south of France. They are called 'bubble houses,' and you can see why!

Cyril Jean is a designer and he loves round things. He collects old records and clocks. He also collects round furniture. And now he has a completely round house for it all.

The centre of the house is one very big bubble. This is both the living room and dining room. There are round armchairs, a round table, and a big round rug in front of a round fireplace. Around the living room are three small bubbles. One bubble is a kitchen with round cupboards, another bubble is the garden room, and the third bubble is a music room for all Cyril's old records. Upstairs there are two more bubbles – a bedroom, and a bathroom.

The doors and windows are also round, of course. The windows are like eyes. There aren't any curtains in the house, because Cyril likes to see the garden all the time.

Bubble houses are the idea of a Hungarian architect, **Antti Lovag**. Lovag thinks that a lot of modern houses are bad for us, especially tall blocks of flats. He thinks that people are happy in round homes because they are more natural. Cyril agrees with this. 'Some people think my house is funny,' he says. 'But for me, this is the perfect home.'

LISTENING AND SPEAKING
Homes around the world

1 Match the places and photos 1–4.

☐ Lisbon ☐ New England ☐ Seoul ☐ Samoa

Candy and Bert

Alise

Kwan

Manola

2 **T 5.5** Listen to the people from these places. Complete the chart.

	Candy and Bert	**Alise**	**Kwan**	**Manola**
House or flat?				
Old or modern?				
Where?				
How many bedrooms?				
Live(s) with?				
Extra information				

3 Work with a partner. Talk about the people.

Candy and Bert live in an old, white house.

Alise lives in a house near the sea.

4 Talk about where you live.

Do you live in a house or a flat?

Where is it?

How many rooms . . . ?

Do you have a garden?

Who . . . ?

►► **WRITING** Describing where you live *p116*

EVERYDAY ENGLISH
Directions 1

1 Look at the street map of Suzie's town. Where can she do these things? Find the places on the map.

- buy: aspirin   some bread
  a book   milk
  a DVD   stamps
- send an email
- go for a walk
- see a film
- have a drink
- catch a bus

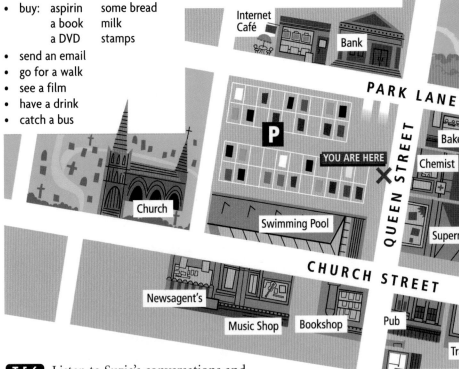

2 **T 5.6** Listen to Suzie's conversations and complete them.

1 **A** _____ me! Is there a _____ near here?
  B Yes. _____ Church Street. Take the first _____
    _____ _____ right. It's _____ _____ the music shop.
  A OK. Thanks.

2 **A** Is there a post office near here?
  B Go straight ahead, and it's _____ _____ left, _____
    _____ the pub.
  A Thanks a lot.

3 **A** Excuse me! Is there a _____ near here?
  B There's an Internet café in Park Lane _____ _____ the
    bank, and there's an Italian restaurant in Church Street next to
    the _____ _____.
  A Is that one _____?
  B No. Just two minutes, that's all.

3 Practise the conversations in exercise 2 with a partner.

4 Make more conversations with your partner. Use the expressions in the box to ask and answer about the places.

| near here   over there   on the corner |
| on the right/left   straight ahead |

- a bookshop   • a bus stop
- a cinema   • a park
- a bank   • a swimming pool
- a supermarket   • a church
- the railway station • a pub
- a car park   • a travel agent's

5 Talk about where you are. Is there a chemist's near here? Is it far? What about a bank/a post office/a supermarket?

Music *of* English

T 5.7 Listen and repeat. Copy the stress and intonation.

Ex cuse me! Is there a chemist's near here? Yes, it's over there.

Ex cuse me! Is there a baker's near here? Yes, it's on the corner.

6 Can you speak English?

can/can't/could/couldn't · was/were · Words that sound the same · On the phone

1 Where do people speak these languages?

French   Spanish   German   Italian
Portuguese   Japanese   English

> They speak French in France and also in Canada.

2 Which languages can you speak?
Tell the class.

> I can speak English and a little Spanish. And of course, I can speak my language.

WHAT CAN YOU DO?
can/can't

1 Match the photos of the Brady family with the sentences.

1 ☐ She can walk now.
2 ☐ We can draw, but we can't write.
3 ☐ I can sing quite well.
4 ☐ 'Can you play the drums?'
   'Yes, I can.' 'No, he can't!'
5 ☐ 'Can they dance?'
   'Yes, they can. My dad's OK, and my mum can dance flamenco really well.'

T 6.1 Listen and check.

a Lucía

b Dominic

c Eva

GRAMMAR SPOT

1 Say all persons of *can* and *can't*.
What do you notice?
I can, you can, he... she... it... we... they...
I can't, you..., etc.

Pronunciation

2 **T 6.2** Listen and repeat these sentences.

I can speak French.
Can you speak French?   = /kən/
Yes, I can.   = /kæn/
No, I can't.   = /kɑːnt/

3 Say these ● ● ●   ● ● ●
sentences. We can draw. She can't write.

▶▶ Grammar Reference 6.1 p141

---

2 [T 6.3] Listen and complete the sentences with *can* or *can't* + verb.

1 I _____ _____ _____, but I _____ _____ _____.
2 He _____ _____, but he _____ _____.
3 '_____ you _____?' 'Yes, I _____.'
4 They _____ _____, but they _____ _____.
5 We _____ _____ and we _____ _____.
6 '_____ she _____?' 'No, she _____.'

[T 6.3] Listen again and repeat.

e | Ben and Ana

d | Philip and Elena

PRACTICE

Lucía can't cook. Can you?

1 [T 6.4] Listen to Lucía and complete the chart. Put ✓ or ✗.

Can . . . ?	Lucía	You	Partner
drive a car	☐	☐	☐
speak French	☐	☐	☐
speak Spanish	☐	☐	☐
cook	☐	☐	☐
play tennis	☐	☐	☐
ski	☐	☐	☐
swim	☐	☐	☐
play the guitar	☐	☐	☐
dance	☐	☐	☐
use a computer	☐	☐	☐

2 Complete the chart about you.

3 Complete the chart about your partner. Ask and answer the questions.

> Can you drive a car? No, I can't.
> Can you ski?
> Yes, I can. But not very well.

Tell the class about you and your partner.

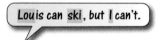

> Louis can ski, but I can't.

What can computers do?

4 What can computers do? Discuss with a partner.

Can they . . . ?

☐ translate
☐ check spellings
☐ write poetry
☐ feel ill
☐ speak English
☐ make music
☐ laugh
☐ think
☐ play chess
☐ have conversations
☐ hear
☐ fall in love

Imagine you live in 2050. What can/can't a computer do?

WHERE WERE YOU YESTERDAY?
was/were, can/could

T 6.5 Read and listen to the questions. Complete the answers.

Present

1 What day is it today?
It's _____ .

2 What month is it now?
It's _____ .

3 Where are you now?
I'm in/at _____ .

4 Are you in England?
_____ , I am.   _____ , I'm not.

5 Can you swim?
_____ , I can.   _____ , I can't.

6 Can your teacher speak three languages?
Yes, _____ can.   No, _____ can't.

Past

What day was it yesterday?
It was _____ .

What month was it last month?
It was _____ .

Where were you yesterday?
I was in/at _____ .

Were you in England in 1999?
_____ , I was.   _____ , I wasn't.

Could you swim when you were five?
_____ , I could.   _____ , I couldn't.

Could your teacher speak English when he/she was seven?
Yes, _____ could.   No, _____ couldn't.

GRAMMAR SPOT

1 Complete the table with the past of *to be*.

	Positive	Negative
I	was	wasn't
You	were	weren't
He/She/It		
We		
They		

Pronunciation

2 **T 6.6** Listen and repeat.
It was /wəz/ Monday yesterday. We were /wə/ at school.
In short answers the pronunciation is different.
Was /wəz/ it hot?   Yes, it was /wɒz/.
Were /wə/ you tired?   but   Yes, we were /wɜː/.

3 What is the past of *can*?

	Positive	Negative
I/You/He/She/It/We/They		

▶▶ **Grammar Reference 6.1 and 6.2 p141**

PRACTICE

Talking about you

1 Ask and answer questions with a partner.

Where were you . . . ?
- at eight o'clock this morning
- at half past six yesterday evening
- at two o'clock this morning
- at this time yesterday
- at ten o'clock last night
- last Saturday evening

2 Complete Emma and Marco's conversation, using *was*, *were*, *wasn't*, *weren't*, or *couldn't*.

E _____ you at Charlotte's party last Saturday?

M Yes, I _____ .

E _____ it good?

M Well, it _____ OK.

E _____ there many people?

M Yes, there _____ .

E _____ Pascal there?

M No, he _____ . And where _____ you? Why _____ you there?

E Oh ... I _____ go because I _____ at Sergio's party! It _____ brilliant!

M Oh!

T 6.7 Listen and check. Listen for the pronunciation of *was* and *were*. Practise with a partner.

Four geniuses!

3 What are these people famous for? Discuss with a partner.

Salvador Dalí | Charlotte Brontë | Tiger Woods | Albert Einstein

4 Look at these sentences.

I was born in London in 1983. I could read when I was four. My sister couldn't read until she was seven.

Match lines in **A**, **B**, and **C** and make similar sentences about the four geniuses.

A	B	C
Salvador Dalí	the USA / 1975	play golf / three
Charlotte Brontë	Germany / 1879	paint / one
Tiger Woods	England / 1816	write stories / four
Albert Einstein	Spain / 1904	couldn't speak / eight

5 Ask and answer questions with a partner about the geniuses.

> When was Salvador Dalí born?   Where was he born?
> How old was he when he could ... ?

6 Work in groups. Ask and answer the questions.
1 Where were you born?
2 When were you born?
3 How old were you when you could ... ?

- walk
- talk
- read
- swim
- ride a bike
- use a computer
- speak a foreign language

Check it

7 Tick (✓) the correct sentence.

1 ☐ I don't can use a computer.
  ☐ I can't use a computer.

2 ☐ I can to speak English very well.
  ☐ I can speak English very well.

3 ☐ I'm sorry. I can't go to the party.
  ☐ I'm sorry. I no can go to the party.

4 ☐ He could play chess when he was five.
  ☐ He can play chess when he was five.

5 ☐ Was they at the party?
  ☐ Were they at the party?

6 ☐ She was no at home.
  ☐ She wasn't at home.

READING AND SPEAKING
Talented teenagers

1 Do you like singing? Can you sing well? Do you like reading? What do you read? Look at the teenagers in the photographs. What can they do?

2 Work in two groups.

Group A Read about the singer.
Group B Read about the writer.

3 Answer the questions about Joss or Christopher.

1 How old is she/he?
2 What can she/he do?
3 Where was she/he born?
4 Where does she/he live?
5 Who does she/he live with?
6 Does she/he go to school?
7 What could or couldn't she/he do when she/he was very young?
8 Why were her/his parents surprised?
9 Where was she/he last month?
10 Why was she/he there?

4 Find a partner from the other group. Tell your partner about your teenager, using your answers.

5 What is the same about Joss and Christopher? What is different? Discuss with your partner.

They're talented teenagers.

Joss is a singer. Christopher's a writer.

Roleplay

6 Work with a partner.

Student A is a journalist.
Student B is Joss or Christopher.

Ask and answer questions, using the questions in exercise 3 to help you.

Hello, Joss! Can I ask you one or two questions?

Of course.

First of all, how old are you?

I'm seventeen.

THE **SOUL SINGER**

CAN A WHITE GIRL SING SOUL? CAN A TEENAGER SING THE BLUES? PEOPLE THINK THAT JOSS STONE CAN.

Joss was born in Devon in the south of England. She lives with her family in a small village in the English countryside. But she also works in New York. She sings at the Beacon Theatre on Broadway. She is a shy seventeen-year-old with a fantastic voice.

Joss could sing very well when she was a little girl. Her parents couldn't believe it. She says 'No-one in our family can sing – only me. My mum can't sing a note!' Later, at school, her friends couldn't understand soul music. 'I love it, but they don't. They prefer pop music.'

Last month she was in New York to make a record. 'I was worried about it. But people like it, so I'm very happy at the moment.'

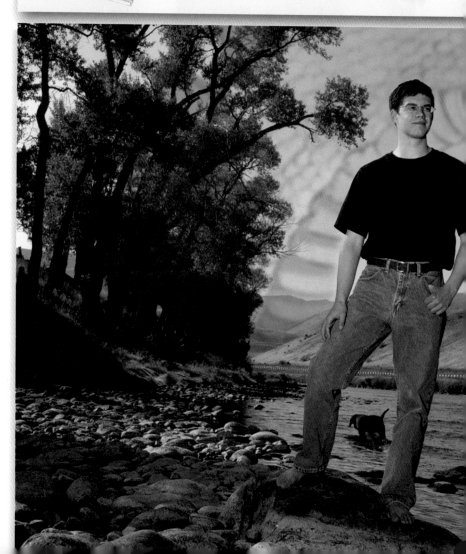

THE FANTASY WRITER

CAN A FIFTEEN-YEAR-OLD WRITE A BESTSELLER?
CAN A TEENAGER'S BOOK SELL MORE THAN HARRY POTTER?
CHRISTOPHER PAOLINI'S ANSWER IS **YES**.

C hristopher was born in Montana, USA. He lives with his family in Paradise Valley. They have a small house by the river. His parents teach him and his sister at home, they don't go to school. Christopher loves language and he loves books. Every day he sits for hours at his computer, he just can't stop writing.

This is surprising because when Christopher was very young he couldn't read very well. Then one day – 'It was magic,' he says, 'I could read, I could see the characters.' Suddenly there were people, conversations and stories in his head. His first book was a fantasy called *Eragon*. His parents were surprised that it was so good.

Last month Christopher was in New York for interviews. Why? Because *Eragon* was number one in the bestseller lists!

VOCABULARY AND PRONUNCIATION
Words that sound the same

1 Look at the sentences. What do you notice about these words?

> I **write** with my **right** hand.
> I have a black **eye**.
> **No**, he doesn't **know** the answer.

2 Find the words in **B** that have the same pronunciation as the words in **A**.

> **A** hear write wear see eye
> there by for hour
> know son four
> too I sun our
> sea where buy here
> right no two their **B**

3 Correct the two spelling mistakes in each sentence.

      hear   **see**
1 I can ~~here~~ you, but I can't ~~sea~~ you.
2 Their are three bedrooms in hour house.
3 I don't no wear Jill lives.
4 My sun lives near the see.
5 Don't where that hat, by a new one!
6 Know, eye can't come to your party.
7 You were write. Sally can't come four dinner.
8 There daughter could right when she was three.
9 I no my answers are write.

T 6.8 Listen and repeat.

4 Look at the phonetic symbols. Write the two words with the same pronunciation.

1 /nəʊ/ _____ _____
2 /sʌn/ _____ _____
3 /tuː/ _____ _____
4 /raɪt/ _____ _____
5 /hɪə/ _____ _____
6 /weə/ _____ _____

▶▶ **Phonetic symbols p159**

EVERYDAY ENGLISH
On the phone

1 Here are the names and addresses of some people you want to phone.

Lisa Jefferson
Freelance Journalist

89 Franklin Street
Cambridge
BOSTON

Cambridge **Herald**

tel [ ]
email ljefferson@usa.net

Yoshi Ishigawa
BUSINESSMAN

659 Tearaimizu-cho
KYOTO 604-8152
JAPAN

Tel: [ ]
email: ishigawa@nkg.or.jp

Travel Peru

Fernando Diaz
Tourist guide

Jiron Junín 612
Lima PERU

Tel: [ ]
email: flmdiaz@travel.co.pe

T 6.9 Listen to the operator. Answer her questions to get Lisa's telephone number.

Operator	International Directory Enquiries. Which country, please?
You	The USA .
Operator	And which town?
You	_____.
Operator	Can I have the last name, please?
You	_____.
Operator	And the initial?
You	_____.
Operator	What's the address?
You	_____.
Recorded message	The number you require is _____.

Roleplay

2 Work with a partner. Take it in turns to be the operator. Make conversations to find out the telephone numbers of Yoshi and Fernando.

Student A Go to p148.   **Student B** Go to p150.

3 Complete conversations 1–3 with these lines. Check answers with a partner.

1 Can I take a message?
2 Great! I'll see you on Sunday at ten, then. Bye!
3 This *is* Jo.
4 Oh, never mind. Perhaps next time. Bye!
5 There's a party at my house on Saturday. Can you come?
6 No, it isn't. I'll just get her.
7 I'll ring back later.
8 Can I speak to the manager, please?

> ! I'll = I will
> will = an offer or promise
> I'll help you

1
A Hello.
B Hello. Can I speak to Jo, please?
A _____.
B Oh! Hi, Jo. This is Nicola. Is Sunday still OK for tennis?
A Yes, that's fine.
B _____!
A Bye!

2
A Hello.
B Hello. Is that Emma?
A _____.
…
C Hello, Emma here.
B Hi, Emma. It's Marco. Listen!
_____?
C Oh sorry, Marco. I can't. It's my sister's wedding.
B _____!
C Bye!

3
A Good morning. Dixons Electrical. How can I help you?
B Good morning. _____?
A I'm afraid Mr Smith isn't in his office at the moment. _____?
B Don't worry. _____.
A All right. Goodbye.
B Goodbye.

4 **T 6.10** Listen and check.

Music of English 🎵🎶

T 6.11 Listen and practise the telephone expressions.

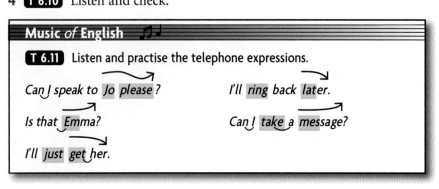

Can I speak to Jo please?

I'll ring back later.

Is that Emma?

Can I take a message?

I'll just get her.

5 Practise the conversations. Make similar conversations with your partner.

▶▶ **WRITING** Formal letters *p117*

7 Then and now

Past Simple 1 – regular verbs · Irregular verbs · Words that go together · What's the date?

STARTER

When were your grandparents and great-grandparents born? Where were they born? Do you know all their names? What were their jobs? If you know, tell the class.

WHEN I WAS YOUNG
Past Simple – regular verbs

1 Look at the photos. Do you know anything about the film star Shirley Temple?

2 **T 7.1** Read and listen to Shirley Temple Black's life now. Complete text **A** with the verbs you hear.

3 **T 7.2** Read and listen to text **B** about Shirley's life a long time ago.

GRAMMAR SPOT

1 Find examples of the past of *is* and *can* in text **B**.

2 Complete the sentences with *work* in the correct form.

Now she _____ at Stanford University. When she was a child she _____ in films.

3 Find the Past Simple of *start*, *dance*, *like*, and *retire* in text **B**. How do we form the Past Simple of regular verbs?

▶▶ **Grammar Reference 7.1 p142**

A *Shirley*
TEMPLE BLACK

Shirley Temple Black _____ a retired politician. She _____ with her husband in California. She _____ cooking and playing with her grandchildren. Also, she sometimes _____ at Stanford University for the Institute of International Studies. She _____ there every month and _____ foreign ministers. They _____ world problems.

B THE CHILD STAR

When she was very young, Shirley was a famous movie star. She started in films when she was only three years old! She could act, she was a good singer and she also danced well. She liked acting very much, and worked in over 50 films. But when she was 20, she retired from the cinema.

C WHY DID SHE STOP ACTING?

From the age of three Shirley _____ very hard for 20th Century Fox.

'I _____ in three or four movies every year. Fortunately I _____ acting!' And the public _____ her and her films. The films _____ over $35 million.

She says, 'I didn't go to school. I _____ at the studio and my mother _____ after me there.'

So why did she stop acting? When she was 12, she finally _____ school. She was a good student and she _____ to go to university. She was still a good actor, but her films weren't so popular, because she wasn't a little girl any more. She _____ to change her career. It was a big change – from actor to politician.

She says, 'I was a politician for 35 years, but people only remember my movies!'

---

4 **T 7.3** What is the past form of these verbs? Listen and practise saying them.

| like look work earn love |
| study act decide want start |

5 **T 7.4** Read and listen to text **C**. Complete the text, using the Past Simple form of the verbs in exercise 4.

GRAMMAR SPOT

1 Find a question with *did* and a negative with *didn't* in text **C**.

2 Look at these questions.
   Where **does** she work now?
   Where **did** she work in 1950?

   Did is the past of *do* and *does*. We use *did* to form a question in the Past Simple.

3 We use *didn't* (= *did not*) to form the negative.
   She **didn't** go to school.

▶▶ **Grammar Reference 7.2 p142**

---

6 Complete the questions about Shirley.

1 When __did__ she __start__ in films?
   When she was only three years old.

2 How many films _____ she _____ in?
   Over 50.

3 Who _____ she _____ for?
   20th Century Fox Film Studios.

4 How much money _____ her films _____?
   Over $35 million.

5 Where _____ she _____?
   At the film studio. She didn't go to school.

6 When _____ she _____ school?
   When she was 12.

7 What _____ she _____ to do?
   Go to university.

8 Why _____ she _____ acting?
   Because her movies weren't so popular any more.

T 7.5 Listen and check. Practise the questions and answers with a partner.

PRACTICE

Talking about you

1 Complete the sentences with *did*, *was*, or *were*.

> 1 Where _____ you born?
>   Where _____ your mother born?
>
> 2 When _____ you start school?
>
> 3 When _____ you learn to read and write?
>
> 4 Who _____ your first teacher?
>
> 5 What _____ your favourite subject?
>
> 6 Where _____ you live when you _____ a child?
>
> 7 _____ you live in a house or a flat?

2 Stand up! Ask two or three students the questions in exercise 1.

3 Tell the class some of the information you learned.

Enrico was born in ...

His mother ...

He started school ...

Pronunciation

1 **T 7.6** Listen to three different pronunciations of *-ed*.

/t/	/d/	/ɪd/
worked	*lived*	*started*

2 **T 7.7** Listen and write the Past Simple verbs on the chart.

/t/	/d/	/ɪd/
_____	_____	_____
_____	_____	_____

Practise saying them.

THE YEAR I WAS BORN

Irregular verbs

1 Look at the list of irregular verbs on p158. Write the Past Simple form of the verbs in the box. Which one isn't irregular?

be _____	begin _____	come _____	get _____	sing _____
leave _____	have _____	die _____	become _____	
win _____	make _____	buy _____	sell _____	

2 **T 7.8** Listen and repeat the Past Simple forms.

3 **T 7.9** James was born in 1984. Listen to his conversation with his parents and complete the sentences. Then listen again and check.

1984
... the year I was born

James was born on 24 January, 1984, in Hong Kong. His parents _____ Hong Kong that year and _____ back to Britain. His father _____ a job in London.

POLITICS

In Britain, Margaret Thatcher _____ Europe's first woman prime minister. US President Ronald Reagan _____ another four years in the White House. The Soviet leader Yuri Andropov _____ after only a year as leader.

SPORTS

American athlete Carl Lewis _____ four gold medals at the Los Angeles Olympics. The Soviet Union didn't go to the Olympics that year. Tiger Woods _____ junior golf champion at the age of eight.

SCIENCE

Apple Macintosh _____ a new personal computer and millions of people _____ one.

MUSIC

Michael Jackson's *Thriller* _____ 43 million albums. Madonna _____ *Holiday*. And Paul McCartney, Tina Turner and David Bowie all _____ hit records that year.

When did it happen?

4 Work with a partner. Ask and answer questions about the year James was born.

1 When/James and his parents leave Hong Kong?
2 Where/his father get a job?
3 How many medals/Carl Lewis win?
4 What/Apple Macintosh make?
5 Which song/Madonna sing?
6 How many albums/Michael Jackson's *Thriller* sell?

5 Make notes about the year you were born. Write about it. Tell the class.

1 Work in groups. Think of important events in history. When did they happen? Make a list, then make questions to ask the other groups.

When did the Second World War begin / end?

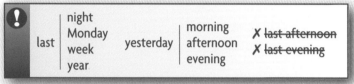

When did the first person walk on the moon?

What did you do?

!	last	night Monday week year	yesterday	morning afternoon evening	✗ last afternoon ✗ last evening

2 Work with a partner. Ask and answer questions with *When did you last … ?* Ask another question for more information.

When did you last have a holiday?

Last August.

Where did you go?

To Spain.

- have a holiday
- watch a DVD
- go shopping
- take a photograph
- go to a party
- talk on a mobile
- write an email
- get a present
- eat in a restaurant

Tell the class some things you learned about your partner.

Yukio had a holiday last August and she went to Italy.

Check it

3 Tick (✓) the correct sentence.

1 ☐ He bought some new shoes.
  ☐ He buyed some new shoes.
2 ☐ Where did you go yesterday?
  ☐ Where you went yesterday?
3 ☐ You see Jane last week?
  ☐ Did you see Jane last week?
4 ☐ Did she get the job?
  ☐ Did she got the job?
5 ☐ I went out yesterday evening.
  ☐ I went out last evening.
6 ☐ He studied French at school.
  ☐ He studyed French at school.
7 ☐ What had you for breakfast?
  ☐ What did you have for breakfast?
8 ☐ I was in New York the last week.
  ☐ I was in New York last week.

▶▶▶ **WRITING** Describing a holiday **p118**

Two

READING AND SPEAKING
Two famous firsts

1 Translate these words.

nouns	**verbs**	**adjectives**
airshow	break a record	excellent
fighter jet	travel	dangerous
flight	disappear	secret
experiences	join	
satellite	survive	
	crash	

2 Look at the texts and complete these sentences.

> Amelia Mary Earhart was the first _____ .
> Yuri Gagarin was the first _____ .

3 Work in two groups.

Group A Read about Amelia Earhart.
Group B Read about Yuri Gagarin.

4 Are the sentences true (✔) or false (✗) about your person?
Correct the false sentences.

1 He/She came from a rich family.
2 He/She had a short but exciting life.
3 He/She fought in a World War.
4 He/She wanted to be a pilot when he/she was a child.
5 He/She flew fighter jets.
6 He/She married, but didn't have any children.
7 He/She travelled to Europe to talk about his/her experiences.
8 He/She died in a plane crash.

5 Find a partner from the other group. Compare Amelia
Earhart and Yuri Gagarin, using your answers.

6 Complete the questions about the other person.
Then ask and answer them with your partner.

About Amelia Earhart
1 Where . . . she born?
2 What . . . she study first?
3 When . . . she first . . . up in a plane?
4 When . . . she . . . her first record?
5 . . . she marry? . . . she . . . any children?
6 What . . . she do in 1935?
7 Where . . . her plane disappear?

About Yuri Gagarin
8 Where . . . he born?
9 When . . . he see his first plane?
10 Why . . . he . . . the Russian Air Force?
11 Why . . . the doctors choose Yuri to be an astronaut?
12 What . . . he do in 1961?
13 Why . . . he . . . around the world?
14 How . . . he die?

What do you think?

Name some famous people from history. What did they do?

famous firsts

Amelia Mary Earhart AMERICAN (1897 – 1937)

The first woman to fly across the Atlantic

Her early years

Amelia was born in her grandparents' house in Kansas. Her parents didn't have any money, but her grandparents were rich and sent her to the best schools. At 20 she decided to study nursing and worked in a hospital in World War I. When she was 23, she visited an airshow and went up in a plane. At that moment, she knew that she wanted to be a pilot.

What she did

In 1920 flying was dangerous and people didn't think it was an activity for women. But Amelia had flying lessons, and a year later, she broke her first record – she flew up to 14,000 feet. She married at 34, but never had children. The next year she became the first woman (and the second person) to fly alone across the Atlantic. She was now famous, and she travelled around the world to talk about her experiences. And in 1935, when she was 38, she became the first person to fly alone across the Pacific.

Her last flight

When she was nearly 40, Amelia wanted to be the first woman to fly around the world. She began the 29,000 mile flight in Miami on 1 June 1937. On 2 July she was nearly at the end of her journey, when she and her plane disappeared near Howland Island in the Pacific Ocean.

Yuri Gagarin RUSSIAN (1934 – 1968)

The first man in space

His early years

Yuri was born on a farm and his family was very poor. As a teenager in World War II, he saw his first plane – a Russian fighter jet. At that moment, he knew that he wanted to be a pilot. He studied hard so that he could join a flying club. His teachers thought he was a natural pilot and told him to join the Russian Air Force.

What he did

He became an excellent pilot. And he was now a husband and father. But when the first Russian satellite went into space, he wanted to become an astronaut. After two years of secret training, the doctors chose Yuri because he was the best in all the tests. On 12 April 1961, when he was 27, he finally went into space. It was very dangerous, because the doctors didn't know if Yuri could survive the journey. When he came back to Earth he was famous, and he travelled around the world to talk about his experiences.

His last flight

He wanted to go into space again, so in 1967 he began training for the next space flight. He was also a test pilot for new Air Force aeroplanes. But the next year he died when his fighter jet crashed on a test flight. He was only 34.

VOCABULARY AND LISTENING
Words that go together

Verbs and nouns

1 Match a verb in **A** with a noun in **B**. Sometimes there is more than one answer.

A	B
become	television
drink	a sandwich
drive	a bike
eat	a pilot
break	a car
cook	a meal
play	a lot of money
watch	the guitar
win	Spanish
speak	a record
ride	a cup of tea
earn	a medal

Ask and answer questions.

> Do you drink tea in the morning?
>> No, I don't. I drink coffee.

> When did you last eat a sandwich?
>> This morning. / Yesterday. / Last week.

Prepositions

2 Fill the gaps with the correct preposition.

1 I like listening ____to____ music.
2 I went _____ the beach _____ my friends.
3 We went to Spain _____ holiday last year.
4 She travelled _____ the world.
5 I get up _____ 11 o'clock _____ Sundays.
6 My father works _____ an office _____ the town centre.
7 Our town has a lot _____ tourists _____ summer.
8 My parents are _____ home _____ the moment.
9 What's _____ television this evening?
10 I wrote an email _____ my daughter.

Compound nouns

3 Match a noun in **A** with a noun in **B**. Do we write one word or two?

post office   homework

A	B
orange	paper
railway	room
swimming	pool
hand	juice
boy	park
news	star
film	card
birthday	station
washing	machine
living	friend
car	bag

T 7.10 Listen, check, and repeat.

4 Test the other students!

> This is where we can go swimming.
>> A swimming pool!

> I buy this every day and read it.
>> A newspaper.

5 **T 7.11** Listen to four conversations. What are they about? Which compound nouns do you hear?

1 _____ _____
2 _____ _____
3 _____ _____
4 _____ _____

Look at the tapescript on p130. Practise the four conversations with a partner.

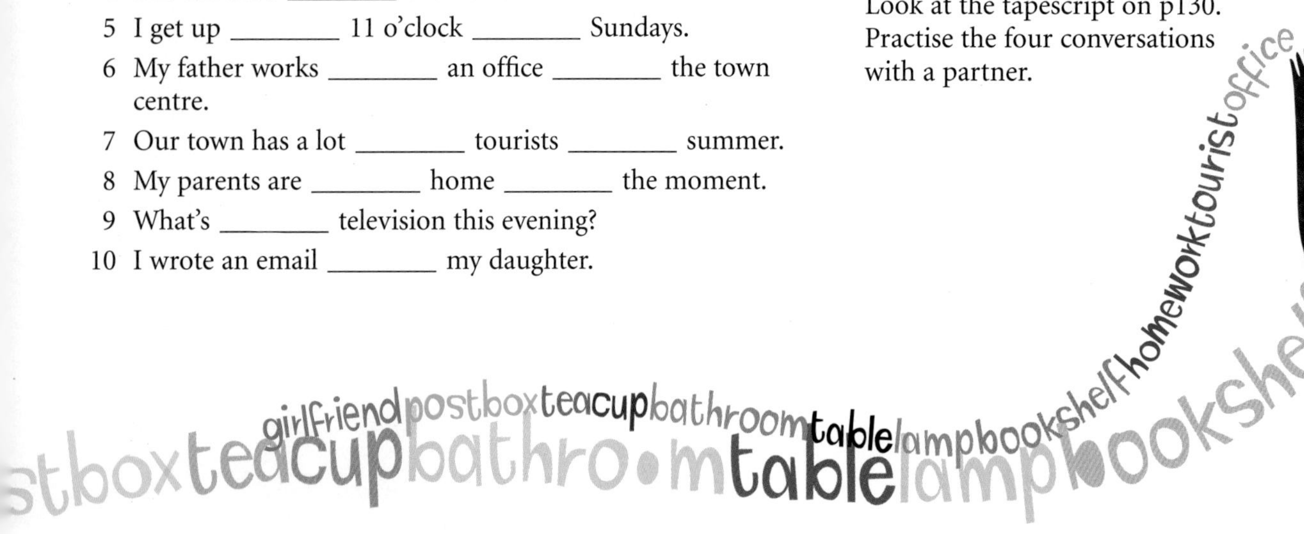

EVERYDAY ENGLISH
What's the date?

1 Write the correct word below the numbers.

> fourth   twelfth   sixth   twentieth   second   thirtieth
> thirteenth   thirty-first   fifth   seventeenth   tenth
> sixteenth   first   third   twenty-first

T 7.12 Listen and practise saying the ordinals.

2 Ask and answer questions with a partner about the months of the year.

> Which is the first month?
>
> January.

> ❗ We write: 3/4/1999 or 3 April 1999
>
> We say: 'The third of April, nineteen ninety-nine.'
> or: 'April the third, nineteen ninety-nine.'
>
> Notice how we say these years:
>
> 1900   'nineteen hundred'
> 1905   'nineteen oh five'
> 2001   'two thousand and one'
> 2012   'two thousand and twelve', or 'twenty twelve'

3 Practise saying these dates.

1 April   19 November   19/12/83
2 March   23 June   3/10/99
17 September 29/2/76   31/5/2000
                              15/7/2007

T 7.13 Listen and check.

4 **T 7.14** Listen and write the dates you hear.

5 Ask and answer the questions with your partner.

1 What's the date today?
2 When did this school course start? When does it end?
3 When's Christmas Day?
4 When's Valentine's Day?
5 When's Mother's Day this year?
6 When's your birthday?
7 What century is it now?
8 What are the dates of public holidays in your country?

8 A date to remember

Past Simple 2 – negatives – *ago* · Spelling and silent letters · Special occasions

STARTER

What is the Past Simple of these verbs? Most of them are irregular.

eat   drink   drive   fly   listen to   make   ride   take   watch   wear

FAMOUS INVENTIONS
Past Simple negatives – *ago*

1 Match the verbs from the Starter with the photos.

2 Work in groups. What year was it a hundred years ago? Ask and answer questions about the things in the photos. What did people do? What didn't they do?

> Did people drive cars a hundred years ago?
>
> Yes, I think they did.
>
> I'm not so sure.
>
> No, they didn't.

3 Tell the class the things you think people did and didn't do.

> We think people drove cars, but they didn't watch TV.

Getting information

4 When were the things in the photos invented? Ask and answer with a partner.

Student A Go to p149.
Student B Go to p150.

> **A** When were cars invented?
> **B** In … .
> **A** That's … years ago.

1 television

2 Coca-Cola

3 phone calls

4 cars

5	records
6	hamburgers
7	photographs
8	planes
9	bikes
10	jeans

BLUE BELL WRANGLERS
are a family affair!

BLUE
BELL

Qualitag

GRAMMAR SPOT

1 Write the Past Simple forms.

Present Simple	Past Simple
I live in London.	I lived in London.
He lives in London.	
Do you live in London?	
Does she live in London?	
I don't live in London.	
He doesn't live in London.	

2 Complete these sentences.

The year 2000 was _____ years ago.

The year 1984 was _____ years ago.

▶▶ **Grammar Reference 8.1 and 8.2 p142**

PRACTICE

Time expressions

1 Make correct time expressions.

in
on
at

___ seven o'clock	___ the morning
___ Saturday	___ Sunday evening
___ night	___ September
___ 2002	___ weekends
___ summer	___ the nineteenth century

2 Work with a partner. Ask and answer questions with *When … ?* Use a time expression and *ago* in the answer.

When did you get up?

At seven o'clock, three hours ago.

When did this term start?

In September, two months ago.

When did . . . ?

- you get up
- you have breakfast
- you arrive at school
- you start learning English
- you start at this school
- this term start
- you last use a computer
- you learn to ride a bicycle
- your parents get married
- you last have a coffee break

3 Tell the class about your day so far. Begin like this.

I got up at seven o'clock and had breakfast. I left the house at ...

PRACTICE

Three inventions

1 Look at the texts. What are the three inventions?

2 **T 8.1** The dates in the texts are *all* incorrect. Read and listen, and correct the dates.

> Daguerre didn't start his experiments in the 1920s He started them in the 1820s.

3 Make these sentences negative. Then give the correct answers.

1 Daguerre invented the bicycle.
   He didn't invent the bicycle.
   He invented the photograph.

2 Daguerre gave his idea to the French government.

3 Mary Anderson lived in New York City.

4 All cars had windscreen wipers by 1916.

5 Leonardo da Vinci made the first bicycle.

6 Kirkpatrick Macmillan came from France.

T 8.2 Listen and check. Practise the stress and intonation.

4 Work with a partner. Make more incorrect sentences about the texts.
Give them to a partner to correct.

Did you know that?

5 **T 8.3** Read and listen to the conversations. Then listen and repeat.

A Did you know that Marco Polo brought spaghetti back from China?
B Really? He didn't! That's incredible!
A Well, it's true!

C Did you know that Napoleon was afraid of cats?
D He wasn't! I don't believe it!
C Well, it's true!

6 Work with a partner.
Student A Go to p149.
Student B Go to p151.
Make similar conversations.

The photograph
LOUIS DAGUERRE FROM FRANCE

Louis Daguerre was a painter for the French opera. But he wanted to make a new type of picture. He started his experiments in the 1920s. Twelve years later he invented the photograph. He sold his idea to the French government in 1935 and the government gave it to the world. Daguerre called the first photographs 'daguerreotypes'. They became popular very fast. By 1940, there were 70 daguerreotype studios in New York City.

The windscreen wiper
MARY ANDERSON FROM THE USA

Mary Anderson often visited New York City by car. In winter she noticed that when it rained or snowed, drivers got out of their cars all the time to clean their windows. In 1893 she began designing something to clean the windows from inside the car. People, especially men, laughed at her idea. But they didn't laugh for long. She invented the windscreen wiper in 1925. And by 1960 all American cars had them.

The bicycle
KIRKPATRICK MACMILLAN FROM SCOTLAND

Long ago in 1540, Leonardo da Vinci drew a design for the modern bicycle. But the first person to make a bicycle was Kirkpatrick Macmillan in 1789. He lived in Scotland, so people didn't hear about his invention for a long time. Twenty years later, another bicycle came from France. In 1825 the bike became cheap and everyone could have one. Now people, especially women, could travel to the next town. It helped them find someone to marry!

LISTENING AND SPEAKING
How did you two meet?

1 Put the sentences in the correct order. There is more than one answer!

- ☐ They got married.
- ☐ They went out for a year.
- ☐ They fell in love.
- ☐ They had two children.
- ☑ Jack and Jill met at a party.
- ☐ They got engaged.
- ☐ They got divorced.

2 Look at the photos of two couples and read the introductions to their stories. What do you think happened next?

3 **T 8.4** Listen to them talking. Were your ideas correct?

4 Answer the questions about Carly and Ned, and Eric and Lori.

1. When did both couples meet?
2. What did Carly think of Ned?
3. What did Ned's girlfriend think of Carly? Why?
4. Where did Eric and Lori's mothers meet?
5. Why didn't Eric and Lori want to meet?
6. What did Eric and Lori think when they met?
7. Do both couples have children?

5 Who said these sentences? What was it about? Write **C**, **N**, **E**, or **L** in the boxes.

a. ☐ I cried and cried.
b. ☐ Our story is easy. We didn't do anything.
c. ☐ It was a big mistake.
d. ☐ I just thought, 'No way.'
e. ☐ … all the old feelings came back.
f. ☐ I took my sister with me.
g. ☐ That was three years ago. Now I'm twenty-four, we're married …
h. ☐ … our wedding is in the fall*.

* **fall** (American English) = autumn (British English)

Speaking

6 Imagine you are one of the people. Tell the story of how you met your husband/wife.

7 Look at these questions. Tell a partner about you and your family.

1. Are you married or do you have a girlfriend/boyfriend? How did you meet?
2. When did your parents or grandparents meet? Where? How?

▶▶ **SONG** *I just called to say I love you*
Teacher's Book **p144**

▶▶ **WRITING** About a friend **p119**

Ned
Michelle
Carly

My very first love

Many people never forget the first person they fall in love with. Carly was 10 years old when she fell in love with sixteen-year-old Ned, but …

Eric
Lori

Do mothers know best?

Parents usually want their children to meet a nice person and get married. Eric's mom wanted to help him meet someone, so …

VOCABULARY AND PRONUNCIATION
Spelling and silent letters

1 There are many silent letters in English words. Practise saying these words.

> know /nəʊ/
>
> talk /tɔːk/
>
> girl /gɜːl/
>
> thought /θɔːt/

Cross out the silent letters in these words.

1	walk	7	work
2	listen	8	hour
3	autumn	9	flight
4	write	10	could
5	eight	11	wrong
6	island	12	daughter

T 8.5 Listen and check. Practise saying the words.

2 Look at the phonetic spelling of these words from exercise 1. Write the words.

1 /wɜːk/   **work**
2 /kʊd/   _____
3 /'lɪsən/   _____
4 /'ɔːtəm/   _____
5 /raɪt/   _____
6 /'aɪlənd/   _____

3 Write the words. They all have silent letters.

1 /bɔːn/   _____
2 /bɔːt/   _____
3 /wɜːld/   _____
4 /'ɑːnsə/   _____
5 /'kʌbəd/   _____
6 /'krɪsməs/   _____

T 8.6 Listen and practise saying the words.

4 Read these sentences aloud.

1 He bought his daughter eight white horses for Christmas.
2 I know you know the answer.
3 They walked and talked for hours and hours on the island.
4 Listen and answer the questions.
5 The girl took the wrong flight.
6 The world is lovely in autumn.

T 8.7 Listen and check.

▶▶ **Phonetic symbols** *p159*

EVERYDAY ENGLISH
Special occasions

1 Look at the list of days. Which are special? Match the special days with the pictures.

birthday	yesterday	Easter Day
Mother's Day	Hallowe'en	New Year's Eve
today	Monday	Valentine's Day
weekend	Thanksgiving	Friday
wedding day	tomorrow	Christmas Day

2 Which days do you celebrate in your country? What do you do?

- make a cake
- give cards and presents
- have a meal
- go out with friends

- wear special clothes
- watch fireworks
- have a party
- give flowers or chocolates

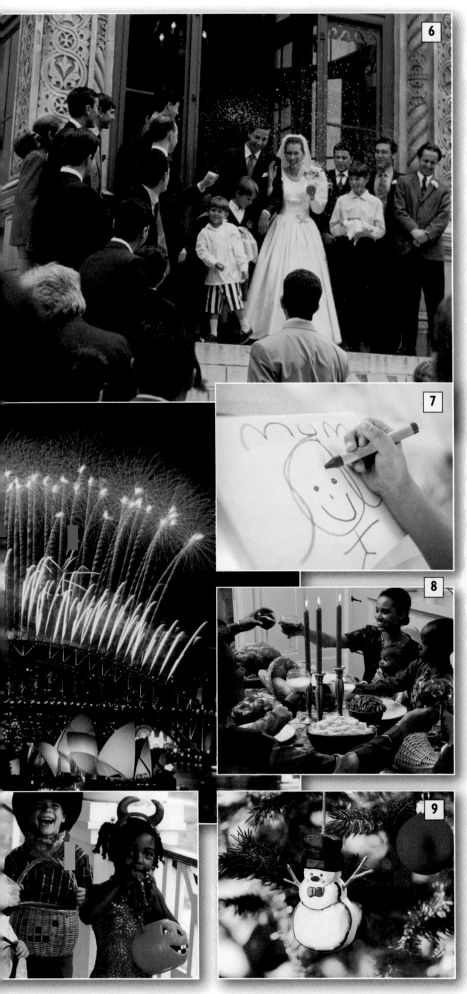

3 Complete the conversations. What are the occasions?

1 Happy _____ to you.
   Happy _____ to you.
   Happy _____, dear Grandma,
   Happy _____ to you.

2 **A** Did you get any _____ cards?
   B Yes, I did. Listen to this.
      Roses are red. Violets are blue.
      You are my _____
      And I love you.
   A Wow! Do you know who it's from?
   B No idea!

3 **A** Wake up, Mummy! Happy _____!
   B Thank you, darling. Oh, what beautiful flowers, and a cup of tea!
   A And I made you a card! Look!
   B It's lovely. What a clever boy!

4 **A** Congratulations!
   B Thank you very much!
   A When's the big day?
   B Pardon?
   A When's your _____ day?
   B The 26th June. Didn't you get your invitation?

5 **A** It's midnight! Happy _____ everybody!
   B Happy _____!
   C Happy _____!

6 **A** Thank goodness! It's Friday!
   B Yeah. Have a nice _____!
   A Same to you.

7 **A** Ugh! Work again. I hate Monday mornings!
   B Me too. Did you have a good _____?
   A Yes, I did. It was great.

T 8.8 Listen and check.

Music of English ♫♪

Work with a partner. Choose a conversation from exercise 3. Learn it by heart. Pay attention to stress and intonation. Act it to the class.

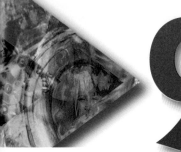

9 Food you like!

Count and uncount nouns · I like/I'd like · some/any · much/many · Food · Polite requests

STARTER

What's your favourite · fruit? · vegetable? · drink?

Write your answers. Compare them with a partner, then with the class.

FOOD AND DRINK
Count and uncount nouns

1 Match the food and drink with the photos. Which list has plural nouns, **A** or **B**?

A		
p ✓ apple juice		pizza
tea		pasta
coffee		cheese
milk		fish
beer		chocolate

B			
apples		peas	
oranges		tomatoes	
bananas		hamburgers	
strawberries		chips	
carrots		biscuits	

2 **T 9.1** Listen to Daisy and Piers talking about what they like and don't like. Tick (✓) the food and drink that Daisy likes. What doesn't Piers like?

3 Who says these things? Write **D** or **P**.

- ☐ I **don't like** coffee **at all**.
- ☐ I **like** orange juice but I **don't like** oranges.
- ☐ I **don't like** fruit **very much at all**.
- ☐ I **quite like** bananas.
- ☐ I **like** all fruit.
- ☐ I **like** vegetables, **especially** carrots and peas.

4 Talk about the lists of food and drink with a partner. What do you like? What do you quite like? What don't you like?

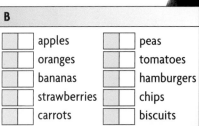

GRAMMAR SPOT

1 Look at the pairs of sentences. What is the difference?

Chocolate **is** delicious.　│　Strawberries **are** delicious.
Apple juice **is** good for you.　│　Apples **are** good for you.

2 Can we count apple juice? Can we count apples?

▶▶ **Grammar Reference 9.1 p143**

I like ... and I'd like ...

1 **T 9.2** Read and listen to the conversation between Piers and Daisy's mum.

M Hello, Piers. Would you like some tea or coffee?
P I'd like a cold drink, if that's OK.
M Of course. Would you like some orange juice?
P Yes, please. I'd love some.
M And would you like a chocolate biscuit?
P Oh, yes, please! Thank you very much.
M You're welcome.

2 Practise the conversation in exercise 1 with a partner. Then have similar conversations about other food and drink.

> Would you like some tea?

> No, thanks. I don't like tea very much.

GRAMMAR SPOT

1 Look at the sentences. What is the difference?

| **Do** you **like** tea? | **Would** you **like** some tea? |
| I **like** biscuits. | I'**d like** a biscuit. (I'd = I would) |

Which sentences mean *Do you want/I want ...*?

2 Look at these sentences.
   I'd like **some** bananas. (plural noun)
   I'd like **some** mineral water. (uncount noun)

We use *some* with both plural and uncount nouns.

3 Look at these questions.

| Would you like **some** chips? | | Are there **any** chips? |
| Can I have **some** tea? | **But** | Is there **any** tea? |

We use *some* not *any* when we request and offer things.
We use *any* not *some* in other questions and negatives.

▶▶ **Grammar Reference 9.2 and 9.3 p143**

PRACTICE

Questions and answers

1 Choose *Would/Do you like ... ?* or *I/I'd like ...* .

   1 *Would/Do* you like a ham sandwich?
     No, thanks. I'm not hungry.

   2 *Do/Would* you like Ella?
     Yes. She's very nice.

   3 *Do/Would* you like a cold drink?
     Yes, cola, please.

   4 Can I help you?
     Yes. *I/I'd* like some stamps, please.

   5 What sports do you do?
     Well, *I'd/I* like swimming very much.

   6 Excuse me, are you ready to order?
     Yes. *I/I'd* like a steak, please.

   T 9.3 Listen and check. Practise with a partner.

2 **T 9.4** Listen and choose the correct answers.

   1 ☐ I like all sorts of fruit.
     ☐ Yes. I'd like some fruit, please.

   2 ☐ I'd like a book by John Grisham.
     ☐ I like books by John Grisham.

   3 ☐ I'd like a new bike.
     ☐ I like riding my bike.

   4 ☐ I'd like a cat but not a dog.
     ☐ I like cats, but I don't like dogs.

   5 ☐ I like Italian wine, especially red wine.
     ☐ We'd like a bottle of Italian red wine.

   6 ☐ No, thanks. I don't like ice-cream.
     ☐ I'd like some ice-cream, please.

   T 9.5 Listen and check. Practise with a partner.

a or some?

3 Write *a*, *an*, or *some*.

1	_a_	strawberry
2	_some_	fruit
3	_____	banana
4	_____	bread
5	_____	milk
6	_____	meat
7	_____	apple
8	_____	toast
9	_____	money
10	_____	dollar
11	_____	notebook
12	_____	homework

4 Write *a*, *an*, or *some*.

1 _____ egg   2 _____ eggs

3 _____ biscuit   4 _____ biscuits

5 _____ (cup of) coffee   6 _____ coffee

7 _____ ice-cream   8 _____ ice-cream

AT THE MARKET
some/any, much/many

1 What can you see at the market? Talk about the photo. Use *some/any* and *not much/not many*.

> There's some cheese.

> There aren't many cakes.

> There isn't much bread.

> There aren't any potatoes.

GRAMMAR SPOT

1 We use *many* with count nouns in questions and negatives.
   How many cake**s** are there?   There **aren't many** cake**s**.

2 We use *much* with uncount nouns in questions and negatives.
   How much bread is there?   There **isn't much** bread.

▶▶ **Grammar Reference 9.4 p143**

2 Read the shopping list. Ask and answer questions about what there is in the market.

Things to buy

bread
eggs
milk
butter
apples
biscuits
potatoes
carrots
strawberries
tomatoes
apple juice
cakes
cheddar cheese
tea

> Is there any bread?

> Yes, there is some.

> How much is there?

> There isn't much.

> Is there any milk?

> No, there isn't.

> Are there any apples?

> Yes, there are.

> How many are there?

> A lot.

3 **T 9.6** Piers and his mum are at the market. Listen and tick (✓) the things they buy from the list above. What don't they buy?

4 Look at the tapescript on p132. Work in groups of three. Practise the conversation.

PRACTICE

much or *many*?

1 Complete the questions using *much* or *many*.

1 How _____ people are there in the room?

2 How _____ petrol is there in the car?

3 How _____ money do you have in your pocket?

4 How _____ eggs are there in the cupboard?

5 How _____ milk is there in the fridge?

6 How _____ apples do you want?

2 Choose an answer for each question in exercise 1.

a A kilo, please.
b There are two bottles.
c There are only two left in the box.
d Just five euros.
e Twenty. Nine men and eleven women.
f It's full.

3 Practise the questions and answers with a partner.

Check it

4 Correct the sentences.

1 How ~~much~~ potatoes do you want? ✗
   How many potatoes do you want?

2 I don't like an ice-cream.
3 Can I have a bread, please?
4 I'm hungry. I like a sandwich.
5 There isn't many milk left.
6 I'd like some fruits, please.
7 How many money do you have?
8 We have lot of homework today.

Roleplay

5 Work with a partner. Make a shopping list each. Buy the things you need in the market. Take turns to be the seller.

Can I help you?

Yes, please. I'd like a/some …

Here you are. Anything else?

Yes. Can I have a/some … ?

How much is that?

That's … , please.

READING AND SPEAKING
Food around the world

1 Which food and drink comes from your country? Which foreign food and drink is popular in your country?

2 Can you identify any places or nationalities in the photos? What food can you see?

3 Read the text. Write the correct question heading for each paragraph.

> **Where does our food come from?**
>
> **What do we eat?**
>
> **How do we eat?**

Find lines in the text that match the photos.

4 Answer the questions.

1 When did human history start? Was it about 10,000 years ago or was it about 1 million years ago?
2 Do they eat much rice in the north of China?
3 Why do the Scandinavians and the Portuguese eat a lot of fish?
4 Where don't people eat much fish?
5 Which countries have many kinds of sausages?
6 How many courses are there in China?
7 How do people eat in the Middle East?
8 Why can we now eat most things at any time of the year?

What do you think?

5 Work in small groups and discuss these questions about your country.

1 What is a typical breakfast?
2 What does your family have for breakfast?
3 Is lunch or dinner the main meal of the day?
4 What is a typical main meal?

Writing

6 Write a paragraph about meals in your country. Use your ideas from exercise 5.

Food around the world

For **99%** of human history, people took their food from the world around them. They ate all that they could find, and then moved on. Then about 10,000 years ago, or for **1%** of human history, people learned to farm the land and control their environment.

The kind of food we eat depends on which part of the world we live in, or which part of our country we live in. For example, in the south of China they eat rice, but in the north they eat noodles. In Scandinavia, they eat a lot of herrings, and the Portuguese love sardines. But in central Europe, away from the sea, people don't eat so much fish, they eat more meat and sausages. In Austria, Germany, and Poland there are hundreds of different kinds of sausages.

In North America, Australia, and Europe there are two or more courses to every meal and people eat with knives and forks. In China there is only one course, all the food is together on the table, and they eat with chopsticks. In parts of India and the Middle East people use their fingers and bread to pick up the food.

Nowadays it is possible to transport food easily from one part of the world to the other. We can eat what we like, when we like, at any time of the year. Bananas come from the Caribbean or Africa; rice comes from India or the USA; strawberries come from Chile or Spain. Food is very big business. But people in poor countries are still hungry, and people in rich countries eat too much.

LISTENING AND SPEAKING
My favourite national food

1 Look at the photos of four national dishes. Which do you like? Match them with the countries.

| Italy   Argentina   England   Austria |

2 Find these things in the photos.

| toast   tomatoes   chilli   onions   egg   bacon   chocolate   beef   sausage |

Bruschetta

Bife de chorizo

Sachertorte

Full English breakfast

3 **T 9.7** Listen to the people. What nationality are they? Match them with their favourite food. What do they say about them?

Anke

Graham

Sergio

Madalena

4 Answer these questions about the people.
1. Who . . . ?
   - travels a lot
   - goes to cafés to eat their favourite food
   - likes sweet things
   - eats their favourite food at home
2. Where is Café Sacher?
3. Who invented *Sachertorte*?
4. When does Graham eat a full English breakfast?
5. How do you make *bruschetta*?
6. Where is Sergio's favourite place to go?
7. How often does Madalena eat beef?
8. Who cooks it for her?

What do you think?

- What are your favourite national foods? When and where do you eat them?
- Describe them to your partner.

EVERYDAY ENGLISH
Polite requests

1 What can you see in the photograph?

2 Match the questions and responses.

1	Would you like some more rice?	Black, no sugar, please.
2	Could you pass the salt, please?	Yes, of course. I'm glad you like it.
3	Could I have a glass of water, please?	Do you want sparkling or still?
4	Does anybody want more wine?	Yes, please. It's delicious.
5	How would you like your coffee?	Yes, of course. Here you are.
6	This is delicious! Can you give me the recipe?	Yes, please. I'd love some.
7	Do you want help with the washing-up?	No, of course not. We have a dishwasher.

T 9.8 Listen and check.

> ❗ We use *Can/Could I . . . ?* to ask for things.
> **Can I** have a glass of water?
> **Could I** have a glass of water?
> We use *Can/Could you . . . ?* to ask other people to do things for us.
> **Can you** give me the recipe?
> **Could you** pass the salt?

Music of English ♪♫

T 9.9 Listen. Notice how the voice goes up at the end of a polite request. Practise the polite intonation.

Could you pass the salt, please?

Could I have a glass of water, please?

Can you give me the recipe?

Can I see the menu, please?

---

3 Complete these requests with *Can/Could I . . . ?* or *Can/Could you . . . ?*

1 _____ have a cheese sandwich, please?
2 _____ tell me the time, please?
3 _____ take me to the station, please?
4 _____ see the menu, please?
5 _____ lend me some money, please?
6 _____ help me with my homework, please?
7 _____ borrow your dictionary, please?

4 Practise the requests with a partner. Give an answer for each request.

> Can I have a cheese sandwich, please?

> Yes, of course. That's £1.75.

T 9.10 Listen and compare your answers.

▶▶ **WRITING** Filling in forms *p120*   Unit 9 · Food you like!   73

10 Bigger and better!

Comparatives and superlatives · *have got* · City and country · Directions 2

STARTER

1 Do you prefer city life or country life? Why? Tell the class.

2 As a class, decide which is the most popular place to live.

> I prefer city life because it's exciting.

> I don't. I prefer country life. It's quiet and relaxing.

CITY LIFE
Comparative adjectives

1 Match an adjective with its opposite. Which adjectives describe city life? Which describe country life?

2 **T 10.1** Listen to Joel and Andy comparing city and country life. Do you agree?

3 **T 10.2** Listen and repeat. Be careful with the sound /ə/.

/ə/   /ə//ə/   /ə/   /ə/   /ə/
The country is slower and safer than the city.

Adjective	Opposite
fast	cheap
modern	slow
expensive	friendly
dangerous	clean
dirty	quiet
unfriendly	old
noisy	safe
exciting	relaxing
busy	boring

4 What do you think? Make sentences comparing city and country life.

The city is   cheaper
The country is   safer
           noisier   than the country.
           dirtier   than the city.
           more expensive
           more exciting

5 Tell the class.

> I think it's safer in the country, but the city's more exciting.

GRAMMAR SPOT

1 Complete these comparatives. What are the rules?

I'm _____ (old) than you.
Your class is _____ (noisy) than my class.
Your car was _____ (expensive) than my car.

2 What are the comparatives of the adjectives in the chart?

3 The comparatives of *good* and *bad* are irregular. What are they?

good _____   bad _____

▶▶ **Grammar Reference 10.1 p144**

PRACTICE

Much more than . . .

1 Write the correct form of the adjectives.

1 A Life in the country is __slower__ __than__ city life. (slow)
   B Yes, the city's much __faster__. (fast)

2 A New York is _____ _____ Los Angeles. (safe)
   B No, it isn't. New York is much _____ _____. (dangerous)

3 A Seoul is _____ _____ Beijing. (big)
   B No, it isn't! It's much _____. (small)

4 A Madrid is _____ _____ _____ Rome. (expensive)
   B No, it isn't. Madrid is much _____. (cheap)

5 A The buildings in Rome are _____ _____ _____ the buildings in Prague. (modern)
   B No, they aren't. They're much _____. (old)

6 A Cafés in London are _____ _____ cafés in Paris. (good)
   B No! Cafés in London are much _____. (bad)

T 10.3 Listen and check. Practise with a partner.

2 Work with a partner. Compare two towns or cities that you both know. Which one do you like better? Why?

COUNTRY LIFE
have got

1 **T 10.4** Close your books. Listen to Andy and Joel's conversation. Who moved to the village of Appleton? Who stayed in London?

2 Complete the conversation with the correct adjectives.

> J So, Andy, tell me, why did you leave London? You had a _____ job.
> A Yes, but I've got a _____ job here.
> J And you had a _____ flat in London.
> A Well, I've got a _____ place here. It's a cottage!
> J Really? How many bedrooms has it got?
> A Three. And it's got a garden. It's _____ than my flat in London and it's _____.
> J But you haven't got any friends!
> A I've got a lot of new friends here. People are much _____ than in London.
> J But the country's so _____.
> A No, it isn't. I've got a surfboard now and I go surfing at weekends. Appleton has got a cinema, restaurants, pubs, and a nightclub. And the air is _____ and the streets are _____.
> J OK. OK. Everything is _____! Can I come next weekend?
> A Of course you can!

3 Practise the conversation with a partner.

GRAMMAR SPOT

1 *Have* and *have got* both express possession. We often use *have got* in spoken British English.

I **have** a dog.	I**'ve got** a dog. (I've = I have)
He **has** a car.	He**'s got** a car. (He's = He has)
Do you **have** a dog?	**Have** you **got** a dog?
Does she **have** a car?	**Has** she **got** a car?
They **don't have** a flat.	They **haven't got** a flat.
It **doesn't have** a garden.	It **hasn't got** a garden.

2 The past of both *have* and *have got* is *had*.

3 Find examples of *have got* and *had* in the conversation.

▶▶ **Grammar Reference 10.2 p144**

PRACTICE

have/have got

1 Write the sentences again, using the correct form of *have got*.

1 London has a lot of parks.
London's got a lot of parks.

2 I don't have much money.
I haven't got much money.

3 I have a lot of homework tonight.

4 Do you have any homework?

5 Our school has a good library, but it doesn't have many computers.

6 My parents have a new DVD player.

7 Does your sister have a boyfriend?

8 I don't have a problem with this exercise.

I've got more than you!

2 Work with a partner. You are both famous film stars. Ask and answer questions to find out who is richer!

Student A
Go to p149.

Student B
Go to p151.

> I've got five boats. How many have you got?

> Twelve. I've got this one, four in the Mediterranean, two in the South Pacific, two in the Caribbean, and three in Asia.

> Well, I've got thirty cars!

> That's nothing! I've got …

PARADISE ISLANDS
Superlative adjectives

1

Coral Club Resort

Barbados, Caribbean Sea
- Built in 1952
- 85 rooms
- $420 to $710 a night
- one bar and restaurant, swimming pool
- 40-minute taxi ride from airport

2

Palm Hotel Resort

Maldives, Indian Ocean
- Built in 1998
- 98 rooms
- $200 to $600 a night
- two bars and two restaurants
- 50-minute boat ride from airport

1 Here are some of the world's most relaxing holiday resorts. Which one do you like best?

2 Correct the false sentences. How many correct sentences (✓) are there? What is the same about them?

1 The Coral Club is cheaper than the Palm Hotel.
2 Bati Island is the most expensive resort.
3 The Coral Club is newer than the Palm Hotel.
4 The Palm Hotel is the newest resort.
5 The Coral Club is bigger than the Palm Hotel.
6 The Palm Hotel is the biggest resort.
7 Bati Island is the smallest resort.
8 The Coral Club has got two restaurants.
9 Bati Island is nearer to the airport than the Palm Hotel.
10 The Coral Club is the nearest to the airport.
11 Bati Island is the furthest from the airport.
12 The Palm Hotel has got a swimming pool.

3 Which is the best hotel in or near your town? What has it got?

PRACTICE

The biggest and best!

1 Complete the conversations using the superlative form of the adjective.

1 That house is very big.
Yes, *it's the biggest house* _____ in the village.

2 The Ritz is a very expensive hotel.
Yes, _____ in London.

3 Appleton is a very pretty village.
Yes, _____ in England.

4 New York is a very cosmopolitan city.
Yes, _____ in the world.

5 Brad Pitt is a very popular film star.
Yes, _____ in America.

6 Miss Smith is a very funny teacher.
Yes, _____ in our school.

7 Anna is a very intelligent student.
Yes, _____ in the class.

8 This is a very easy exercise.
Yes, _____ in the book.

T 10.5 Listen and check.

2 **T 10.6** Close your books. Listen to the first lines in exercise 1 and give the answers.

Talking about your class

3 How well do you know the other students in your class? Describe them using these adjectives and others.

> tall small old young intelligent funny

> I think Ivan is the tallest in the class. He's taller than Karl.

> Sofia's the youngest.

> I'm the most intelligent!

4 Write the name of your favourite film star. Read it to the class. Compare the people. Which film star is the most popular in your class?

Check it

5 Correct the sentences.

1 Yesterday was more hot than today.
2 She's taller that her brother.
3 I'm the most young in the class.
4 Last week was busyer than this week.
5 He doesn't got any sisters.
6 Do you got any bread?
7 My homework is the worse in the class.
8 This exercise is most difficult in the book.

READING AND SPEAKING
Viva la danza!

1 **T 10.7** Do you know any Latin dances? Listen to three types of Latin dance music – flamenco, tango, and salsa. Which music goes with which city?

Buenos Aires   Havana   Seville

2 Where are these cities? What do you know about them? Each sentence is about one of them. Write **BA**, **H**, or **S**.

1 **BA** It is called 'the Paris of the South'.
2 ☐ It became independent from Spain in 1816.
3 ☐ It is the capital city of Andalucía.
4 ☐ In 1960 Fidel Castro led a socialist revolution.
5 ☐ The Arabs ruled the city from 711 to 1248.
6 ☐ It is one of Europe's largest historical centres.
7 ☐ African slaves came to work in the sugar and tobacco fields.
8 ☐ It was Spain's most important port in Latin America.
9 ☐ More than 4 million European immigrants came to work there.

3 Work in three groups.

Group 1 Read about **Buenos Aires**.
Group 2 Read about **Havana**.
Group 3 Read about **Seville**.

Which sentences in exercise 2 are about your city?

4 Answer the questions about your city.
1 How many people live there?
2 Does it have a river? If yes, what is its name?
3 Why is it a tourist centre?
4 What are some important dates in its history?
5 Which famous people lived there?
6 What kind of music and dance is it famous for?
7 What or who were the influences on its music?
8 Which of these things can you do in the city you read about?
 • buy things in its beautiful shops
 • visit Ernest Hemingway's house
 • see a famous fiesta
 • learn to dance in a club
 • hear music by Piazzolla in his home country
 • visit the Alcazar Palace

5 Find partners from the other two groups. Compare the cities, using your answers.

Viva la danza!

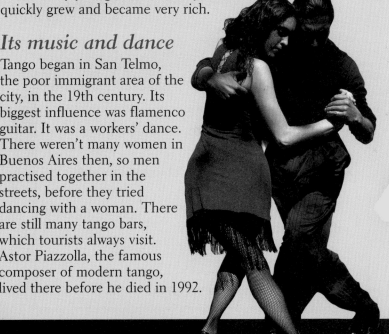

Buenos Aires

Buenos Aires is the capital city of Argentina. It stands on the banks of the River Plate, the world's widest river. It has a population of 3 million, or 10 million, including Gran Buenos Aires. It is called 'the Paris of the South' because of its lovely European buildings. It is also a big commercial centre and visitors love its beautiful shops.

Its history

For a long time, Buenos Aires was a small port in the furthest corner of the Spanish Empire. It became independent from Spain in 1816. Then the British arrived to build railways across Argentina. More than 4 million European immigrants came between 1840 and 1940 to work on the railways. They were mostly young men. The city quickly grew and became very rich.

Its music and dance

Tango began in San Telmo, the poor immigrant area of the city, in the 19th century. Its biggest influence was flamenco guitar. It was a workers' dance. There weren't many women in Buenos Aires then, so men practised together in the streets, before they tried dancing with a woman. There are still many tango bars, which tourists always visit. Astor Piazzolla, the famous composer of modern tango, lived there before he died in 1992.

Havana

Havana is the capital of Cuba, the largest island in the Caribbean. It has a population of 2.2 million. It is one of the oldest cities in Latin America. It is a very cultural city and has lots of beautiful old Spanish buildings. In the 1990s Cuba became the second most popular tourist attraction in the Caribbean .

Its history

In the 16th century, Havana was Spain's most important port and city in Latin America. Later, African slaves came here to work in the country's sugar and tobacco fields. At the beginning of the 19th century, it was one of the richest cities in the West. Ernest Hemingway, the famous US writer, lived there from 1940. In 1960 Fidel Castro led a socialist revolution and became president.

Its music and dance

Havana was the birthplace of many Afro-Cuban dance styles, including salsa. The music was an exciting mixture of Spanish guitar and African drums. Salsa's original name was 'Casino' because of the clubs (casinos) that people danced in. Later, Latin Americans in New York gave it the name 'salsa', meaning 'spice'. Today tourists go to Havana to learn to salsa and to dance in the famous clubs.

Seville

Seville is the capital of Andalucía, and the largest city of Southern Spain, with a population of 750,000. It stands on the banks of the Guadalquivir river. It is one of Europe's largest historical centres with many beautiful old buildings. Tourists also come for its famous fiesta in April.

Its history

The Arabs ruled the city from 711 to 1248. They built the Alcazar Palace and the Giralda tower. In 1503 Seville became the most important port in Spain for ships sailing to South America, and it was a very rich cultural centre. The famous painter Diego Velázquez was born here in 1599. Last century, there were two international exhibitions in Seville in 1929 and 1992.

Its music and dance

Flamenco began in the 17th century as a song and dance with very fast hand clapping. Arabs and gypsies were the biggest influence on flamenco. The guitar music came later. In the 18th century, one of the first flamenco schools began in the famous Triana district in Seville. Visitors can still find real flamenco here in the music cafés, but the music and dancing doesn't start before midnight!

VOCABULARY AND PRONUNCIATION
City and country words

1 Match these words with the pictures. Which things do you usually find only in the country?

wood park museum church cathedral farm bridge car park port factory pub field theatre lake village hill mountain cottage building river	

2 Complete the sentences with a word from exercise 1.

1 Everest is the highest _____ in the world.
2 The Golden Gate _____ in San Francisco is the longest _____ in the USA.
3 The Caspian Sea isn't a sea, it's the largest _____ in the world.
4 Rotterdam is the busiest _____ in Europe. Ships from all over the world stop there.
5 The Empire State _____ in New York was the tallest _____ in the world for over 40 years.
6 A church is much smaller than a _____ .

T 10.8 Listen and check.

3 Write these words from exercise 1.

/wʊd/ _____   /fɑːm/ _____   /'fæktri/ _____
/fiːld/ _____   /'θɪətə/ _____   /'vɪlɪdʒ/ _____
/'kɒtɪdʒ/ _____   /tʃɜːtʃ/ _____   /'bɪldɪŋ/ _____

T 10.9 Listen and repeat.

4 Divide into two groups. Play the game. Which group can continue the longest?

Group 1 A walk in the country
Continue one after the other.

> I went for a walk in the country and I saw a farm.

> I went for a walk in the country and I saw a farm, and some cows.

> I went for ...

Group 2 A walk in the city
Continue one after the other.

> I went for a walk in the city and I saw some shops.

> I went for a walk in the city and I saw some shops, and a cathedral.

> I went for ...

▶▶ **WRITING** Describing a place *p121*

EVERYDAY ENGLISH
Directions 2

1 **T 10.10** Listen to Andy's directions to his cottage. Mark the route on the map. Then complete the directions.

> Leave the A34 at Apple Cross. _____ left at the traffic lights. Then go _____ the hill, and _____ the first bridge. OK? Then go _____ the second bridge, and _____ the road by the river. Go _____ the pub, and _____ right _____ the hill. Go _____ the corner past the farm, and my cottage is _____ _____ right. It's easy!

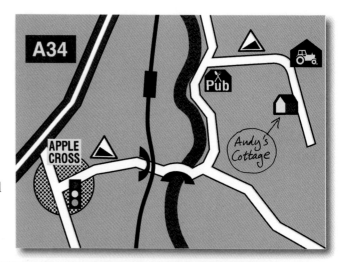

2 **T 10.11** Complete the text with the prepositions. Listen to Joel and Andy's conversation. Check your answers.

along	down	into	round	over	past	through	under	up

Joel drove _____ the hill, _____ the first bridge, and _____ the second bridge.

Then he drove _____ the road by the river, _____ the pub, and _____ the hill.

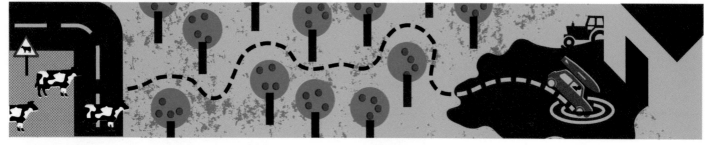

Next he drove _____ the corner, off the road, _____ some apple trees, and _____ a lot of mud!

3 Cover the text. Look at the pictures and tell Joel's story.

4 Work with a partner. **Student A** Think of a place near your school. Give your partner directions, but do not say what the place is.
Student B Listen to the directions. Where are you?

11 Looking good!

Present Continuous · *Whose?* · Clothes · Words that rhyme · In a clothes shop

STARTER

1 Look around the classroom. Can you see any of these clothes?

> a hat   a coat   a jumper   a shirt   a T-shirt   a dress   a skirt   a jacket
> a suit   shorts   trousers   jeans   shoes   boots   trainers

2 What are you wearing?
What is your teacher wearing?
Tell the class.

> I'm wearing blue jeans and a white T-shirt.

> You're wearing a dress.

DESCRIBING PEOPLE
Present Continuous

1 Look at the photos. Describe the people.

Who . . . ?
- is pretty
- is good-looking   • is tall
- is handsome   • isn't very tall

> Poppy's pretty.

Who's got . . . ?

long	
short	
fair	hair
dark		blue	
grey		brown	eyes

> Sofia's got dark hair and brown eyes.

2 What are they doing?

Who . . . ?
- is smiling
- is laughing   • is playing the guitar
- is eating   • is sitting down
- is standing up   • is using a computer
- is drawing   • is painting
- is reading   • is walking

> Ella's smiling.

3 What are they wearing?

> Andy's wearing glasses.

> Simon's wearing a black jacket.

Andy

Alison, Ella, and Alfie

Poppy

GRAMMAR SPOT

1 *Am/is/are* + adjective describes people and things.

She **is** young/tall/pretty.

2 *Am/is/are* + verb + *-ing* describes activities happening *now*. Complete the table.

I	
You	learning English.
He/She	sitting in a classroom.
We	listening to the teacher.
They	

This is the Present Continuous tense. What are the questions and the negatives?

3 What is the difference between these sentences?

He **speaks** Spanish.
He's **speaking** Spanish.

▶▶ **Grammar Reference 11.1 and 11.2 p145**

PRACTICE

Talking about you

1 Write sentences that are true for you at the moment.

1 I/wearing a jacket   *I'm not wearing a jacket, I'm wearing a jumper.*
2 I/wearing jeans
3 I/standing up   6 teacher/writing
4 I/looking out of the window   7 we/working hard
5 it/raining   8 I/chewing gum

Tell a partner about yourself.

2 Work with a partner.
Student A Choose someone in the classroom, but don't say who.
Student B Ask *Yes/No* questions to find out who it is!

Is it a girl?   Yes, it is.
Is she sitting near the window?
No, she isn't.
Has she got fair hair?
No, she hasn't.

3 Look out of the window. What can you see? Buildings? Hills? Fields? Can you see any people? What are they doing? Describe the scene.

Kate and Sofia

Naomi

Dan, John, Clifford, and Albert

Simon

Colin

Who's at the party?

4 **T 11.1** Oliver is at the party, but he doesn't know anyone. Monica is telling him about the other guests. Listen and write the people's names on the picture.

5 Listen again and complete the table.

	Present Continuous	**Present Simple**
Harry	He's sitting down and he's talking to Mandy.	He works in LA.
Mandy		
Fiona		
George		
Roz and Sam		

Getting information

6 Work with a partner.

Student A Look at the picture of a party on p149.
Student B Look at the picture of a party on p151.

Don't show your picture! There are *ten* differences. Talk about the pictures to find them.

> In my picture three people are dancing.
>
> In my picture four people are dancing.
>
> There's a girl with fair hair.
>
> Is she wearing a black dress?

THE HOUSE IS A MESS!
Whose is it?

1 Find these things in the room. Then find them on the people on p85.

> a baseball cap   boots   a baby   a plant   trainers
> a coat   sunglasses   a tie   a bag   a football   a briefcase

2 **T 11.2** Listen to the questions. Complete the answers with *his*, *hers*, or *theirs*.

1 Whose is the baseball cap?   It's _____.
2 Whose are the boots?   They're _____.
3 Whose is the baby?   It's _____.

Practise the questions and answers with a partner. Then ask about the other things in exercise 1.

3 Give something of yours to the teacher. Ask and answer questions about the objects. Use these possessive pronouns.

> mine   yours   his   hers   ours   theirs

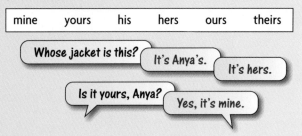

> Whose jacket is this?
>
> It's Anya's.
>
> It's hers.
>
> Is it yours, Anya?
>
> Yes, it's mine.

PRACTICE

who's or whose?

1 Choose the correct word. Compare your answers with a partner.

1 I like *your/yours* house.
2 *Ours/Our* house is smaller than *their / theirs*.
3 And *their/theirs* garden is bigger than *our/ours*, too.
4 *My/Mine* children are older than *her/hers*.
5 *Whose/Who's* talking to *your/yours* sister?
6 This book isn't *my/mine*. Is it *your/yours*?
7 '*Whose/Who's* dictionary is this?' 'It's *his/him*.'
8 '*Whose/Who's* going to the party tonight?' 'I'm not.'
9 '*Whose/Who's* dog is running round *our/ours* garden?'

2 **T 11.3** Listen to the sentences. If the word is **Whose?** shout 1! If the word is **Who's?** shout 2!

Who's on the phone? ⟨ **2** ⟩   **Whose** is it? ⟨ **1** ⟩

What a mess!

3 **T 11.4** Complete the conversation. Listen and check.

A _____ is this tennis racket?
B It's _____.
A What's it doing here?
B I'm _____ tennis this afternoon.

> ❗ The Present Continuous can also describe activities happening in the near future.
>
> I**'m playing** tennis this afternoon.
> We**'re having** pizza for dinner tonight.

4 Make more conversations with a partner.

1 these football boots? / John's / playing football later
2 these ballet shoes? / Mary's / going dancing tonight
3 this suitcase? / mine / going on holiday tomorrow
4 this coat? / Jane's / going for a walk soon
5 this plane ticket? / Jo's / flying to Rome this afternoon
6 all these glasses? / ours / having a party tonight

T 11.5 Listen and check.

Check it

5 Correct the sentences.

1 Alice is tall and she's got long, black hairs.
2 Who's boots are these?
3 I'm wearing a jeans.
4 Look at Roger. He stands next to Jeremy.
5 He's work in a bank. He's the manager.
6 What is drinking Suzie?
7 Whose that man in the garden?
8 Where you going tonight?
9 What you do after school today?

GRAMMAR SPOT

1 Complete the table.

Subject	Object	Adjective	Pronoun
I	me	my	mine
You	you	_____	_____
He	_____	his	_____
She	_____	_____	hers
We	us	our	_____
They	them	_____	_____

2 *Whose . . . ?* asks about possession.

Whose hat is this?
Whose is this hat?   It's my hat. = It's mine.
Whose is it?

3 Careful!

Who's your teacher?   Who's = Who is

▶▶ **Grammar Reference 11.3 p145**

LISTENING AND SPEAKING
Looking for that something

1 What makes you happy? Think of five things that make you happy. Write them down. Compare them with a partner.

2 What makes you happiest? Choose one thing only. Compare with the class.

3 **T 11.6** Close your books and listen to the song.

4 Read the song by an Irish band called *Westlife*.

Can you match these words from the song and their meanings?

joy	to love
to cherish	happiness
to deny	when the sun comes up
solitary	to say no to something
the sunrise	alone, lonely

5 **T 11.6** Look at the words on the right. Choose the correct word to complete the lines. Listen again and check.

What do you think?

- In the song, what does 'flying without wings' mean?
- Did you find any of the things on your list in the song?

Everybody's _____ for that something	**looking / finding**
One thing that makes it all complete	
You find it in the strangest _____	**places / houses**
Places you never knew it could be	
Some find it in the faces of their _____	**parents / children**
Some find it in their lover's _____	**hair / eyes**
Who can deny the joy it brings	
When you find that _____ thing	**special / interesting**
You're flying without wings	
Some find it sharing every _____	**breakfast / morning**
Some in their solitary lives	
You find it in the words of others	
A simple line can make you _____ or cry	**dance / laugh**
You find it in the deepest _____	**friendship / water**
The kind you cherish all your life	
And when you know how _____ that means	**many / much**
You've found that special thing	
You're flying without wings	
So impossible as it may seem	
You've got to _____ for every dream	**fight / sleep**
'Cause who's to _____ which one you let go	**say / know**
Would have made you complete	
Well, for me it's waking up beside _____	**her / you**
To watch the sunrise on your face	
To know that I can say I _____ you	**like / love**
At any given time or place	
It's little things that only I know	
Those are the things that make you _____	**mine / theirs**
And it's like flying without wings	
'Cause you're my special _____	**person / thing**
I'm flying without wings	
You're the place my life _____	**begins / stops**
And you'll be where it ends	
I'm flying without wings	
And that's the joy you _____	**take / bring**
I'm flying without wings	

Flying
without wings

Speaking

6 Read the questionnaire and answer the questions. Stand up. Ask students in the class the questions. Find people with the same answers as yours.

My favourite things

1 What's your favourite food?

_____

2 What's your favourite drink?

_____

3 What's your favourite colour?

_____

4 What are your favourite clothes?

_____

5 What are your favourite shoes?

_____

6 Who's your favourite singer or band?

_____

7 What are your favourite things to do at weekends?

_____

8 Who's your favourite person?

_____

9 Where's your favourite place?

_____

10 Who's your favourite film star or actor?

_____

7 Tell the class which people like the same things as you.

Johann and I both like blue.

Stella and I both like trainers.

▶▶ **WRITING** Describing people *p122*

VOCABULARY AND PRONUNCIATION

Words that rhyme

1 Read these lines. Which words rhyme?

> **A** Who knows whose roses those are?
> **B** Those flowers are ours, thank you.

T 11.7 Listen and check. Practise saying the lines.

2 Match the words that rhyme.

red	kissed
green	dark
hat	mean
short	shoes
park	said
list	that
whose	bought

eyes	beer
those	pay
ours	wear
hair	knows
near	size
grey	flowers

3 Write two of the words on each line according to the sound.

Vowels

1 /e/ ___red___ ___said___
2 /æ/ _____ _____
3 /ɪ/ _____ _____
4 /iː/ _____ _____
5 /ɑː/ _____ _____
6 /uː/ _____ _____
7 /ɔː/ _____ _____

Diphthongs

1 /aɪ/ ___eyes___ _____
2 /ɪə/ _____ _____
3 /eɪ/ _____ _____
4 /eə/ _____ _____
5 /əʊ/ _____ _____
6 /aʊ/ _____ _____

T 11.8 Listen and check.

4 Can you add any more words to the lists? Practise saying them.

> red said bed head ...
> hat that cat ...

▶▶ **Phonetic symbols** *p159*

Tongue twisters

5 **T 11.9** Tongue twisters are sentences that are difficult to say. They are good pronunciation practice. Listen, then try saying these quickly to a partner.

Four fine fresh FISH for you

If a dog chews shoes, whose shoes does he choose?

Six Silly Sisters selling Shiny Shoes

I'm looking back to see if she's looking back to see if I'm looking back to see if she's looking back at me!

6 Choose two tongue twisters and learn them. Say them to the class.

EVERYDAY ENGLISH

In a clothes shop

1 Read the lines of a conversation in a clothes shop. Who says them, the customer or the shop assistant? Write **SA** or **C**.

a ☐ Can I help you? **SA**

b ☐ Oh yes. I like that one much better. Can I try it on? **C**

c ☐ £39.99. How do you want to pay?

d ☐ Yes, please. I'm looking for a shirt to go with my new jeans.

e ☐ Blue.

f ☐ Yes, of course. The changing rooms are over there. … Is the size OK?

g ☐ OK. I'll take the green. How much is it?

h ☐ Can I pay by credit card?

i ☐ What colour are you looking for?

j ☐ No, it isn't the right blue.

k ☐ No, it's a bit too big. Have you got a smaller size?

l ☐ That's the last blue one we've got, I'm afraid. But we've got it in green.

m ☐ Well, what about this one? It's a bit darker blue.

n ☐ What about this one? Do you like this?

o ☐ Credit card's fine. Thank you very much.

2 Can you match any lines with the photos?

Photo 1 SA Can I help you?
        C Yes, please. I'm looking for a shirt to go with my new jeans.

3 Work with a partner and put the all the lines in the correct order.

T 11.10 Listen and check.

Music of English ♪♩

Practise the conversation with your partner. Pay attention to stress and intonation.

---

4 Make more conversations in a clothes shop. Buy some different clothes.

▶▶▶ **SONG** *Wonderful tonight*
Teacher's Book **p149**

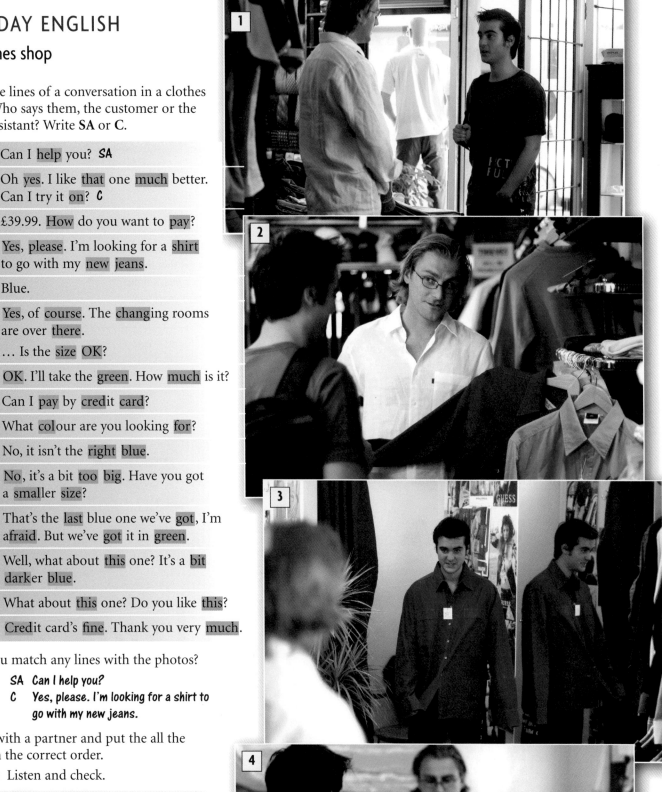

12 Life's an adventure!

going to future · Infinitive of purpose · The weather · Making suggestions

STARTER

1 How many sentences can you make?

2 Make similar true sentences about you. Tell the class.

I'm going to Brazil I went to Brazil	soon. when I was a student. next month. in a year's time. two years ago. when I retire.

FUTURE PLANS

going to

1 Jack and his sports teacher, Danny Carrick, both have plans for the future. Read their future plans. Which do you think are Jack's? Which are Danny's? Write **J** or **D**.

1 [J] I'm going to be a footballer.
2 [ ] I'm going to travel all over the world.
3 [ ] I'm going to train very hard.
4 [ ] I'm going to try new things.
5 [ ] I'm going to play for Manchester United.
6 [ ] I'm not going to marry until I'm very old.
7 [ ] I'm not going to stay at home and watch TV.
8 [ ] I'm going to learn to scuba-dive.
9 [ ] I'm going to write a book.
10 [ ] I'm going to be famous.

When I grow up ...
Jack, age 11

T 12.1 Listen and check. Were you correct?

2 Talk first about Jack, then about Danny. Use the ideas in exercise 1.

> Jack's going to be a footballer.
> He's going to ...
> He isn't going to ...

Which two plans are the same for both of them?

> They're both going to ...

3 **T 12.2** Listen and repeat the questions and answers about Jack.

> Is he going to be a footballer?
> Yes, he is.
> What's he going to do?
> Train very hard.

When I retire...

Danny Carrick, age 58

PRACTICE

Questions about Jack

1 With a partner, make more questions about Jack. Then match them with an answer.

Questions
1 Why/he/train very hard?
2 How long/play football?
3 When/marry?
4 How many children/have?
5 Who/teach to play?

Answers
a Until he's 35.
b Two.
c His sons.
d Not until he's very old – about 25!
e Because he wants to be a footballer.

2 **T 12.3** Listen and check. Practise the questions and answers with your partner.

Questions about you

3 Are you going to do any of these things after the lesson? Ask and answer the questions with a partner.

1 watch TV
2 have a coffee
3 catch a bus
4 eat in a restaurant
5 meet some friends
6 cook a meal
7 go shopping
8 wash your hair
9 do your homework

Are you going to watch TV?

Yes, I am./ No, I'm not.

4 Tell the class some of the things you and your partner *are* or are *not* going to do.

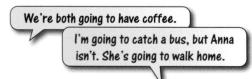

We're both going to have coffee.

I'm going to catch a bus, but Anna isn't. She's going to walk home.

GRAMMAR SPOT

1 The verb *to be* + *going to* expresses future plans. Complete the table.

I		
You		
He/She		going to leave tomorrow.
We		
They		

What are the questions and the negatives?

2 Is there much difference between these two sentences?
   I'm **leaving** tomorrow.   I'm **going to** leave tomorrow.

▶▶ **Grammar Reference 12.1 p146**

I'm going to sneeze!

> ! We also use *going to* when we can see *now* that something is sure to happen soon.

5 What is going to happen? Use these verbs.

| have   sneeze   win   jump   be late   kiss   rain   fall |

1 It _____

2 I _____

3 She _____

4 He _____

5 You _____

6 They _____

7 They _____ a baby.

8 He _____

6 Put a sentence from exercise 5 into each gap.

1 Take an umbrella. _____ .
2 Look at the time! _____ for the meeting.
3 Anna's running very fast. _____ the race.
4 Look! Jack's on the wall! _____ .
5 Look at that man! _____ .
6 _____ . It's due next month.
7 There's my sister and her boyfriend! _____ .
8 'Oh dear. _____ . Aaattishooo!' 'Bless you!'

T 12.4 Listen and check.

I WANT TO SEE THE WORLD!
Infinitive of purpose

1 Match the places and activities. Can you find them in the photos?

Nepal	fly over the Grand Canyon
Brazil	climb Mount Everest
The Great Barrier Reef	take photographs of the lions
China	walk along the Great Wall
Hawaii	go scuba-diving
Alaska	visit the rainforest
the USA	watch whales
Kenya	go surfing

2 Danny Carrick is going to visit all the countries in exercise 1. He is telling his friend, Harold, about his plans. Read their conversation and complete the last sentence.

Danny   First I'm going to Nepal.
Harold   Why?
Danny   To climb Mount Everest!
Harold   Oh my goodness! Where are you going after that?
Danny   Well, then I'm going to Kenya to …

T 12.5 Listen and check. Practise the conversation with a partner.

3 Would you like to try any of these activities?

GRAMMAR SPOT

1 With the verbs *to go* and *to come*, we usually use the Present Continuous for future plans.

> I**'m going** to Nepal tomorrow.
> ✗ I'm going to go to Nepal soon.

> She**'s coming** this evening.
> ✗ She's going to come this evening.

2 Do these sentences mean the same?

> I'm going to Nepal **to climb Mount Everest**.
> I'm going to Nepal **because I want to climb Mount Everest**.

The infinitive can tell us *why* something happens.

> I'm going to America **to learn English**.

▶▶ **Grammar Reference 12.2 p146**

PRACTICE

Roleplay

1 Work with a partner. **Student A** is Harold, **Student B** is Danny. Ask and answer questions about the places.

> **Harold** Why are you going to Nepal?
> **Danny** To climb Mount Everest!
> **Harold** Oh my goodness!

2 Talk about Danny Carrick's journey. Use *first*, *then*, *next*, *after that*.

> First he's going to Nepal to climb Mount Everest.
> Then he's ...

Why . . . ? and *When . . . ?*

3 Write down the names of some places you went to in the past. Ask and answer questions about the places with a partner.

> Why did you go to England? — To learn English.
> When did you go? — Two years ago.

> Why did you go to Switzerland? — To visit my cousins.
> When did you go? — Last year.

Tell the class about your partner.

4 Use your imagination! Write down the names of some places you are going to in the *future* and do the same.

> Why are you going to Paris? — To go shopping.
> When are you going? — In two weeks' time.

Check it

5 Tick (✓) the correct sentence.

1. ☐ Is going to rain.
   ☐ It's going to rain.
2. ☐ Do you wash your hair this evening?
   ☐ Are you going to wash your hair this evening?
3. ☐ She's going to have a baby.
   ☐ She's going to has a baby.
4. ☐ I'm going to the post office to buy some stamps.
   ☐ I'm going to the post office for buy some stamps.
5. ☐ I'm going home early this evening.
   ☐ I'm go home early this evening.
6. ☐ I opened the window to get some fresh air.
   ☐ I opened the window for to get some fresh air.

READING AND SPEAKING
Born free

1 Which of these sports do you think is the most dangerous? Put them in order 1–6. 1 is the *most* dangerous. Compare your ideas with a partner and then the class.

- ☐ skiing
- ☐ football
- ☐ mountain-climbing
- ☐ windsurfing
- ☐ golf
- ☐ scuba-diving

2 Match a verb with a noun or phrase.

jump	a medal
join	over a wall
win	underwater
swim	a record
break	oxygen
breathe	a class

3 Look at the photos of Tanya Streeter and David Belle. Do you know what the sport is? Work in two groups.

Group A Read about Tanya.
Group B Read about David.

Answer the questions about your person.
Check your answers with your group.

1 Where did he/she grow up?
2 What did he/she like doing as a child?
3 How did he/she become interested in the sport?
4 How does he/she feel when he/she does the sport?
5 How dangerous is the sport?
6 Does he/she teach the sport?
7 What did he/she do last year?
8 What are his/her future plans?

4 Work with a partner from the other group. Compare Tanya and David, using your answers.

Speaking

5 **Group A** Make questions to ask David.

1 Why/like the countryside?
2 What/like doing at school?
3 What sport/invent?
4 What/do in Lisses?
5 What/do next?

Group B Make questions to ask Tanya.

1 What/like doing as a child?
2 When/join a diving class?
3 How long/can/swim underwater?
4 What record/break?
5 What/do next?

6 Work with a partner from the other group. Interview each other.

Free-diving

As a child, **Tanya Streeter** always loved swimming in the sea – she grew up in the Cayman Islands in the Caribbean. She could always dive the deepest for seashells. But she didn't know then that she could dive deeper than anyone else in the world.

Tanya discovered her diving abilities in 1997, when she joined a class in free-diving. Free-diving is a new sport. It's very dangerous, because you dive with no oxygen. There were only men in the class and no-one wanted to dive with her because she was a girl. But her class was surprised when they saw how long she could swim underwater. Her teachers immediately wanted to train her. A few months later, Tanya started breaking records. She can swim underwater for nearly six minutes with just one breath! Last year she broke the world free-diving record. She dived 121 metres with one breath.

She says: 'At the bottom of the sea I'm calm. I love the peace and quiet down there. Coming up again is very difficult. You can't think about the pain!

I'm not planning to break any more records for a while. I'm going to wait and see if anyone breaks my last record! In the future I'm going to teach free-diving and work for sea-life conservation.'

Free-running

David Belle grew up in the countryside, and he always loved the feeling of freedom there. He liked running, jumping, and climbing trees in the woods when he was a child. At the age of nine, he and his family went to live in Lisses, a town outside Paris. But he continued to jump and climb there. He loved doing gymnastics at school.

As a teenager in 1989, David invented the sport of *Le Parkour* or 'free-running'. The idea of *Le Parkour* is to find new and often dangerous ways to travel across the town. The runners or 'traceurs' work in groups. They run and jump over walls, roofs and buildings – everything! They try to move like cats. David and his friend Sebastian spent ten years in Lisses practising their moves and jumps and teaching other people. Last year they were on television for the first time. David says that *Le Parkour* is an art and a philosophy, not a sport. They are not trying to win medals. They just want to learn new moves and do them well. They like to feel free.

David says: 'We do it because we need to move. We are going to take our art to the world and show people how to move. And we are going to go where no human ever went before.'

VOCABULARY AND SPEAKING
The weather

1 Match the words and symbols.

| sunny | rainy | windy | snowy | cloudy | foggy |

1 FOG **2** ❄ **3** 🌬 **4** ☁💧 **5** ☀ **6** ☁

Which symbols can the following adjectives go with?

| hot | warm | cold | cool | wet | dry |

2 **T 12.6** Listen and complete the answers.

A What's the weather like today?
B It's _____ and it's very _____ .
A What was it like yesterday?
B Oh, it was _____ and _____ .
A What's it going to be like tomorrow?
B I think it's going to be _____ .

> **!** The question *What . . . like?* asks for a description.
> *What's the weather like?* = Tell me about the weather.

Practise the questions and answers. Ask and answer about the weather where *you* are today, yesterday, and tomorrow.

3 Work with a partner. Find out about the weather round the world yesterday.

Student A Look at the information on this page.
Student B Go to p151.

Ask and answer questions to complete the information.

WORLD WEATHER
NOON YESTERDAY

		°C
Athens	S	18
Berlin	R	7
Bombay		
Edinburgh	C	5
Geneva		
Hong Kong	S	29
Lisbon		
London	R	10
Los Angeles		
Luxor	S	40
Milan		
Moscow	Sn	-1
Oslo		

S = sunny
C = cloudy
Fg = foggy
R = rainy
Sn = snowy

> **What was the weather like in Athens?**
>
> **It was sunny and warm. 18 degrees.**

4 Which city was the hottest? Which was the coldest? Which month do you think it is?

EVERYDAY ENGLISH
Making suggestions

1 Make a list of things you can do in good weather and things you can do in bad weather. Compare your list with a partner.

Good weather	Bad weather
go to the beach	watch TV

2 **T 12.7** Read and listen to the beginning of two conversations. Complete **B**'s suggestions.

1 **A** It's a lovely day! What shall we do?
B Let's _____!

2 **A** It's raining again! What shall we do?
B Let's _____ and _____.

> **!** **1** We use *shall* to ask for and make suggestions.
> What **shall** we do?
> **Shall** we go swimming? = I suggest that we go swimming.
>
> **2** We use *Let's* to make a suggestion for everyone.
> **Let's** go! = I suggest that we all go. (Let's = Let us)
> **Let's** have a pizza!

3 Continue the two conversations in exercise 2 with these lines. Put them in the correct order a–c.

		Well, let's go swimming.
		OK. Which film do you want to see?
1	a	Oh no! It's too hot to play tennis.
		Oh no! We watched a DVD last night.
		OK. I'll get my swimming costume.
		Well, let's go to the cinema.

T 12.8 Listen and check.

> **Music *of* English** ♫
>
> Practise the two conversations with your partner. Pay attention to stress and intonation.

4 Have more conversations suggesting what to do when the weather is good or bad. Use your lists of activities in exercise 1 to help you.

▶▶ **WRITING** Writing a postcard *p123*

13 Storytime

Question forms · Adjectives and adverbs · Describing feelings · At the chemist's

1 Match a question word with an answer.

2 Look at the answers. What do you think the story is?

When . . . ?	Six.
Where . . . ?	1991.
What . . . ?	Paris.
Who . . . ?	Because I love him.
Why . . . ?	John.
Which . . . ?	Some roses.
How . . . ?	€50.
How much . . . ?	The red ones.
How many . . . ?	By plane.

A QUIZ
Question words

1 Look at the pictures. Which stories do you know?

2 Work in groups and answer the questions in the quiz.

3 **T 13.1** Listen and check your answers. Listen carefully to the intonation of the questions.

4 In groups, answer these questions.

1 Which of the stories in the quiz do you like best?

2 When you were a child, did you read a lot? Did your parents tell you stories? Which stories did you like best?

3 Are there any famous stories from your country or culture?

STORYTIME

1 When did Shakespeare die? In the ...
a 15th century   b 17th century   c 19th century

2 What happens at the end of *Romeo and Juliet*?

3 How many dwarfs are there in *Snow White*?
a 4   b 7   c 11

4 How much money do Hansel and Gretel's parents have?
a a lot   b not much   c none

5 How long does Sleeping Beauty sleep?

6 Who does Cinderella marry?
a the handsome Prince
b the King
c Aladdin

7 Who created Mickey Mouse?

1 <u>Underline</u> all the question words in the quiz. **When**

Pronunciation

2 **T 13.2** Listen to the two questions. Notice the difference in intonation. Practise saying them.

'Where do you live?' 'In London.'

'Do you live in London?' 'Yes, I do.'

3 Make *two* similar questions for each of these statements. What are the short answers?

1 She's wearing jeans. (what)
2 She works in the bank. (where)
3 He's leaving tomorrow. (when)
4 I visited my aunt. (who)
5 We came by taxi. (how)
6 They're going to have a party. (why)

4 **T 13.3** Listen and check.

▶▶ **Grammar Reference 13.1 p146**

QUIZ

8 Where did Hans Christian Andersen come from?
   a Russia   b Denmark   c Poland

9 What nationality are Don Quixote and Sancho Panza?

10 Whose lamp is magic?
   a Aladdin's   b Dracula's   c Harry Potter's

11 Why does Pinocchio's nose grow long?

12 What kind of animal is Walt Disney's Dumbo?
   a an elephant   b a dog   c a horse

13 Which city does Sherlock Holmes live in?
   a New York   b London   c Paris

14 How old is Harry Potter in the first story *Harry Potter and the Philosopher's Stone*?
   a 8   b 11   c 17

PRACTICE

Questions and answers

1 Look at the question words in **A** and the answers in **C**. Choose the correct question from **B**.

A	B	C
Where		To the shops.
When		This morning.
Who	did you buy?	A friend from work.
How	did you go?	We drove.
Whose car	did you go with?	Joe's.
Why	did you go in?	To buy some new clothes.
What	did you pay?	A new jacket.
How many		Only one.
Which one		The black leather one.
How much		£180.99.

T 13.4 Listen and check.

Listening and pronunciation

2 **T 13.5** Tick (✓) the sentence you hear.

1 ☐ Where do you want to go?
  ☐ Why do you want to go?

2 ☐ How is she?
  ☐ Who is she?

3 ☐ Where's he staying?
  ☐ Where's she staying?

4 ☐ Why did they come?
  ☐ Why didn't they come?

5 ☐ How old was she?
  ☐ How old is she?

6 ☐ Does he play the guitar?
  ☐ Did he play the guitar?

7 ☐ Where did you go at the weekend?
  ☐ Where do you go at the weekend?

Asking about you

3 Put the words in the correct order to make questions.

1 like learning do English you?
2 do you night what did last?
3 languages mother many does how your speak?
4 last go you shopping did when?
5 football which you do team support?
6 come car today school by you to did?
7 much do homework have you how?
8 usually who sit you do next class in to?
9 English want learn to you do why?

4 Work with a partner. Ask and answer the questions.

DO IT CAREFULLY!
Adjectives and adverbs

1 Are the words in *italics* adjectives or adverbs?

1 Smoking is a *bad* habit.
The team played *badly* and lost the match.

2 Please listen *carefully*.
Jane's a *careful* driver.

3 The homework was *easy*.
Peter's very good at tennis. He won the game *easily*.

4 I know the Prime Minister *well*.
My husband's a *good* cook.

5 It's a *hard* life.
Teachers work *hard* and don't earn much money.

GRAMMAR SPOT

1 Look at these sentences.
Lunch is a **quick** meal for many people.
(*quick* = adjective. It describes a noun.)
I ate my lunch **quickly**.
(*quickly* = adverb. It describes a verb.)

2 How do we make regular adverbs? What happens when the adjective ends in *-y*?

3 There are two irregular adverbs in exercise 1. Find them.

▶▶ **Grammar Reference 13.2 p146**

---

2 Match the verbs and phrases with an adverb. Usually more than one answer is possible. Which are the irregular adverbs?

get up
walk
work
run
speak
speak English
pass the exam
do your homework

slowly
quietly
early
fluently
carefully
easily
hard
fast/quickly

PRACTICE
Order of adjectives/adverbs

1 Put the adjective in brackets in the correct place in the sentence. Where necessary, change the adjective to an adverb.

1 We had a holiday in Spain, but unfortunately we had weather. (terrible)
2 Maria dances. (good)
3 When I saw the accident, I phoned the police. (immediate)
4 Don't worry. Justin is a driver. (careful)
5 Jean-Pierre is a Frenchman. He loves food, wine, and rugby. (typical)
6 Please speak. I can't understand you. (slow)
7 We had a test today. (easy)
8 We all passed. (easy)
9 You speak English. (good)

Telling a story

2 Complete these sentences in a suitable way.

1 It started to rain. **Fortunately** …
2 Ali invited me to his party. **Unfortunately** …
3 I was fast asleep when **suddenly** …
4 I saw a man with a gun outside the bank. **Immediately** …

3 **T 13.6** Listen to a man describing what happened to him in the middle of the night. Number the adverbs in the order you hear them.

Noises in the night

☐ quickly
☐ quietly
☐ slowly
☐ immediately
☐ carefully
☐ suddenly
☐ fortunately
☐ really

4 Work with a partner and tell the story again. Use the order of the adverbs to help you.

Check it

5 Correct the mistake in each sentence.

1 Where does live Anna's sister?
2 The children came into the classroom noisyly.
3 What means *comb*?
4 I always work hardly.
5 Do you can help me, please?
6 When is going Peter on holiday?
7 You did this exercise good.

VOCABULARY
Describing feelings

1 Match the feelings to the pictures.

bored	tired	worried	excited	annoyed	interested

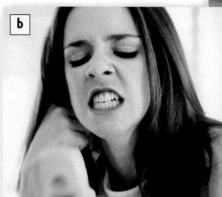
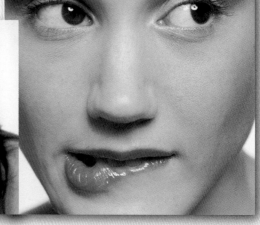
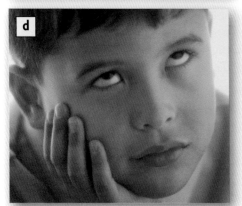

2 Match the feelings and reasons to make sentences.

	Feelings		Reasons
I am	bored tired worried excited annoyed interested	because	I'm going on holiday tomorrow. we have a good teacher. I worked very hard today. I can't find my keys. I have nothing to do. I want to go to the party but I can't.

> **!** Some adjectives can end in both *-ed* and *-ing*.
> The book was **interesting**.
> I was **interested** in the book.
> The lesson was **boring**.
> The students were **bored**.

3 Complete each sentence with the correct adjective.

1. | excited
   | exciting

   Life in New York is very …
   The football fans were very …

2. | tired
   | tiring

   The marathon runners were very …
   That game of tennis was very …

3. | annoyed
   | annoying

   The child's behaviour was really …
   The teacher was … when nobody did the homework.

4. | worried
   | worrying

   The news is very …
   Everybody was very … when they heard the news.

4 Answer your teacher's questions using adjectives from exercises 1 and 2.

Did you like doing exercise 2?

No, we didn't. It was very boring!

How did you feel?

Very bored!

READING AND LISTENING

A short story

1 Do you give presents at Christmas? What are some of the best/worst presents you have given or received?

2 Work with a partner. Look at the pictures. Where and when does the story take place? Who do you think the people are?

3 **T 13.7** Read and listen to part one of the story.

4 Answer the questions.

1 Where does Della live?
2 Is she married?
3 What's her job?
4 What time of year is it?
5 What does she want to do for Jim?
6 Why do you think she is going into town? What is she going to do?
7 Which of these adjectives best describe Della? Why?

> happy   sad   tired   tiring   worried
> worrying   bored   careful   annoying
> excited   angry

5 **T 13.8** Read and listen to part two.

6 Answer the questions.

1 Where did Della go? What did she do? Did you guess correctly?
2 How much money does she have for Jim's present?
3 What does she buy for him? Why?
4 What does she think of her hair now?
5 What does Jim think of her hair? What do you think the problem is?
6 What adjectives best describe Della in part two of the story? Why?

> happy   sad   tired   tiring   worried
> worrying   bored   careful   annoying
> excited   angry   surprised

7 How do you think the story is going to end? Discuss your ideas with the class.

Read part three on p104 and check your ideas.

The Christmas Presents

Part One

One dollar and eighty-seven cents. That was all. Della carefully counted the money again. There was no mistake. Every day, when she went to the shops, she didn't spend much money. She bought the cheapest meat and the cheapest vegetables. It was very tiring – she walked for hours around the shops to find the cheapest food. She saved every cent possible. Only one dollar and eighty-seven cents. The next day was Christmas, and she couldn't do anything about it. So she sat there in her little room and cried quietly.

Della lived in this poor little room in New York with her husband, James Dillingham Young. James (Jim to his friends) was lucky because he had a job, but it wasn't a good job. Times were bad and there was no work for Della. But when Jim came home, she immediately put her arms around him. And that was good.

Della wanted to buy Jim a Christmas present – something really good to show how much she loved him. Suddenly she ran to the mirror and looked at her beautiful long hair. Then she put on her old brown hat and coat and quickly went into town.

Part Two

She stopped when she came to a door with 'Madame Eloise – Hair' on it. Inside was a small fat woman. 'Do you buy hair?' Della asked.

'I buy hair,' Madame answered. 'Take your hat off, then, and show me your hair.'

Madame slowly touched the hair with her hand. 'Twenty dollars,' she said.

'Quick! Cut it off! Give me the money!' Della said.

The next two hours went quickly. Della was happy, because she was at the shops with money for a present for Jim. At last she found him the perfect present. Jim had one special thing. He had a beautiful gold watch that once belonged to his father, and before that to his grandfather. Jim loved his watch, but it had no chain. When Della saw the gold watch chain, she knew immediately that it was right for Jim. It cost twenty-one dollars.

Della ran home excitedly with the eighty-seven cents. When she arrived, she looked at her very short hair in the mirror. 'Oh dear. I look like a schoolboy! What is Jim going to say when he sees me?'

At seven o'clock Jim came in. His eyes were on Della. She could not understand the look on his face. He was not angry or surprised. He just looked at her sadly. Della ran to him.

'Jim, don't look at me like that! I sold my hair because I wanted to give you a present.'

'You sold your hair?' he said quietly.

'Yes. I told you. But don't worry. It grows so fast. But don't you love me any more, Jim?'

Part Three

Suddenly Jim put his arms around Della. 'I love you, Della. It doesn't matter if your hair is long or short. But open this. Then you can see why I was unhappy at first.'

Della opened the present excitedly. Then she gave a little scream of happiness. But a second later there was a cry of unhappiness. There were the combs – for her beautiful hair. When she first saw these lovely, expensive combs in the shop window, she wanted them. And now they were hers. But she no longer had her hair! Della held them in her hand and her eyes were full of love.

Then Della remembered. She ran to get Jim's present. 'Isn't it lovely, Jim? Give me your beautiful watch, and let's see it with its new chain!'

But Jim sat down and smiled.

'Della, you see, I sold the watch to buy your combs.'

And this was the story of two young people who were very much in love.

Adapted from a short story by O. Henry

8 **T 13.9** Read and listen to part three.

9 Answer the questions.

1 What did Jim think of Della's hair? What was his problem? Did you guess correctly?

2 Does Della like her present?

3 What's the problem with Della's present for Jim?

4 Which of these do you think is the moral of the story?

You don't need to spend a lot of money on a nice present.

Thinking carefully about a present is important.

The best present of all is love.

Language work

10 Put some adjectives and adverbs from the story into the correct box.

Adjectives	Adverbs

11 Write questions about the story using these question words. Ask and answer the questions across the class.

| ~~when~~   how much   what |
| why   where   how |

When did the story take place?

A long time ago, at Christmas.

▶▶ **WRITING** Writing a story **p124**

EVERYDAY ENGLISH
At the chemist's

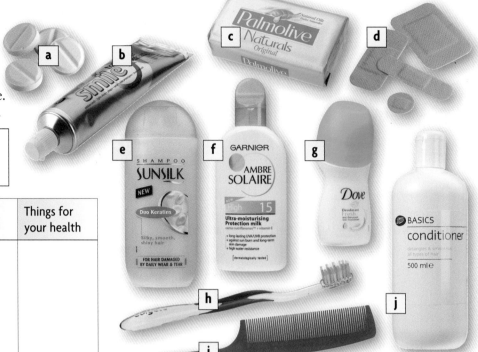

1 Match a word in the box with a picture.
Write the words in the correct column.

> a comb   suncream   aspirin   shampoo
> deodorant   plasters   a toothbrush
> conditioner   soap   toothpaste

Things for your hair	Things for your teeth	Things for your skin	Things for your health

2 **T 13.10** Listen and complete the conversation at the chemist's.

A Hello. Can I help you?

B Yes, please. I'm not (1)_____ very well.
I'm (2)_____ for some aspirin. (3)_____
can I find them?

A Right here. What (4)_____ do you want?
Small or (5)_____ ?

B Large, please. And I (6)_____ _____
some shampoo, as well.

A What (7)_____ of shampoo? For dry hair?
Normal hair?

B Um … for dry hair, please.

A There's Sunsilk or Palmolive. (8)_____ one
do you want?

B Sunsilk's fine, thanks.

A (9) _____ else?

B No, that's all. (10)_____ _____ is that?

A Four pounds twenty.

B (11)_____ you are.

A Ten pounds. Thank you. And here's five pounds
eighty (12)_____ .

B Thanks. Bye.

A Bye-bye. Thank you very much.

Music of English ♪♫

T 13.10 Listen again. Practise the conversation with a partner, paying particular attention to
stress and intonation.

3 With your partner, make more conversations in the chemist's. Use the words in exercise 1.

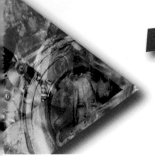

14 Have you ever?

Present Perfect + *ever, never, yet,* and *just* • At the airport

1 Match the countries and flags.

| Australia Brazil France |
| Germany Great Britain |
| Italy Japan Canada |
| Spain the USA |

1   2   3   4   5

6   7   8   9   10

2 Tick (✓) the countries that you have visited.

IN MY LIFE
Present Perfect + *ever* and *never*

1 **T 14.1** Listen to Steve and Ryan's conversation. What are they talking about? Who's Tara?

2 **T 14.2** Read and listen to Ryan's answers. Then listen and repeat.

> I've been to Paris. (I've = I have)
> I haven't been to Barcelona.
> I've been to Italy.
> I've never been to Venice.
> She's been to Mexico. (She's = She has)
> She hasn't been anywhere in Europe!

Work in groups. Look at the flags. Tell each other which countries you have or haven't been to. Have you been to any other countries?

3 **T 14.3** Read and listen to Tara and Steve's conversation. Practise with a partner.

> **T** Have you ever been to Barcelona?
> **S** No, I haven't.
> **T** Have you ever been to Paris?
> **S** Yes, I have.
> **T** When did you go?
> **S** Two years ago.
> **T** Did you like it?
> **S** Yes, it was beautiful.

4 Write down the names of four cities in your country or another country that you have been to. Have similar conversations with your partner.

5 Tell the class about your partner.

> Maria's been to Berlin.   (Maria's = Maria has)
>
> She went there two years ago.
>
> But she hasn't been to Paris. /
> She's never been to Paris.   (She's = She has)

Unit 14 · Have you ever? 107

GRAMMAR SPOT

1 We use the Present Perfect to talk about experiences at some time in our lives.

> **Have** you **ever** (at any time in your life) **been** to Paris?

2 We use the Past Simple to say exactly *when* something happened.

> **When** did you go to Paris?
>
> I **went** there | two years ago.
> | in 1998.

3 We make the Present Perfect tense with *has/have* + the past participle. Complete the table.

	Positive	Negative	
I You We They			been to Paris.
He She It			

4 Write *ever* and *never* in the right place in these sentences.

> Has he _____ been to Barcelona?
> He's _____ been to Barcelona.

▶▶ **Grammar Reference 14.1 p147**

PRACTICE

Past participles

1 Here are the past participles of some verbs. Write the infinitive.

eaten	_eat_	made	_____	given	_____
seen	_____	taken	_____	won	_____
met	_____	ridden	_____	had	_____
drunk	_____	cooked	_____	stayed	_____
flown	_____	bought	_____	done	_____

2 Which are the two regular verbs?

3 What are the Past Simple forms of the verbs?

4 Look at the list of irregular verbs on p158 and check your answers.

What has Ryan done?

1 **T 14.4** • Listen to Ryan talking about his life and tick (✓) the things he has done.

- ☐ lived in a foreign country
- ☐ worked for a big company
- ☐ stayed in an expensive hotel
- ☐ flown in a jumbo jet
- ☐ cooked a meal for a lot of people
- ☐ met a famous person
- ☐ seen a play by Shakespeare
- ☐ ridden a motorbike
- ☐ been to hospital
- ☐ won a competition

2 Tell your teacher about Ryan and answer your teacher's questions.

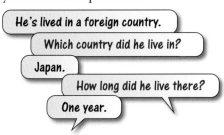

> He's lived in a foreign country.
> Which country did he live in?
> Japan.
> How long did he live there?
> One year.

3 Ask your teacher the questions from exercise 1.

> Have you ever lived in a foreign country?
> Which country did you live in?

4 Ask a partner the questions. Tell the class about your partner.

A HONEYMOON IN VENICE
Present Perfect + *yet* and *just*

1 Ryan and Tara are on honeymoon in Venice. Before they went, they made a list of things they wanted to do there. Read the list below.

> ### VENICE
>
> Things to do ...
> - have a coffee in St Mark's Square
> - climb up the Bell Tower
> - see the paintings in the Doge's Palace
> - go on a gondola
> - have a boat ride along the Grand Canal
> - walk across the Rialto Bridge
> - visit the glass factories on Murano Island
> - go to the beach at the Lido

2 **T 14.5** Tara is phoning her sister Amy back home in the USA. Listen to their conversation. Tick (✓) the things in the list she and Ryan have done.

GRAMMAR SPOT

1 Complete the sentences.
  1 Have you _____ on a gondola **yet**?
  2 We _____ climbed up the Bell Tower **yet**.
  3 We've **just** _____ a boat ride along the Grand Canal.

2 Where do we put *yet* in a sentence? Where do we put *just* in a sentence?

3 We can only use *yet* with **two** of the following. Which two?
  ☐ Positive sentences
  ☐ Questions
  ☐ Negative sentences

▶▶ **Grammar Reference 14.2 p147**

---

3 With a partner, talk about what Ryan and Tara have done and haven't done yet.

> They've had a coffee in St Mark's Square.
> They haven't climbed up the Bell Tower yet.

T 14.5 Listen again and check.

Venice

PRACTICE

I've just done it

1 Work with a partner. Make questions with *yet* and answers with *just*.

> **Have you done the washing-up yet?**
>> **Yes, I've just done it.**

1 do the washing-up
2 do the shopping
3 wash your hair
4 clean the car
5 make the dinner
6 meet the new student
7 check your email
8 give your homework to the teacher
9 finish the exercise

Check it

2 Tick (✓) the correct sentence.

1 ☐ I saw Ryan yesterday.
　☐ I've seen Ryan yesterday.

2 ☐ Did you ever eat Chinese food?
　☐ Have you ever eaten Chinese food?

3 ☐ Tara won £5,000 last month.
　☐ Tara has won £5,000 last month.

4 ☐ I've never drank champagne.
　☐ I've never drunk champagne.

5 ☐ Steve has ever been to America.
　☐ Steve has never been to America.

6 ☐ Has your sister yet had the baby?
　☐ Has your sister had the baby yet?

7 ☐ I haven't done my homework yet.
　☐ I've done my homework yet.

8 ☐ Did she just bought a new car?
　☐ Has she just bought a new car?

READING AND SPEAKING
We've never learnt to drive!

1 Work with a partner. Ask and answer the questions. Compare answers with the class.

Have you ever ...?	Never	Once or more When? Where? Who with?
... walked a long way		
... cycled a long way		
... ridden a motorbike		
... hitch-hiked/ thumbed a lift		
... ridden a horse		
... ridden in a horse and cart		

2 These words are in the texts. Translate them.

> a gun   a hearse   a locust   a tornado

3 Look at the pictures and read the introductions. What have Tudor Bowen-Jones and Josie Dew *never* learnt to do? How do they travel?

4 Work in two groups.

Group A Read about Tudor.
Group B Read about Josie.

5 Answer the questions.

1 Does he/she have a job?
2 When did he/she start travelling?
3 Which year did he/she go abroad for the first time?
4 Does he/she always travel alone?
5 How many countries has he/she been to?
6 Has he/she been to Egypt?
7 Has he/she been to the USA?
8 Has he/she ever been frightened? What happened?
9 Tell your partner three more interesting things that have happened to him/her.
10 What is he/she going to do next?

6 Find a partner from the other group. Compare Tudor and Josie, using your answers.

What do you think?

- Would you like to travel like Tudor or Josie? Why/Why not?
- Do people cycle a lot or hitch-hike in your country? Why/Why not?
- What's your favourite way to travel? Why?

Tudor Bowen-Jones is going to spend his 90th birthday doing what he loves best – hitch-hiking.

Tudor, a retired teacher from South Wales, has spent 60 years hitch-hiking all over the world. He is now on his seventh passport, and wants to be in Vienna for his birthday. Tudor's first journey abroad was to France and Belgium in 1947. Now he likes to make two or three journeys a year. But he has never learnt to drive.

Tudor says: 'I started hitch-hiking round Britain in the 1940s when I didn't have any money. It was the only way to travel. I've been to 40 countries, and I think it's an excellent way to visit places and meet people. People are usually very surprised when I tell them what I am doing!'

His journeys have taken him across Europe, the Middle East, and America, and he has taken all kinds of interesting lifts. He has hitched-hiked with a horse and cart in Hungary, ridden a motorbike across Spain, sat in the back of a hearse in France, and enjoyed the comfort of a Rolls-Royce in Germany. The longest he has waited for a lift is twelve hours.

He has been to the Pyramids in Egypt, where the driver took out a gun. Tudor was frightened, but the driver cleaned the gun and put it back again! Tudor says that hitch-hiking is not dangerous, if you are careful.

He has made friends all over Europe. They come and visit him in his little home in Wales. 'I'm always going to hitch-hike,' Tudor says.

When Josie Dew was young, she fell out of a car, so she has never learnt to drive.

She was still at primary school when she decided she wanted to travel. So when she was eleven, she decided to go for long bike rides, and cycled 40 or 50 miles every day.

Josie says: 'The only good thing about secondary school was cycling there and back. I left when I was 16. I love cooking, so I started a business. I cooked three-course meals, and delivered them by bike! In 1985, as soon as I had some money, I cycled to Africa and back.'

Josie has been to 40 countries and has had all kinds of interesting experiences. She has cycled through the Himalayan mountains in Nepal, then down into India. She has cycled through millions of locusts in the Moroccan desert. She has travelled through tornados in the USA. She was in Romania on Christmas Day in 1989 when President Ceaușescu was executed by the Government. And she hasn't been to Egypt yet, because when she was in Turkey, a war started nearby. So she went to Greece instead.

She has sometimes travelled with friends, boyfriends and even her mother, but she has often cycled alone. She had only one really frightening experience – a man attacked her in Bulgaria.

In 1997 she hurt her knee very badly, so she started writing books about her journeys. She's written five books, and now she's on her bike again! At the moment she's planning to cycle around New Zealand.

LISTENING AND VOCABULARY
All around the world

1 **T 14.6** Close your books and listen to a song by Lisa Stansfield. What is the song about? Who is her 'baby'? What does *gonna* mean?

2 Match the words in **bold** with their meanings. Use a dictionary, if necessary.

We had a **quarrel**.	He was really angry.
He **gave** a **reason**.	We disagreed/fought.
He was **so mad**.	He explained it.
I **lied** to him.	I did nothing with my time.
I **wasted time**.	I didn't tell him the truth.

3 **T 14.6** Read the words of the song. Can you complete any of the lines? Listen to the song again and write the words you hear.

What do you think?

• Make a list of your favourite English songs.
• Compare your list with a partner.

All around the world

Chorus

I've _____ around the world and I
I can't _____ my baby
I don't know when, I don't know _____
Why he's _____ away
And I don't know _____ he can be, my baby
But I'm gonna find _____

We had a quarrel and I let myself go
I said so _____ things, things he didn't know
And I was oh so _____
And I don't think he's _____ back

He gave the reason, the reasons he should _____
And he said so many things he's never said _____
And he was oh so mad
And I don't _____ he's coming, coming back
I did too much lying, wasted too _____ time
Now I'm _____ crying.

Chorus

So open-hearted, he never did me _____
I was the one, the weakest one of _____
And now I'm oh so _____
And I don't _____ he's coming back, coming back
I did too much lying, wasted too much time
Now I'm _____ crying.

Chorus

I've _____ around the world _____ for my baby
_____ around the world and I'm gonna
I'm gonna find _____

EVERYDAY ENGLISH
At the airport

1 What do you do at an airport? Read the sentences and put them in the correct order.

- [ ] You wait in the departure lounge.
- [ ] You board the plane.
- [ ] You get a trolley for your luggage.
- [1] You arrive at the airport.
- [ ] You check in your luggage and get a boarding pass.
- [ ] You go through passport control.
- [ ] You check the departures board for your gate number.

2 **T 14.7** Listen to the airport announcements and complete the chart.

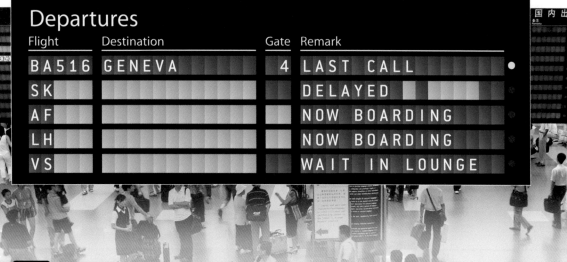

Departures			
Flight	Destination	Gate	Remark
BA516	GENEVA	4	LAST CALL
SK			DELAYED
AF			NOW BOARDING
LH			NOW BOARDING
VS			WAIT IN LOUNGE

3 **T 14.8** Listen to the conversations. Who are the people? What are they doing?

- meeting people
- checking in luggage
- waiting in the departure lounge
- saying goodbye

4 Complete each conversation with the correct question.

> When can we see each other again?
> Did you have a good honeymoon?
> Did the announcement say gate 4 or 14?
> Have you got much hand luggage?

1
A Listen! . . . BA 516 to Geneva. That's our flight.
B _____?
A I couldn't hear. I think it said 4.
B Look! There it is on the departure board. It *is* gate 4.
A OK. Come on! Let's go.

2
A Can I have your ticket, please?
B Yes, of course.
A Thank you. How many suitcases have you got?
B Just one.
A And _____?
B Just this bag.
A That's fine.
B Oh . . . can I have a seat next to the window?
A Yes, that's OK. Here's your boarding pass. Have a nice flight!

3
A Ryan! Tara! Over here!
B Hi! Amy! Great to see you!
A It's great to see you too. You look terrific! _____?
B Fantastic. Everything was fantastic.
A Well, you haven't missed anything here. Nothing much has happened at all!

4
A There's my flight. It's time to go.
B Oh no! It's been a wonderful two weeks. I can't believe it's over.
A I know. _____?
B Soon, I hope. I'll email every day.
A I'll phone too. Goodbye, my darling. Give my love to your family.
B Goodbye, Lukas.

T 14.8 Listen again and check.

▶▶ **WRITING** Writing an email – Saying thank you **p125**

▶▶ **SONG** *Summertime* Teacher's Book **p153**

Music *of* English ♫♪

Work with a partner. Choose a conversation from exercise 4. Learn it by heart. Pay attention to stress and intonation. Act it to the class.

Writing

UNIT 3 NATURAL WRITING Using pronouns

1 <u>Underline</u> the pronouns and possessive adjectives in these sentences.

1 <u>She</u> likes <u>my</u> brother and he likes her.
2 Our mother works hard. Her job is interesting.
3 We listen to our teachers. They help us.

2 Complete the table.

Subject pronouns	Object pronouns	Possessive adjectives
I	me	my
	you	
he	him	his
	her	
it	it	its
we	us	
	them	their

3 Complete the sentences with the correct pronoun.

1 My sister has a new car, but <u>she</u> doesn't drive <u>it</u>.
2 Luc has two sons. _____ plays football with _____ in his free time.
3 That's my dictionary. Can I have _____ back, please?
4 Irma's new teacher is Mr Banks. _____ likes _____ a lot.
5 Rosa and I are good students. _____ like our teacher Estella and she likes _____.
6 Our teacher gives _____ a lot of homework.
7 Kate knows Joanna, but Maria doesn't know _____ at all.
8 Mike buys a newspaper every day. _____ reads _____ on the train.
9 Look! This is a photo of _____ with my family.
10 Sally lives near Paul and Sue. _____ goes to work with _____ every day in their car.

> **!** Subject pronouns come *before* the verb.
> **He** knows them. **I** love him. **She** wants it.
>
> Object pronouns come *after* the verb.
> He knows **them**. I love **him**. She wants **it**.

4 Read about István's family.
Who is István? Who is in the photo?

5 The text is not very natural. Which nouns can you replace with pronouns or possessive adjectives? Underline them.

István's family

István Kis is Hungarian, but István lives in the USA because István is married to an American. István is a music professor. István likes his job because his job is interesting, and István loves playing in concerts. István travels around the world to play, but István's wife, Stacey, doesn't go with István because Stacey doesn't like travelling.

István and Stacey have a nine-year-old daughter. István and Stacey's daughter's name is Mary-Jane. Mary-Jane goes to school, and Mary-Jane also plays the piano every day. Mary-Jane wants to be a pianist, too, and travel with Mary-Jane's father. Stacey doesn't want to go with István and Mary-Jane. When István and Mary-Jane travel round the world, Stacey says she wants a dog!

6 Work with a partner and rewrite the text to make it more natural. Begin like this.

István Kis is Hungarian, but he lives in the USA ...

1 Do you have friends from different countries? Who? Where from? Talk to a partner.

2 Read Becky's letter to her penfriend, Tiago.
- Where is she?
- Where is he?
- What does Becky write about?

20 Holland Street,
Brighton BN2 2WB

5 April

We begin all letters
with *Dear …*

Dear Tiago,

Thank you for your address in Brazil! My name's Becky
and I'm nineteen years old. I'm a language student at
Brighton University. I live in a house near the centre of
Brighton with my mother and father, my brother James,
and my Polish friend Danka.

I speak French, Spanish and a little German, but I
don't speak Portuguese. Sorry! My favourite subject at
university is Spanish, but I don't like German.

I like listening to music and swimming. At weekends
I go out with my friends. Sometimes we go to the
cinema and sometimes we go to a café or a nightclub.

What about you? What do you do in Brazil? Please write to me.

We end letters to a
friend with *Best wishes.*
We use *Love* if we know
the person very well.

Best wishes,

Becky

3 Read the letter again.
- How does it begin and end?
- What is the date?
- What is Becky's address?
- What is the postcode?
- Do you write addresses in the same way?

4 Write a similar letter to a penfriend about you.

Tiago Costa
Rua Bellavista 118
Fortaleza
Brazil

UNIT 5 DESCRIBING WHERE YOU LIVE Linking words – *and, so, but, because*

1 Join **A, B** and **C** to make sentences.

A	B	C
I like New York	and so but because	I don't like Los Angeles. it's an exciting city. I go there a lot. I like Chicago.

2 Write similar sentences about where you live.
Start *I like/don't like* (your town)…

3 Complete the sentences with *and, so, but,* or *because*.

1 In my bedroom there's a television __and__ a DVD player.
2 We live on the top floor, _____ we don't have a garden.
3 I like living here _____ it's near the shops.
4 I like Mexican food, _____ my husband doesn't like it.
5 We both like sailing, _____ we live near the sea.
6 London is expensive, _____ I like it.

4 Read about Suzie's new flat. Complete the text with one of the linking words in exercise 1.

Where I live

I live in a new flat near the centre of Oxford. It's very small (1)_____ it's lovely! There's a sunny living room, a kitchen, a bedroom (2)_____ a bathroom. The living room has a big window (3)_____ a nice comfortable sofa in front of it. There isn't a very big garden, (4)_____ there is a park at the end of the road, (5)_____ in summer I often go there to read or sunbathe.

I live alone with my cat, Marmalade, (6)_____ I never feel lonely (7)_____ I have a lot of visitors. My friends come to see me a lot, (8)_____ we sometimes watch a film or cook a meal.

I love my flat for many reasons: the sunny living room, the good times with friends, (9)_____ best of all (10)_____ it is my first home.

5 Make notes about where you live. Use these questions.

- Where is it?
- Is it old or new?
- How many rooms are there?
- Who do you live with?
- What is near your home?
- Do you like it? What do you like best of all?

Talk to a partner about your notes.

6 Write a description of your home.

UNIT 6 FORMAL LETTERS Applying for a job

1 Read the advertisement for a job. What is the job? Where is it?

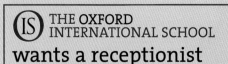

(IS) THE OXFORD INTERNATIONAL SCHOOL

wants a receptionist

- Do you like working with people?
- Can you speak two foreign languages?
- Can you use a computer?
- Do you know Oxford well?

Please write to: Anne Watson, Director
The Oxford International School
16 College Street, Oxford OX2 7PT
or email: awatson@oxfordint.co.uk

2 Carol is interested in the job. Read the information about her. Do you think she is the right person for the job?

Name	Carol Barnes
Age	28
Address	4 Hope Road, Oxford OX6 5PP
Present job	Tourist guide
Last job	Hotel receptionist
Languages	French, Spanish

3 Look at Carol's letter and complete it with the information from her chart.

The name and address of the person you are writing to goes here.

The date goes here.

We use *Ms*, *Miss*, or *Mrs* for a woman.
We use *Mr* for a man.

We end formal letters with *Yours sincerely*.

Sign the letter and print your name.

Anne Watson, Director
The Oxford International School
16 College (2)_____
Oxford OX2 7PT

4 Hope (1)_____
Oxford OX6 5PP

19 August

Dear Ms Watson,

I am interested in the job of (3)_____ in your school.

I (4)_____ years old and I (5)_____ in Oxford. At the moment I (6)_____ guide, but last year I (7)_____ a hotel receptionist. I (8)_____ working with people very much and I (9)_____ speak two (10)_____, French and a little Spanish. I can also (11)_____ a computer. I (12)_____ born in Oxford, so I know it very well.

I look forward to hearing from you.

Yours sincerely,

Carol Barnes

Carol Barnes

Paragraph 1
Introduction

Paragraph 2
The main part of the letter

Paragraph 3
Ending

4 Read this advertisement for another job. What is the job? Answer the questions about you. Now write a similar letter to Carol's.

Happy Holidays want **TOURIST GUIDES**

- Are you over 18?
- Do you like talking to people?
- Do you know your town well?
- Can you speak English?
- Are you free from July to September?

Please write to: Peter Mann, Happy Holidays, Central Office, 89 Brook Street, LONDON W1 5PW

UNIT 7 DESCRIBING A HOLIDAY

1 Read the information about Robert and Daniella. Make notes about your last holiday.

Questions	Robert	Daniella	Me
Where/go?	Wales	Japan	
When/go?	last June	last October	
How long/stay?	a week	three weeks	
How/travel?	train	plane	
Where/stay?	a bed and breakfast	with friends	
What/do?	went walking in the countryside	visited Tokyo and Kyoto	
What/see?	some beautiful mountains and rivers; *not* any people!	some beautiful temples; *not* Mount Fuji	
Enjoy the holiday?	Yes	Yes	

2 Ask and answer the questions about Robert with a partner.

> **Where did he go?**
> **To Wales.**
> **How long did he stay?**
> **For a week.**

3 Complete the questions about Daniella and write short answers.

1 Where ____did she go____ ?   To Japan._____
2 When _____ ?   _____
3 How long _____ ?   _____
4 How _____ ?   _____
5 Where _____ ?   _____
6 What _____ ?   _____
7 What _____ ?   _____
8 Did _____ ?   Yes, she did.

4 Read about Daniella's holiday. Put the verbs in the Past Simple.

My exciting holiday

Last October I (1) _____ (have) a very exciting holiday.
I (2) _____ (go) to Japan for three weeks to stay with friends.
I (3) _____ (travel) by plane. It (4) _____ (be) a long journey but fortunately my friends
(5) _____ (meet) me at the airport and (6) _____ (drive) me straight to their house near
Tokyo. I (7) _____ (stay) with my friends for the first week. In the second week I (8) _____
(visit) Tokyo and then in the third week I (9) _____ (take) the train to Kyoto where I (10)
_____ (see) some beautiful temples and gardens. I (11) _____ (enjoy) the holiday very much
indeed but I (12) _____ (not see) Mount Fuji. Next time I want to climb it with my friends.

5 Talk to a partner about your last holiday. Then write about it.

1 Make sentences with a line in **A**, a word in **B**, and a line in **C**.

A	B	C
1 I left the party early		a she was thirty.
2 Peter couldn't speak		b they came for dinner.
3 Tim didn't see the Colosseum	because	c I was at school.
4 Eva didn't start learning English	when	d she couldn't afford them.
5 I didn't enjoy maths lessons	until	e after midnight.
6 Sally didn't buy the red shoes		f he was nearly four.
7 They didn't go to bed		g I didn't feel well.
8 We met Ken's wife last Saturday		h he was in Rome.

2 Write notes about an old friend. Use these questions to help.

- What is his/her name?
- Where did you meet?
- What did you do together?
- How often do you meet now?
- What do you do when you meet?

Talk to a partner about your notes.

3 Read the text about 'My oldest friend.' Complete the text with words from the box.

and but because so when until

My oldest friend

My oldest friend is called Sandy. We met thirty years ago (1)_____ we were both five years old. It was my first day at school (2)_____ I was very unhappy (3)_____ I wanted my mother. Sandy gave me a sweet (4) _____ we became friends immediately. We were together nearly every day (5) _____ we left school twelve years later.

Then I went to university, (6) _____ Sandy didn't. She married (7) _____ she was just eighteen (8) _____ had three children. I studied for eight years (9) _____ I wanted to be an accountant. I had a lot of new friends, (10) _____ I didn't see Sandy very often. Sometimes we didn't meet for months, (11) _____ we often talked on the telephone.

Now I'm married, too. I live near Sandy (12) _____ we meet every week. She's a student now, (13) _____ I have a baby, (14) _____ we can give each other a lot of advice!

4 Write about your friend. Use your notes to help.

1 Read the email.

- Who is it from?
- What is it about?
- Who is it to?
- How does it begin and end?

2 These lines are from the email. Where do they go?

a Could you tell me what time the restaurant closes?
b I look forward to hearing from you.
c Could I possibly have a quiet room at the back of the hotel?

From: p.west@uktel.com
To: bookings@liverpoolarms.co.uk
Date: 17 March
Subject: Booking a room

Dear Sir or Madam,

I would like to book a single room at your hotel for the nights of 12, 13, and 14 April.
(1)_____

I understand you have a restaurant.
(2)_____

My details are: 15 Monarch Road, London, NW1 2TS. Tel: (0207) 566 4945. Please let me know if you need a deposit or a credit card number.

Thank you very much.
(3)_____

Yours faithfully,

Peter West

3 Look at the hotel's online booking form. Complete the form with information about Peter West in exercise 1.

LIVERPOOL • ARMS • HOTEL
ONLINE BOOKING

Please complete this form. All rooms have bath and shower en suite. Room prices include breakfast.

Name	
Email	
Tel/Fax	
Address	
Country	

Number of guests
☐ Adults   ☐ Children

Number of rooms
☐ Single   ☐ Twin   ☐ Double   ☐ Family

Check-in [_____] dd/mm/yy
Check-out [_____] dd/mm/yy

Additional information

Reset
Send

4 Write an email to book a room at the hotel.

- Book a double room for four nights next month.
- Ask for a room with a view of the sea.
- Ask about Internet and other facilities (phone, television, room service, car parking etc.).
- Give your personal details.

> We can use *which* and *where* to join sentences.
>
> We use *which* for things:
>
> This is the book. **It** has the information.
>
> This is the book **which** has the information.
>
> We use *where* for places:
>
> There's the house. John and Mary live **in it**.
>
> There's the house **where** John and Mary live.

1 Join the sentences with *which* or *where*.

1 Jack wrote the letter. It arrived this morning.
_____

2 There's the park. We play football in it.
_____

3 This is the hotel. I always stay here.
_____

4 Barbara's got a car. It's faster than yours.
_____

2 What is your capital city? What do you know about it? Talk to a partner.

3 Read about London and complete the text using the words in the box.

a where the Queen lives
b which is the biggest
c which are much bigger
d where the Romans landed
e where you can buy anything
f where you can see

MY CAPITAL CITY

London has a population of about 7,000,000. It lies on the River Thames, (1)_____ nearly 2,000 years ago. From about 1800 until World War II, London was the biggest city in the world, but now there are many cities (2)_____.

London is famous for many things. Tourists come from all over the world to visit its historic buildings, such as Buckingham Palace, (3)_____, and the Houses of Parliament, (4)_____ and hear the famous clock, Big Ben. They also come to visit its theatres, its museums, and its many shops, such as Harrods, (5)_____. And, of course, they want to ride on the big wheel next to the river!

Like many big cities, London has problems with traffic and pollution. Over 1,000,000 people a day use the London Underground, but there are still too many cars on the streets. The air isn't clean, but it is cleaner than it was 100 years ago.

For me, the best thing about London is the parks. There are five in the city centre. But my children's favourite place is Hamleys, (6)_____ toy shop in the world!

4 Write four paragraphs about your capital city. Begin each paragraph with the same words as in the text about London. Write 100–150 words.

Paragraph 1 How big is it? Where is it?
Paragraph 2 What is it famous for?

Paragraph 3 Does it have any problems?
Paragraph 4 What do you like best about it?

> ❗ These two sentences have the same meaning. How are they different? Which is more formal?
>
> I like him a lot, **but** I don't love him.
> **Although** I like him a lot, I don't love him.

1 Complete the sentences with a word from the box.

although   because   but
too   both   for example

1 My father loves skiing, _____ my mother hates it.

2 We stopped playing tennis _____ it started to rain.

3 _____ it was cold and wet, we still played tennis.

4 My two sisters are very similar. They _____ love dancing and skiing.

5 Rosa loves dancing and Hannah loves it_____.

6 There's so much to do at the weekend. _____ you can go skiing or swimming.

2 Complete the text with the correct linking word from exercise 1.

3 Work with a partner. Talk about your brothers, sisters, parents, or children. Are you/they similar? Do you/they like doing the same things?

4 Write about two people in your family and compare them. Describe …

- what they look like
- their likes and dislikes
- their personalities

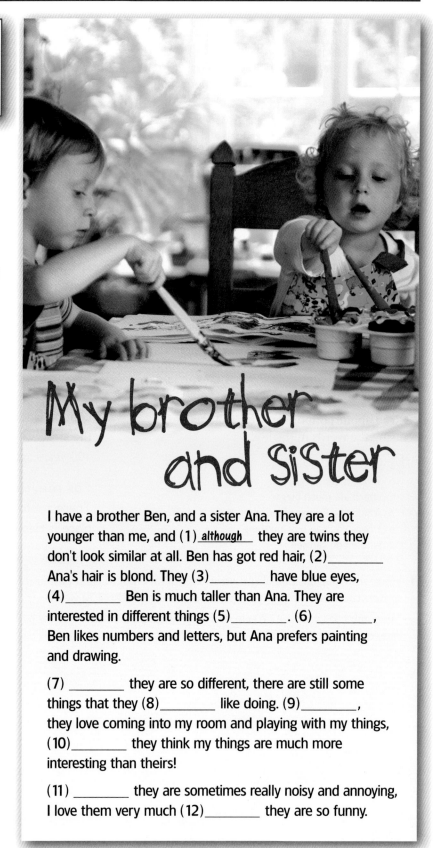

My brother and sister

I have a brother Ben, and a sister Ana. They are a lot younger than me, and (1) _although_ they are twins they don't look similar at all. Ben has got red hair, (2)_____ Ana's hair is blond. They (3)_____ have blue eyes, (4)_____ Ben is much taller than Ana. They are interested in different things (5)_____. (6) _____, Ben likes numbers and letters, but Ana prefers painting and drawing.

(7) _____ they are so different, there are still some things that they (8)_____ like doing. (9)_____, they love coming into my room and playing with my things, (10)_____ they think my things are much more interesting than theirs!

(11) _____ they are sometimes really noisy and annoying, I love them very much (12)_____ they are so funny.

1 Discuss these questions with a partner.
- Do you often receive postcards? Who from? Where from? Give examples.
- What was the last postcard you sent? Who to? Where from?

2 Read the postcard. Find words for good weather and bad weather.

3 Underline the descriptions for a good holiday *or* a bad holiday. Read your postcard to your partner.

Friday, April 14th

Dear Mum and Dad,

We're having | a wonderful / quite a good | time here in Corsica,
| and fortunately / but unfortunately | the weather is | glorious / not very good |. They say
that the weather here in April is often quite changeable
so we're | just unlucky / very lucky |. It is | warm and sunny / cold and cloudy | nearly
every day so most of the time we | stay in the hotel / go to the beach | and
| play cards / swim and sunbathe |. Yesterday it was so | hot / foggy | that we
couldn't | see the sea / lie in the sun |. Tomorrow we're not going to
| the beach / stay in the hotel |, we're going to drive round the island
and go sightseeing.

See you soon

Love, Lara and Mick

Mr and Mrs Binchey
20 Model Farm Road
Cork City
Ireland

Corsica

4 Write a postcard to a friend. Write about …
- where you are on holiday
- the weather
- something you do often
- something you did yesterday
- something you are going to do tomorrow

1 Do you know the story of *The Emperor's New Clothes*? Discuss what you know.

2 Read the story and complete it with the adjectives and adverbs from the box. Use each word once only.

3 What stories do you know that begin *Once upon a time …* ? Which is your favourite? Discuss as a class.

4 Write your favourite story. Use adjectives and adverbs.

Begin: *Once upon a time …*   End: *… and they lived happily ever after.*

Adjectives	Adverbs
~~expensive~~	angrily
beautiful	immediately
embarrassed	loudly
naked	naturally
new	quickly
pleased	suddenly
wonderful	unfortunately
worried	unhappily

The Emperor's New Clothes

Once upon a time there was an Emperor who loved to spend his money on **(1)** _expensive_ clothes. One day, two tailors arrived at his palace. They said they could make him the most **(2)**_____ suit, with magic cloth that only clever people could see. 'What a **(3)**_____ suit to have,' thought the Emperor. 'I'll know **(4)**_____ who is clever and who is stupid in my palace.'

The Emperor gave the tailors a lot of money and a room in the palace. He was very excited, but he was also **(5)**_____. 'Oh dear' he thought, 'I hope I can see the magic cloth.' He sent one of his ministers to look first.

The minister went into the tailors' room. 'Oh no! I can't see anything,' he thought **(6)**_____. 'What can I say to the Emperor?'
'Well?' said one tailor. 'Do you like the suit?'
'Oh, it is excellent!' he said.
'We're very **(7)**_____ to hear that,' said the tailors.
The minister told the Emperor and the Emperor was delighted. He went to the tailors' room with his minister.

'Look,' said the minister. 'Aren't the colours lovely?' **(8)**_____ the poor Emperor couldn't see anything at all, but he said 'Oh yes, the suit is wonderful. Thank you.'

(9)_____ everybody wanted to see the suit, so the Emperor put on his **(10)**_____ clothes and went into the city with his ministers. All the people clapped and cheered **(11)**_____. The Emperor felt better.

Then **(12)**_____ a little boy ran out. 'The Emperor isn't wearing any clothes!' he shouted.
'Oh, it's true!' the people said. 'He's as **(13)**_____ as the day he was born!'

The Emperor was so **(14)**_____. He ran **(15)**_____ back to the palace and called **(16)**_____ for the tailors but they were gone.

UNIT 14 WRITING AN EMAIL Saying thank you

1 Have you ever been to another country to study the language? Where did you go? How long for? What language did you study? Did you have a good time?

2 Do you remember Danka who went to study English in Brighton? Look quickly at the email.
- Where is Danka now?
- Where are they?
- Who is Jacek?
- Who is she writing to?
- Why is she writing?

3 Read the email again and complete it with the words from the box. Check with a partner.

lot	going x2	couldn't
visit	just	has
quickly	much	but
had	like	

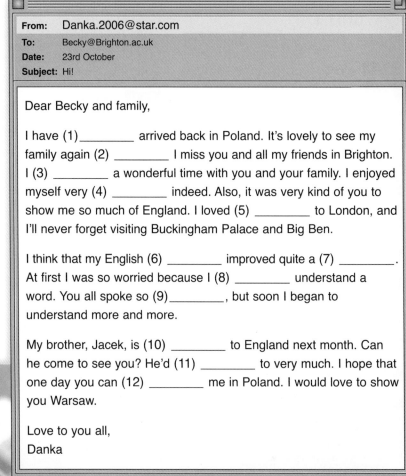

From: Danka.2006@star.com
To: Becky@Brighton.ac.uk
Date: 23rd October
Subject: Hi!

Dear Becky and family,

I have (1)_____ arrived back in Poland. It's lovely to see my family again (2) _____ I miss you and all my friends in Brighton. I (3) _____ a wonderful time with you and your family. I enjoyed myself very (4) _____ indeed. Also, it was very kind of you to show me so much of England. I loved (5) _____ to London, and I'll never forget visiting Buckingham Palace and Big Ben.

I think that my English (6) _____ improved quite a (7) _____. At first I was so worried because I (8) _____ understand a word. You all spoke so (9)_____, but soon I began to understand more and more.

My brother, Jacek, is (10) _____ to England next month. Can he come to see you? He'd (11) _____ to very much. I hope that one day you can (12) _____ me in Poland. I would love to show you Warsaw.

Love to you all,
Danka

4 Write a similar email to someone who you have stayed with.

Tapescripts

UNIT 1

1.1   see p6

1.2

A   Hello. My name's Lisa. What's your name?
B   Mike.
A   Where are you from, Mike?
B   I'm from Boston. Where are you from?
A   I'm from Boston, too!

1.3

1   This is Marco. He's from Italy.
2   This is Emma. She's from England.
3   This is Lisa and Mike. They're from the USA.

1.4   see p8

1.5

1   He's from Spain.
2   What's her name?
3   They're from Japan.
4   Where's she from?
5   He's a teacher in Italy.

1.6   see p9

1.7

Tiago
My name's Tiago Costa and I'm a student. I'm 18. I'm not married. I have one sister and two brothers. I live in a house in Fortaleza, Brazil. I want to learn English because it's an international language.

1.8

The alphabet song
A B C D E F G H I J K L M N O P Q R S T U V W X Y Z
That is the English alphabet!

1.9   see p10

T 1.10   see p11

1.11

1   My brother has four children.
2   I have 10 stamps in my bag.
3   Hello, extension 4177.
4   I live at number 19.
5   Goodbye. See you at five.
6   Hello. 01913 786 499?

1.12

1   A   Hello, Lisa Jefferson.
    B   Hello, Lisa. It's Mike.
    A   Mike! How are you?
    B   I'm fine, thank you. And you?
    A   I'm OK, thanks.
2   A   Bye, Marco! Have a nice day!
    B   Thanks, and you. See you later!
    A   Yes, at 7.00 at the cinema.
    B   Great! Bye, Emma!

3   A   Hello. 270899.
    B   Hi, Alice! It's me, Charles. How are you?
    A   Not bad, thanks. And you?
    B   Very well, thanks. How are the children?
    A   They're fine.

T 1.13   see p11

UNIT 2

T 2.1

1   A   What's her surname?
    B   Jefferson.
2   A   What's her first name?
    B   Lisa.
3   A   Where's she from?
    B   The USA.
4   A   What's her job?
    B   She's a journalist.
5   A   What's her address?
    B   89, Franklin Street, Cambridge, Boston
6   A   What's her phone number?
    B   (616) 326 1204.
7   A   How old is she?
    B   Twenty-six.
8   A   Is she married?
    B   No, she isn't.

T 2.2

1   A   What's his surname?
    B   Jefferson.
2   A   What's his first name?
    B   Rudi. That's R-U-D-I.
3   A   Where's he from?
    B   The USA.
4   A   What's his job?
    B   He's an actor.
5   A   What's his address?
    B   82, Beacon Street, Boston. That's Beacon, B-E-A-C-O-N Street. Boston.
6   A   What's his phone number?
    B   (617) 227 5930.
7   A   How old is he?
    B   Twenty-eight.
8   A   Is he married?
    B   No, he isn't.

T 2.3   see p13

T 2.4   see p14

T 2.5

1   It's small. It's big.
2   It's easy. It's difficult.
3   He's old. She's young.
4   They're old. They're new.
5   It's lovely. It's horrible.
6   It's fast. It's slow.
7   They're hot. They're cold.
8   It's cheap. It's expensive.

T 2.6   see p17

T 2.7

D=Danka, K=Klaus
1   D   Hello. My name's Danka.
    K   Hello, Danka. I'm Klaus.
    D   Where are you from, Klaus?
    K   I'm from Germany, from Hamburg. And you? Where are you from?
    D   I'm from Poland.
    K   From Warsaw?
    D   Yes, that's right.

S=Simon, C=Class, D=Danka
2   S   Good morning everybody.
    C   Good morning, Simon.
    S   How are you all?
    C   Fine. Good. OK.
    S   How are you Danka?
    D   I'm fine, thank you. And you?
    S   Very well. Now listen everybody …

B=Becky, D=Danka, V=Valerie
3   B   Bye, Danka. Have a nice day.
    D   Pardon?
    B   Have a good day at the language school.
    D   Ah, yes. Thank you.
    B   What's your teacher called?
    D   My teacher called?
    V   What's his name?
    D   Oh, yes. His name's Simon.
    B   And is he good?
    D   My teacher good?
    V   Yes. Simon, your teacher, is he a good teacher?
    D   Oh yes, yes. Very good, very nice.

T 2.8   see p18

T 2.9

1   That's five pounds fifty, please.
2   Look, it's only twelve pounds.
3   Here you are. Twenty p change.
4   Pizza is three pounds seventy-five.
5   One hundred pounds for that is very expensive.
6   Nine pounds *fifteen*, not nine pounds fifty.

T 2.10   see p18

T 2.11

1   A   Good morning.
    B   Good morning. Can I have a coffee, please?
    A   Here you are. Anything else?
    B   No, thanks.
    A   One pound fifty, please.
    B   Thanks.
    A   Thank you.
2   A   Hi. Can I help?
    B   Yes. Can I have a tuna and egg salad, please?
    A   Anything to drink?
    B   Yeah. A mineral water, please.
    A   OK. Here you are.
    B   How much is that?
    A   Six pounds thirty-five, please.
    B   Thanks.

T 2.12   see p19

UNIT 3

see p20 & 21

is	works	likes
comes	speaks	flies
lives	has	loves

1 István's a music professor. Pamela's a doctor.
2 He comes from Hungary. She comes from Canada.
3 He lives in a big city, but she lives in a small town.
4 He works four days a week. She works 16 hours a day non-stop.
5 He speaks three languages. She speaks to sick people on her radio.
6 He loves his job and she loves her job, too.
7 He has a daughter. She isn't married.
8 He likes playing tennis in his free time. She never has free time.

1 A Where does István come from?
  B Budapest, in Hungary.
2 A What does he do?
  B He's a music professor.
3 A Does he speak German?
  B Yes, he does.
4 A Does he speak Spanish?
  B No, he doesn't. He doesn't speak Spanish or French.

see p22

A Where does Pamela come from?
B Canada.
A What does she do?
B She's a doctor.
A Does she live in Canada?
B No, she doesn't.
A Does she like her job?
B Yes, she does.

Iman
1 Iman comes from Somalia.
2 Iman lives and works in Somalia.
3 She's a tourist guide.
4 She speaks five languages.
5 She likes playing tennis in her free time.
6 She isn't married.

Giorgio
7 Giorgio works in an office in London.
8 He is Italian.
9 He has three sons.
10 He likes relaxing with his family in his free time.

1 She likes her job.
2 She loves walking.
3 He isn't married.
4 Does he have three children?
5 What does he do?

T 3.9

1 A Good afternoon. Can I have two ice-creams, please?
  B Chocolate or vanilla?
  A One chocolate, one vanilla, please.
  B That's one pound eighty. Anything else?
  A No, thank you.
2 A Only two letters for you this morning, Mrs Craig.
  B Thank you very much, Mr McSporran. And how's Mrs McSporran this morning?
  A Oh, she's very well, thank you. She's busy in the shop.
3 A A glass of wine before bed, my dear?
  B Oh, yes please.
  A Here you are.
  B Thank you, my dear. I'm very tired this evening.
4 A Hello, Mr McSporran.
  B Good morning, boys and girls. Hurry up, we're late.
  A Can I sit here, Mr McSporran?
  C No, no, I want to sit there.
  B Be quiet all of you, and SIT DOWN!

T 3.10

a A pilot flies planes.
b A chef cooks in a restaurant.
c A nurse looks after people in hospital.
d A lawyer helps people in court.
e An actor makes films.
f A journalist writes for a newspaper.
g A model wears beautiful clothes.
h An architect designs buildings.
i A shop assistant sells things.

T 3.11 see p26

T 3.12

It's five o'clock. It's eight o'clock.
It's half past five. It's half past eleven.
It's quarter past five. It's quarter past two.
It's quarter to six. It's quarter to nine.
It's five past five. It's ten past five.
It's twenty past five. It's twenty-five past five.
It's twenty-five to six. It's twenty to six.
It's ten to six. It's five to six.

T 3.13 see p27

UNIT 4

T 4.1

Ceri is 28 years old and lives in Cardiff, Wales. She works hard as a lawyer from Monday to Friday, but she doesn't relax at weekends. She plays rugby for the Women's Welsh Rugby team. On Saturdays she trains with her team at the Rugby Club, and on Sundays she plays in a match. She has no free time, but she loves her job and playing rugby.

T 4.2

I love my job as a family lawyer, because I like helping people. But I love playing rugby, too, so my life is very busy!
Every lunchtime I go running in the park near my office. On Monday and Thursday evenings I go to the swimming pool with my boyfriend Alex. On Tuesday and Friday mornings I get up at 5.30 and go to the gym before work. And on Wednesday evenings I train with my team at the club.
On Friday evenings I just relax because I'm usually very tired! I sometimes visit my sister. She lives in the centre of Cardiff, too. Or I cook a nice dinner at home with Alex. We love cooking. After dinner we often watch a DVD.
We never go out on Saturday evenings, because I always play in a match on Sundays. I want our team to win the next World Cup!

T 4.3

Q=Question, C=Ceri
Q Where do you work?
C In Cardiff.
Q Do you like your work?
C Yes, I do.
Q Do you relax at weekends?
C No, I don't.
Q Why don't you relax at weekends?
C Because I play rugby.

T 4.4

1 A What time do you go to bed?
  B At eleven o'clock.
2 A Where do you go on holiday?
  B To Spain or Portugal.
3 A What do you do on Sundays?
  B I always relax.
4 A When do you do your homework?
  B After dinner.
5 A Who do you live with?
  B My mother and sisters.
6 A Why do you like your job?
  B Because it's interesting.
7 A How do you travel to school?
  B By bus.
8 A Do you go out on Friday evenings?
  B Yes, I do sometimes.

T 4.5

1 What does she do on Sundays?
2 Do you stay at home on Thursday evenings?
3 He lives here.
4 What do you do on Saturday evenings?
5 I read a lot.
6 Why don't you like your job?

T 4.6 see p32 & 33

T 4.7

1 A So, do you like Norway, Mick?
   B Yes, it's beautiful. Look at the mountains and blue sky! I love skiing here.
   A Yes, I love it too. I ski here every winter and spring.
   B You are lucky.
   A I know! Do you want a coffee now?
   B Yes, please. Good idea.

2 D Phew! It's hot today.
   M It is. Daniella, here are the drinks.
   D OK, Mum!
   M Bob, how are the hamburgers?
   B They're ready!
   M Lovely. And here's the salad. Daniella, can you tell your brother that lunch is ready?
   D Sure, Mum.
   M Thanks. Bob, come and have a drink!
   B Great!

3 T Hello! Can you help me? Can you speak English?
   S Yes. A little.
   T Can you tell me – what festival is this?
   S It's our Flower Festival. We have it every February.
   T It's so beautiful! I love the small pink and white flowers.
   S They are orchids.
   T Wow! There are hundreds!
   S Do you like dancing? We have Thai dancing here this evening.
   T Oh yes. I want to see that!

Song: Teacher's Book p139

T 4.8

1 A I'm sorry I'm late. The traffic is bad today.
   B Don't worry. Come and sit down. We're on page 25.

2 A Excuse me.
   B Yes?
   A Do you have a dictionary?
   B I'm sorry, I don't. It's at home.
   A It doesn't matter.

3 A It's very hot in here. Can I open the window?
   B Pardon?
   A The window, can I open it?
   B Yes, of course.

4 A Excuse me!
   B Oh, good morning Marco. Can I help you?
   A Yes, please. Can I have a ticket for the trip to York?
   B Yes, of course. It's eighty pounds. Do you want to pay twenty pounds deposit now?
   A Sorry. What does 'deposit' mean?
   B It means you can pay twenty pounds now and sixty pounds later.
   A Ah! I see. Yes, please.

T 4.9

I'm sorry I'm late.
Don't worry.
Excuse me.
I'm sorry.
It doesn't matter.
Pardon?
Yes, of course.
I see.
Excuse me!
What does 'deposit' mean?

 UNIT 5

T 5.1

A Is there a television?
B Yes, there is.
A Is there a computer?
B No, there isn't.
A Are there any books?
B Yes, there are.
A How many books are there?
B There are a lot.
A Are there any pictures?
B No, there aren't.

T 5.2

What's in your picture?
There are three people in the living room. A man and a woman on the sofa and a little girl in the armchair. There's a radio on the coffee table and a rug under it. There's a cat on the rug in front of the fire. There are a lot of pictures on the walls but there aren't any photographs. There are two plants on the floor next to the television and some flowers on the small table next to the sofa.

T 5.3

Suzie's kitchen
S=Suzie, M=Matt
S And this is the kitchen.
M Mmm, it's very nice.
S Well, it's not very big, but there are a lot of cupboards. And there's a new fridge, and a cooker. That's new, too.
M But what's in all these cupboards?
S Well, not a lot. There are some cups, but there aren't any plates. And I have some knives and forks, but I don't have any spoons!
M Do you have any glasses?
S No. Sorry.
M Never mind. We can drink this champagne from those cups! Cheers!

T 5.4

Yoshi's briefcase
What's in my briefcase? Well, there's a newspaper – a Japanese newspaper – and there's a dictionary – my Japanese/English dictionary. I have some pens, three, I think. Also I have a notebook for vocabulary. I write words in that every day. And of course I have my keys – my car keys and my house keys. Oh yes, very important, there are some photos of my family, my wife, and my daughter. And there's my mobile. I phone home to Tokyo every night. That's all, I think. I don't have any stamps and my address book is in my hotel.

T 5.5

Homes around the world
Candy and Bert from New England
C Our house is quite old, about fifty years old. It's in the centre of the village near the church. All the houses here are white. We have a living room, quite a big kitchen and three bedrooms, and a big verandah all around the house.
B Our children aren't at home now. They both have jobs in the city, so most of the time it's just Candy and me.

C Yes, so in summer we do bed and breakfast for tourists. We have lovely visitors from all over the world.

Alise from Samoa
I live with my family in a house near the sea. We have an open house, … er … that is … er … our house doesn't have any walls. Houses in Samoa don't have walls because it is very, very hot, but we have blinds to stop the rain and sun. Our house is in the old style. We have only one room for living and sleeping, so it is both a bedroom and a living room. We have rugs and we sit and sleep on the floor.

Kwan from Korea
I live and work in Seoul, the capital city of Korea. It's a big, modern, exciting city, but it is quite expensive. My flat is very, very small. I have three rooms: a small kitchen, a bathroom, and a room for sitting, eating and sleeping. But I live in the centre of the city, and there are a lot of shops, restaurants and bars near my flat. My work place is near too. I live alone at the moment, but I want to marry my girlfriend next year.

Manola from Lisbon
I live in the old town near the sea. It is called the Alfama. I have a very beautiful flat. There's just one room in my flat, one very big room with one very big window. My bed's next to the window so I see the sea and all the lights of the city when I go to sleep. I live alone, but I have a cat and I'm near the shops and lots of friends come to visit me. I love my flat.

T 5.6

1 A Excuse me! Is there a newsagent's near here?
   B Yes. It's in Church Street. Take the first street on the right. It's next to the music shop.
   A OK. Thanks.

2 A Is there a post office near here?
   B Go straight ahead, and it's on the left, next to the pub.
   A Thanks a lot.

3 A Excuse me! Is there a café near here?
   B There's an Internet café in Park Lane next to the bank, and there's an Italian restaurant in Church Street next to the travel agent's.
   A Is that one far?
   B No. Just two minutes, that's all.

T 5.7 see p43

UNIT 6

6.1 see p44

6.2 see p44

6.3

1   I can speak French, but I can't speak German.
2   He can't dance, but he can sing.
3   'Can you cook?' 'Yes, I can.'
4   They can ski, but they can't swim.
5   We can dance and we can sing.
6   'Can she drive?' 'No, she can't.'

6.4

Lucia

Well, there are a lot of things I can't do. I can't drive a car, of course, I'm only 14. Languages? Well, I can't speak French, but I can speak Spanish. My mother's Spanish, and we often go to Spain. My mum's a really good cook. She can cook really well, not just Spanish food, all kinds of food, but I can't cook at all. I just love eating! What about sports? Er … I think I'm good at quite a lot of sports. I can play tennis, and I can ski. Sometimes we go skiing in the Spanish Pyrenees. And of course I can swim. But musical instruments – no – I can't play any at all. But I can dance! I dance flamenco with my mum sometimes. I love it. And I can use a computer, of course. All my friends can.

6.5 see p46

6.6 see p46

6.7

E=Emma, M=Marco

E   Were you at Charlotte's party last Saturday?
M   Yes, I was.
E   Was it good?
M   Well, it was OK.
E   Were there many people?
M   Yes, there were.
E   Was Pascal there?
M   No, he wasn't. And where were you? Why weren't you there?
E   Oh … I couldn't go because I was at Sergio's party! It was brilliant!
M   Oh!

6.8

1   I can hear you, but I can't see you.
2   There are three bedrooms in our house.
3   I don't know where Jill lives.
4   My son lives near the sea.
5   Don't wear that hat, buy a new one!
6   No, I can't come to your party.
7   You were right. Sally can't come for dinner.
8   Their daughter could write when she was three.
9   I know my answers are right.

T 6.9

Operator

International Directory Enquiries. Which country, please?
…
And which town?
…
Can I have the last name, please?
…
And the initial?
…
What's the address?
…
The number you require is 00 1 616 326 1204.

T 6.10

1   A   Hello.
    B   Hello. Can I speak to Jo, please?
    A   This *is* Jo.
    B   Oh! Hi, Jo. This is Nicola. Is Sunday still OK for tennis?
    A   Yes. That's fine.
    B   Great! I'll see you on Sunday at ten, then. Bye!
    A   Bye!
2   A   Hello.
    B   Hello. Is that Emma?
    A   No it isn't. I'll just get her.
    C   Hello, Emma here.
    B   Hi, Emma. It's Marco. Listen! There's a party at my house on Saturday. Can you come?
    C   Oh sorry, Marco. I can't. It's my sister's wedding.
    B   Oh, never mind. Perhaps next time. Bye!
    C   Bye!
3   A   Good morning. Dixons Electrical. How can I help you?
    B   Good morning. Can I speak to the manager, please?
    A   I'm afraid Mr Smith isn't in his office at the moment. Can I take a message?
    B   Don't worry. I'll ring back later.
    A   All right. Goodbye.
    B   Goodbye.

T 6.11 see p51

UNIT 7

T 7.1

A   Shirley Temple Black

Shirley Temple Black is a retired politician. She lives with her husband in California. She likes cooking and playing with her grandchildren. Also, she sometimes works at Stanford University for the Institute of International Studies. She goes there every month and meets foreign ministers. They discuss world problems.

T 7.2 see p52

T 7.3

liked	studied
looked	acted
worked	decided
earned	wanted
loved	started

T 7.4

C   Why did she stop acting?

From the age of three Shirley worked very hard for 20th Century Fox.
'I acted in three or four movies every year. Fortunately I liked acting!' And the public loved her and her films. The films earned over $35 million.
She says, 'I didn't go to school. I studied at the studio and my mother looked after me there.'
So why did she stop acting? When she was 12, she finally started school. She was a good student and she wanted to go to university. She was still a good actor, but her films weren't so popular, because she wasn't a little girl any more. She decided to change her career. It was a big change – from actor to politician.
She says, 'I was a politician for 35 years, but people only remember my movies!'

T 7.5

1   A   When did she start in films?
    B   When she was only three years old!
2   A   How many films did she act in?
    B   Over 50.
3   A   Who did she work for?
    B   20th Century Fox Film Studios.
4   A   How much money did her films earn?
    B   Over $35 million.
5   A   Where did she study?
    B   At the film studio. She didn't go to school.
6   A   When did she start school?
    B   When she was 12.
7   A   What did she want to do?
    B   Go to university.
8   A   Why did she stop acting?
    B   Because her movies weren't so popular any more.

T 7.6 see p54

T 7.7

wanted	danced
loved	retired
acted	earned
looked	liked

T 7.8

was	died
began	became
came	won
got	made
sang	bought
left	sold
had	

T 7.9

1984 The year I was born
J=James, D=Dad, M=Mum

J Dad, tell me about when I was born. When did you leave Hong Kong?

D Erm … you were born in January, and we left later that year and came back to Britain.

M Yes, you got a job in London, didn't you, Robert?

D That's right. Remember Margaret Thatcher was Prime Minister, then.

M Of course. She was Europe's first woman Prime Minister, James.

J I know that, Mum. But who was in the White House?

D Ronald Reagan. Actually, he began his second four years then?

M He was an actor before. Did you know that, James?

J No, I didn't, Mum!

D And that was the year that the Soviet leader, Yuri Andropov, died.

M Oh, yes. He was only leader for a year. Oh, and I remember – the Soviet Union didn't go to the Olympic Games that year. Isn't that right, Robert? The 1984 Games – were they in Los Angeles?

D Yes, they were. Remember Carl Lewis won four gold medals that year.

J That was in athletics, wasn't it?

M That's right.

D Oh, and remember little Tiger Woods?

J The golfer?

D Yes. He became junior champion that year. He was only eight years old.

J Wow. Hey, 1984 was a busy year. Did anything else happen?

M Well … Apple Macintosh made a new computer. I remember because I bought one. Millions of people bought one.

J And what about music? Was Michael Jackson famous then?

D Yes, he was. His album *Thriller* came out that year. It sold millions.

J 43 million, actually. It's the best-selling album of all time!

D Really?

M Oh, and remember, Robert? Madonna sang *Holiday!* (sings)

J Oh, no! Stop it, Mum! You sing that every time we go on holiday!

M I know. I like it. Anyway, who else was famous, then, Robert?

D Let's see. Paul McCartney … Tina Turner, David Bowie – they all had hit records that year.

J Wow, that's amazing! They're all still famous today.

T 7.10

orange juice
railway station
swimming pool
handbag
boyfriend
newspaper
film star
birthday card
washing machine
living room
car park

T 7.11

1 **A** I can't find my handbag.
   B Here it is!
   A Oh yes, thank you. Where did you find it?
   B In the living room where you left it!

2 **A** Would you like some chocolate cake?
   B No, thanks, just orange juice for me.
   A But I made this cake for you.
   B Did you? I'm sorry! I don't like chocolate cake.

3 **A** I have nothing to wear for your boyfriend's party.
   B What about your white jeans?
   A They aren't clean.
   B Well, wash them. You have a washing machine, don't you?

4 **A** Do you want anything from the shops?
   B A newspaper, please. *The Times*, I think.
   A OK.
   B Oh, and can you take this letter to the post office?
   A Sure.

T 7.12

first	thirteenth
second	sixteenth
third	seventeenth
fourth	twentieth
fifth	twenty-first
sixth	thirtieth
tenth	thirty-first
twelfth	

T 7.13

1 The first of April
   April the first
2 The second of March
   March the second
3 The seventeenth of September
   September the seventeenth
4 The nineteenth of November
   November the nineteenth
5 The twenty-third of June
   June the twenty-third
6 The twenty-ninth of February, nineteen seventy-six
7 The nineteenth of December, nineteen eighty-three
8 The third of October, nineteen ninety-nine
9 The thirty-first of May, two thousand
10 The fifteenth of July, two thousand and seven

T 7.14

1 The fourth of January
2 May the seventh, 1997
3 The fifteenth of August, 2001
4 **A** It was a Friday.
   B No, it wasn't. It was a Thursday.
   A No, I remember. It was Friday the thirteenth. The thirteenth of July.
5 **A** Oh no! I forgot your birthday.
   B It doesn't matter, really.
   A It was last Sunday, wasn't it? The thirtieth. November the thirtieth.
6 **A** Hey! Did you know that Shakespeare was born and died on the same day?
   B That's not possible!
   A Yes, it is. He was born on April the twenty-third, fifteen sixty-four and he died on April the twenty-third, sixteen sixteen.

UNIT 8

T 8.1

The photograph
Louis Daguerre from France

Louis Daguerre was a painter for the French opera. But he wanted to make a new type of picture. He started his experiments in the 1820s. Twelve years later he invented the photograph. He sold his idea to the French government in 1839 and the government gave it to the world. Daguerre called the first photographs 'daguerreotypes'. They became popular very fast. By 1850, there were 70 daguerreotype studios in New York City.

The windscreen wiper
Mary Anderson from the USA

Mary Anderson often visited New York City by car. In winter she noticed that when it rained or snowed, drivers got out of their cars all the time to clean their windows. In 1903 she began designing something to clean windows from inside the car. People, especially men, laughed at her idea. But they didn't laugh for long. She invented the windscreen wiper in 1905. And by 1916 all American cars had them.

The bicycle
Kirkpatrick Macmillan from Scotland

Long ago in 1490, Leonardo da Vinci drew a design for the modern bicycle. But the first person to make a bicycle was Kirkpatrick Macmillan in 1839. He lived in Scotland, so people didn't hear about his invention for a long time. Twenty years later, another bicycle came from France. In 1895 the bike became cheap and everyone could have one. Now people, especially women, could travel to the next town. It helped them find someone to marry!

T 8.2

1 He didn't invent the bicycle. He invented the photograph.
2 He didn't give his idea to the French government. He sold it to them.
3 She didn't live in New York City. She often visited New York City.
4 All cars didn't have windscreen wipers by 1916. Only American cars had them.

5 Leonardo da Vinci didn't make the first bicycle. Kirkpatrick Macmillan made it.
6 He didn't come from France. He came from Scotland.

T 8.3 see p62

T 8.4

My very first love
C=Carly, N=Ned
C I first met Ned when I was just ten years old. He was sixteen, er, very good-looking, and of course he had a girlfriend … a really beautiful girlfriend. I hated her.
N Hmm. I can remember Carly when she was only ten. She played in the street. She played on the corner near my house. I was sixteen. I had a girlfriend – she didn't like you, did she, Carly?
C Hmm, no … because she knew I liked you!!! You married her, didn't you? Four years later … I was fourteen, I cried and cried … I remember it well.
N Yeah – I was only twenty. I wasn't ready. It was a big mistake – a big mistake.
C You moved to London and had Michelle, your daughter.
N Yeah – my little Michelle, she's great …
C Yeah, she's lovely… And I finished school and then I went to college. I didn't marry … I had one or two boyfriends but nobody special. And two or three years later, my brother had a party. He invited you, and you came … And when I saw you, all the old feelings came back, and you told me you were divorced …
N Yeah, I was divorced and at my parents' house again. You were twenty-one, and just … wonderful. And we just fell in love.
C Yes, that's what happened. That was three years ago – now I'm twenty-four, we're married and we have a new baby, and Michelle is with us too. I'm so lucky … I married my very first love.

Do mothers know best?
E=Eric, L=Lori
E Our story is easy. We didn't do anything. It was our mothers who did it all!
L Yes. You see, our mothers are friends. They met one summer by the lake. They both have little summer houses there. And, of course, they talked a lot about their children.
E … and they decided that they wanted us to meet.
L We both thought this wasn't a very good idea!
E When my mom said to me 'I know a nice girl for you,' I just thought, 'No way.'
L Me, too! You see, my mom did this a lot, and it was usually terrible.
E But we finally said 'OK' – just for some peace.
L I took my sister with me …
E … and I took my best friend, Steve.
L But I was so surprised! Eric was wonderful!

E And of course, I thought the same about Lori. We all had a great time by the lake that summer. And at the end of the summer I knew I was in love with Lori.
L That was four years ago, and our wedding is in the fall. Our mothers are very happy, and we are, too!
E Yes. Sometimes mothers know best!

Song: Teacher's Book p144

T 8.5 see p64

T 8.6

1	born	4	answer
2	bought	5	cupboard
3	world	6	Christmas

T 8.7 see p64

T 8.8

1 Happy birthday to you.
Happy birthday to you.
Happy birthday, dear Grandma,
Happy birthday to you.

2 A Did you get any Valentine cards?
B Yes, I did. Listen to this.
Roses are red. Violets are blue.
You are my Valentine
And I love you.
A Wow! Do you know who it's from?
B No idea!

3 A Wake up, Mummy! Happy Mother's Day!
B Thank you, darling. Oh, what beautiful flowers, and a cup of tea!
A And I made you a card! Look!
B It's lovely. What a clever boy!

4 A Congratulations!
B Thank you very much!
A When's the big day?
B Pardon?
A When's your wedding day?
B The 26th June. Didn't you get your invitation?

5 A It's midnight! Happy New Year everybody!
B Happy New Year!
C Happy New Year!

6 A Thank goodness! It's Friday!
B Yeah. Have a nice weekend!
A Same to you.

7 A Ugh! Work again. I hate Monday mornings!
B Me, too. Did you have a good weekend?
A Yes, I did. It was great.

UNIT 9

T 9.1

D = Daisy, P = Piers
D Mmm, I love apple juice. Do you like it Piers?
P No – it's disgusting. I like Cola, … and I love beer.
D Yuck! You don't! You don't drink beer!
P Yes, I do. Sometimes my dad gives me some of his beer – and I love it.
D Well, that's different … My dad drinks coffee – I don't like coffee at all. But my mum drinks tea and I love tea – with lots of milk and sugar.
P No, I don't like tea or coffee, just cola – oh and orange juice. It's funny – I like orange juice, but I don't like oranges. I don't like fruit very much at all. Except bananas – I quite like bananas.
D Really? I like all fruit – apples, oranges, bananas, and I love strawberries. And … what about vegetables, do you like them?
P No – I don't eat vegetables.
D What? Never? Not even potatoes? You eat chips – I know you do.
P Yeah – OK, I eat potatoes – especially chips. Chips and hamburgers. I love that for my dinner.
D I don't like hamburgers – my favourite dinner is fish and chips with peas.
P Fish – yuk! Peas – yuk!
D I like vegetables – especially carrots and peas, oh and tomatoes. Hey, are tomatoes fruit or vegetable?
P I don't know. Anyway, I don't like tomatoes – except on pizza or with pasta and cheese. I love pizza and pasta.
D Me too.
P Anyway, I know your favourite food.
D No, you don't!
P Yes, I do. It's chocolate – all girls like chocolate!
D Boys like chocolate too! You ate all those chocolate biscuits at my house last week.
P They were biscuits. That's different. Anyway – you ate more than me …
D No, I didn't!
P Yes, you did!
D Didn't!
P Did!

T 9.2 see p67

T 9.3

1 Would you like a ham sandwich?
No, thanks. I'm not hungry.
2 Do you like Ella?
Yes. She's very nice.
3 Would you like a cold drink?
Yes, cola, please.
4 Can I help you?
Yes. I'd like some stamps, please.
5 What sports do you do?
Well, I like swimming very much.
6 Excuse me, are you ready to order?
Yes. I'd like a steak, please.

T 9.4

1 Good afternoon. Can I help you?
2 Who's your favourite writer?
3 What would you like for your birthday?
4 Do you like animals?
5 Here's the wine list, sir.
6 Have some ice-cream with your strawberries.

T 9.5

1 A Good afternoon. Can I help you?
  B Yes. I'd like some fruit, please.
2 A Who's your favourite writer?
  B I like books by John Grisham.
3 A What would you like for your birthday?
  B I'd like a new bike.
4 A Do you like animals?
  B I like cats, but I don't like dogs.
5 A Here's the wine list, sir.
  B We'd like a bottle of Italian red wine.
6 A Have some ice-cream with your strawberries.
  B No, thanks. I don't like ice-cream.

T 9.6

At the market
M = Mum, P = Piers, S = Stallholder
M Piers! Hurry up!
P Aw, Mum, I don't like shopping.
M Come on, Piers. I need your help.
P OK.
    ….
S Good morning Madam. How can I help you today?
M Well, I'd like some apple juice, please.
S How many bottles?
M Two, please.
P But Mum, … I don't like apple juice.
M Shh Piers. It's good for you. Thank you. Here … You can carry them.
P Oh no!
M And a kilo of tomatoes, please.
S No problem. Lovely and fresh these tomatoes are. There we are.
M And I'd like some of that cheddar cheese, please.
S This one? How much? Is this much OK?
M That's fine, thanks. And … is there any brown bread? I can't see any.
S Sorry, no, there isn't – but there's some nice white bread. Look! It's homemade.
M Erm …
P Mum, I really like white bread. Please can we have it?
M Oh, OK then. Yes, thanks.
S Anything else?
P Oh yeah! Mum! Look at those cakes!
M Shh Piers. … Um … oh yes, some apples.
S How many – one bag or two?
M Two bags, please.
P Oh yuck. Can't we have bananas?
M No, we can't. Here. Take these bags for me.
P Oh Mum! They're heavy!
M Thanks. … How much is all that?
S Let's see, that's ten pounds and eighty-five pence.
M Here you are.
S Thanks. And here's your change.
M Thanks. Bye!
    ….
P Phew! Is that everything?
M No, erm, … I still need erm …

P Mum, not more. I hate shopping!
M … need to buy your new trainers, but if you don't want to …
P New trainers – cool!
M … But I thought you didn't like shopping …
P Yeah, but …

T 9.7

My favourite national food
Anke
One dish that is very famous in my country is 'Sachertorte'. It is a kind of chocolate cake and you eat it with cream. I love it! The famous Café Sacher is in the centre of Vienna. They say a chef called Franz Sacher invented it there. When I am in Vienna, I always go to Café Sacher for some of their cake and a nice black coffee.

Graham
Now in my job, I travel the world, and I like all kinds of food … but my favourite, my favourite is … er … I always have it as soon as I come home … is a full English breakfast. Bacon, eggs, sausage, mushrooms, tomatoes, and of course, toast. I love it, not every day, but when I'm at home we have it every Sunday. Mmmm! I'd like it right now. Delicious.

Sergio
We love eating in my country! One of my favourite national dishes is called 'bruschetta'. This is actually toast, but you make it with special bread. You can eat it with a lot of things, but my favourite bruschetta has tomatoes, garlic, and olive oil on it. In my town there is a 'bruschetteria'. This is a small café – selling only toast! It's my favourite place to go.

Madalena
One kind of food that my country is very famous for is meat, especially beef. Everybody eats a lot of meat here. My family eats beef three or four times a week. There are a lot of different beef dishes, but my favourite is 'bife de chorizo.' This is a big steak! My mum cooks it with tomatoes and chilli. Delicious!

T 9.8

1 Would you like some more rice?
  Yes, please. It's delicious.
2 Could you pass the salt, please?
  Yes, of course. Here you are.
3 Could I have a glass of water, please?
  Do you want sparkling or still?
4 Does anybody want more wine?
  Yes, please. I'd love some.
5 How would you like your coffee?
  Black, no sugar, please.
6 This is delicious! Can you give me the recipe?
  Yes, of course. I'm glad you like it.
7 Do you want help with the washing-up?
  No, of course not. We have a dishwasher.

T 9.9 see p73

T 9.10

1 A Can I have a cheese sandwich, please?
  B Yes, of course. That's £1.75.
2 A Could you tell me the time, please?
  B It's just after ten.
3 A Can you take me to the station, please?
  B Jump in.

4 A Can I see the menu, please?
  B Here you are. And would you like a drink to start?
5 A Could you lend me some money, please?
  B Not again! How much would you like this time?
6 A Can you help me with my homework, please?
  B What is it? French? I can't speak a word of French.
7 A Can I borrow your dictionary, please?
  B Yes, if I can find it. I think it's in my bag.

 UNIT 10

T 10.1

J = Joel, A = Andy
J I prefer city life. It's faster, more modern, and more exciting than country life.
A Yes, but city life's also more dangerous. The country's slower and safer than the city. I prefer the country. It's more relaxing.
J Well, it's certainly more relaxing, but that's because it's more boring!

T 10.2 see p74

T 10.3

1 A Life in the country is slower than city life.
  B Yes, the city's much faster.
2 A New York is safer than Los Angeles.
  B No, it isn't. New York is much more dangerous.
3 A Seoul is bigger than Beijing.
  B No, it isn't! It's much smaller.
4 A Madrid is more expensive than Rome.
  B No, it isn't. Madrid is much cheaper.
5 A The buildings in Rome are more modern than the buildings in Prague.
  B No, they aren't. They're much older.
6 A Cafés in London are better than cafés in Paris.
  B No! Cafés in London are much worse.

T 10.4

Country life
J = Joel, A = Andy
J So, Andy, tell me, why did you leave London? You had a good job.
A Yes, but I've got a better job here.
J And you had a nice flat in London.
A Well, I've got a nicer place here. It's a cottage!
J Really? How many bedrooms has it got?
A Three. And it's got a garden. It's bigger than my flat in London and it's cheaper.
J But you haven't got any friends!
A I've got a lot of new friends here. People are much friendlier than in London.
J But the country's so boring!
A No, it isn't. I've got a surfboard now and I go surfing at weekends. Appleton has got a cinema, restaurants, pubs, and a nightclub. And the air is cleaner and the streets are safer.
J OK. OK. Everything is better! Can I come next weekend?
A Of course you can!

T 10.5

1 That house is very big.
   Yes, it's the biggest house in the village.
2 The Ritz is a very expensive hotel.
   Yes, it's the most expensive hotel in London.
3 Appleton is a very pretty village.
   Yes, it's the prettiest village in England.
4 New York is a very cosmopolitan city.
   Yes, it's the most cosmopolitan city in the world.
5 Brad Pitt is a very popular film star.
   Yes, he's the most popular film star in America.
6 Miss Smith is a very funny teacher.
   Yes, she's the funniest teacher in our school.
7 Anna is a very intelligent student.
   Yes, she's the most intelligent student in the class.
8 This is a very easy exercise.
   Yes, it's the easiest exercise in the book.

T 10.6 see p77

T 10.7

Musical excerpts: flamenco; tango; salsa

T 10.8

1 Everest is the highest mountain in the world.
2 The Golden Gate Bridge in San Francisco is the longest bridge in the USA.
3 The Caspian Sea isn't a sea, it's the largest lake in the world.
4 Rotterdam is the busiest port in Europe. Ships from all over the world stop there.
5 The Empire State Building in New York was the tallest building in the world for over 40 years.
6 A church is much smaller than a cathedral.

T 10.9

wood	village
farm	cottage
factory	church
field	building
theatre	

T 10.10

J = Joel, A = Andy

J So how do I find your cottage, then?
A Have you got a pen and paper?
J Erm … yes, I have.
A OK. Well, leave the A34 at Apple Cross. Turn left at the traffic lights. Then go down the hill, and under the first bridge. OK? Then go over the second bridge, and along the road by the river. Go past the pub, and turn right up the hill. Go round the corner past the farm, and my cottage is on the right. It's easy!
J OK. Got that. See you tomorrow afternoon!
A Bye. Safe journey. Oh, don't forget your surfboard!

T 10.11

J = Joel, A = Andy

A Look at you! What happened? Where's your car?
J I had a small problem …
A What? How?
J Well, I did what you said. I drove down the hill, under the first bridge, and over the second bridge, then I drove along the road by the river, past the pub, and up the hill. Next I drove round the corner, but I saw some big cows in front of me. So I turned quickly, drove off the road through some apple trees, and into a lot of mud.
A Oh no! Are you all right?
J I'm fine. But now I can't move the car. Come and help me.
A Of course. But why didn't you just stop?
J Well, there were a lot of cows and they didn't look very friendly.
A But cows aren't dangerous.
J OK, OK! … I still don't like the country very much …

UNIT 11

T 11.1

Who's at the party?
O = Oliver, M = Monica

O Oh dear, Monica! I don't know any of these people. Who are they?
M Don't worry, Oliver. They're all very nice. Can you see that man over there? He's sitting down. That's Harry. He's a musician. He works in LA.
O Sorry, where?
M You know, LA. Los Angeles.
O Oh, yeah.
M And he's talking to Mandy. She's wearing a red dress. She's very nice and very rich! She lives in a beautiful old house in the country.
O Rich, eh?
M Yes. Rich and married! Next to her is Fiona. She's drinking a glass of red wine. Fiona's my oldest friend, she and I were at school together.
O And what does Fiona do?
M She's a writer. She writes children's stories – they're not very good but … anyway, she's talking to George. He's laughing and smoking a cigar. He's a pilot. He travels the world, thousands of miles every week.
O And who are those two over there? They're dancing. Mmmm. They know each other very well.
M Oh, that's Roz and Sam. They're married. They live in the flat upstairs.
O So … um … that's Harry and Mandy and … um … it's no good, I can't remember all those names.

T 11.2

1 A Whose is the baseball cap?
   B It's his.
2 A Whose are the boots?
   B They're hers.
3 A Whose is the baby?
   B It's theirs.

T 11.3

1 Who's on the phone?
2 I'm going to the pub. Who's coming?
3 Wow! Look at that sports car. Whose is it?
4 Whose dictionary is this? It's not mine.
5 There are books all over the floor. Whose are they?
6 Who's the most intelligent in our class?
7 Who's got my book?
8 Do you know whose jacket this is?

T 11.4

A Whose is this tennis racket?
B It's mine.
A What's it doing here?
B I'm playing tennis this afternoon.

T 11.5

1 A Whose are these football boots?
   B They're John's. He's playing football later.
2 A Whose are these ballet shoes?
   B They're Mary's. She's going dancing tonight.
3 A Whose is this suitcase?
   B It's mine. I'm going on holiday tomorrow.
4 A Whose is this coat?
   B It's Jane's. She's going for a walk soon.
5 A Whose is this plane ticket?
   B It's Jo's. She's flying to Rome this afternoon.
6 A Whose are all these glasses?
   B They're ours. We're having a party tonight.

T 11.6

Flying without wings
Everybody's looking for that something
One thing that makes it all complete
You find it in the strangest places
Places you never knew it could be

Some find it in the faces of their children
Some find it in their lover's eyes
Who can deny the joy it brings
When you find that special thing
You're flying without wings

Some find it sharing every morning
Some in their solitary lives
You find it in the words of others
A simple line can make you laugh or cry

You find it in the deepest friendship
The kind you cherish all your life
And when you know how much that means
You've found that special thing
You're flying without wings

So impossible as it may seem
You've got to fight for every dream
'Cause who's to know which one you let go
Would have made you complete

Well, for me it's waking up beside you
To watch the sunrise on your face
To know that I can say I love you
At any given time or place

It's little things that only I know
Those are the things that make you mine
And it's like flying without wings
'Cause you're my special thing
I'm flying without wings

You're the place my life begins
And you'll be where it ends
I'm flying without wings
And that's the joy you bring
I'm flying without wings

T 11.7 see p88

T 11.8

Vowels	Diphthongs
1 /e/ red said	1 /aɪ/ eyes size
2 /æ/ hat that	2 /ɪə/ near beer
3 /ɪ/ list kissed	3 /eɪ/ grey pay
4 /iː/ green mean	4 /eə/ hair wear
5 /ɑː/ park dark	5 /əʊ/ those nose
6 /uː/ whose shoes	6 /aʊ/ ours flowers
7 /ɔː/ short bought	

T 11.9 see p88

T 11.10

SA Can I help you?
C Yes, please. I'm looking for a shirt to go with my new jeans.
SA What colour are you looking for?
C Blue.
SA What about this one? Do you like this?
C No, it isn't the right blue.
SA Well, what about this one? It's a bit darker blue.
C Oh yes. I like that one much better. Can I try it on?
SA Yes, of course. The changing rooms are over there.
...
 Is the size OK?
C No, it's a bit too big. Have you got a smaller size?
SA That's the last blue one we've got, I'm afraid. But we've got it in green.
C OK. I'll take the green. How much is it?
SA £39.99. How do you want to pay?
C Can I pay by credit card?
SA Credit card's fine. Thank you very much.

Song: Teacher's Book p149

UNIT 12

T 12.1

Future plans
Jack
When I grow up I'm going to be a footballer – a really good one. I'm in the school team and I play three times a week. But I'm going to train very hard, every day, so I can be really, really good. First I'm going to play for Manchester United, then Inter Milan, and then Real Madrid. Those are my favourite teams. I'm going to travel all over the world and I'm going to be famous. I'm not going to marry until I'm very old – about 25. Then I want to have two sons. I'm going to play football until I'm 35 – that's a very long time. And I'm going to teach my sons to play. I want them to be famous footballers, too!

Danny Carrick
When I retire next year ... I'm going to retire early ... I'm not going to stay at home and watch TV. I'm going to try lots of new things. First I want to go mountain-climbing. In fact, I want to climb Mount Everest, so I'm going to train very hard for that. I'm going to learn to scuba-dive, too, because I want to go scuba-diving in Australia. There are so many things I want to do!

I'm going to travel all over the world, then I'm going to write a book about my adventures. I want to call it 'Life begins at 60!' In my book, I'm going to tell other retired people to try new things, too. You are only as old as you feel!

T 12.2 see p90

T 12.3

1 A Why is he going to train very hard?
 B Because he wants to be a footballer.
2 A How long is he going to play football?
 B Until he's 35.
3 A When is he going to marry?
 B Not until he's very old – about 25!
4 A How many children is he going to have?
 B Two.
5 A Who is he going to teach to play?
 B His sons.

T 12.4

1 Take an umbrella. It's going to rain.
2 Look at the time! You're going to be late for the meeting.
3 Anna's running very fast. She's going to win the race.
4 Look! Jack's on the wall. He's going to fall.
5 Look at that man! He's going to jump.
6 They're going to have a baby. It's due next month.
7 There's my sister and her boyfriend! They're going to kiss.
8 A Oh dear. I'm going to sneeze. Aaattishooo!
 B Bless you!

T 12.5 see p92

T 12.6

A What's the weather like today?
B It's snowy and it's very cold.
A What was it like yesterday?
B Oh, it was cold and cloudy.
A What's it going to be like tomorrow?
B I think it's going to be warmer.

T 12.7

1 A It's a lovely day! What shall we do?
 B Let's play tennis!
2 A It's raining again! What shall we do?
 B Let's stay at home and watch a DVD.

T 12.8

1 A It's a lovely day! What shall we do?
 B Let's play tennis!
 A Oh no! It's too hot to play tennis.
 B Well, let's go swimming.
 A OK. I'll get my swimming costume.
2 A It's raining again! What shall we do?
 B Let's stay at home and watch a DVD.
 A Oh no! We watched a DVD last night.
 B Well, let's go to the cinema.
 A OK. Which film do you want to see?

UNIT 13

T 13.1

Storytime quiz
1 When did Shakespeare die?
 b In the 17th century
2 What happens at the end of *Romeo and Juliet*?
 They both die. They kill themselves.
3 How many dwarfs are there in *Snow White*?
 b 7
4 How much money do Hansel and Gretel's parents have?
 c None
5 How long does Sleeping Beauty sleep?
 100 years
6 Who does Cinderella marry?
 a The handsome Prince
7 Who created Mickey Mouse?
 Walt Disney
8 Where did Hans Christian Andersen come from?
 b Denmark
9 What nationality are Don Quixote and Sancho Panza?
 Spanish
10 Whose lamp is magic?
 a Aladdin's
11 Why does Pinocchio's nose grow long?
 Because he tells lies
12 What kind of animal is Walt Disney's Dumbo?
 a an elephant
13 Which city does Sherlock Holmes live in?
 b London
14 How old is Harry Potter in the first story *Harry Potter and the Philosopher's Stone*?
 b 11

T 13.2 see p99

T 13.3

1 A What's she wearing?
 B Jeans.
 A Is she wearing jeans?
 B Yes, she is.
 C No, she isn't.
2 A Where does she work?
 B In a bank.
 A Does she work in a bank?
 B Yes, she does.
 C No, she doesn't.
3 A When's he leaving?
 B Tomorrow.
 A Is he leaving tomorrow?
 B Yes, he is.
 C No, he isn't.
4 A Who did you visit?
 B My aunt.
 A Did you visit your aunt?
 B Yes, I did.
 C No, I didn't.
5 A How did you come?
 B By taxi.
 A Did you come by taxi?
 B Yes, we did.
 C No, we didn't.
6 A Why are they going to have a party?
 B Because it's her birthday. (sample answer)
 A Are they going to have a party?
 B Yes, they are.
 C No, they aren't.

T 13.4

A Where did you go?
B To the shops.
A When did you go?
B This morning.
A Who did you go with?
B A friend from work.
A How did you go?
B We drove.
A Whose car did you go in?
B Joe's.
A Why did you go?
B To buy some new clothes.
A What did you buy?
B A new jacket.
A How many did you buy?
B Only one.
A Which one did you buy?
B The black leather one.
A How much did you pay?
B £180.99.

T 13.5

1 Why do you want to go?
2 Who is she?
3 Where's he staying?
4 Why didn't they come?
5 How old was she?
6 Does he play the guitar?
7 Where did you go at the weekend?

T 13.6

Noises in the night

It was about two o'clock in the morning, and … suddenly I woke up. I heard a noise. I got out of bed and went slowly downstairs. There was a light on in the living room. I listened carefully. I could hear two men speaking very quietly. 'Burglars!' I thought. 'Two burglars!' Immediately I ran back upstairs and phoned the police. I was really frightened. Fortunately the police arrived quickly. They opened the front door and went into the living room. Then they came upstairs to find me. 'It's all right now, sir,' they explained. 'We turned the television off for you!'

T 13.7 see p102

T 13.8 see p103

T 13.9 see p104

T 13.10

A Hello. Can I help you?
B Yes, please. I'm not feeling very well. I'm looking for some aspirin. Where can I find them?
A Right here. What size do you want? Small or large?
B Large, please. And I'd like some shampoo, as well.
A What kind of shampoo? For dry hair? Normal hair?
B Um … for dry hair, please.
A There's Sunsilk or Palmolive. Which one do you want?
B Sunsilk's fine, thanks.
A Anything else?
B No, that's all. How much is that?
A Four pounds twenty.

B There you are.
A Ten pounds. Thank you. And here's five pounds eighty change.
B Thanks. Bye.
A Bye-bye. Thank you very much.

UNIT 14

T 14.1

S = Steve, R = Ryan

S Ryan, where are you and Tara going for your honeymoon?
R Somewhere in Europe, we think. France, maybe, or Spain. I've been to Paris, but I haven't been to Barcelona.
S Yes, Paris is beautiful. But what about Venice? It's very romantic.
R Mmm, that's an idea. I've been to Italy, but I've never been to Venice.
S What about Tara? Where does she want to go?
R Oh, Tara doesn't mind where we go. She's been to Mexico and Brazil, but she hasn't been anywhere in Europe!

T 14.2 see p106

T 14.3 see p106

T 14.4

What has Ryan done?

Yes, I've lived in a foreign country. In Japan, actually. I lived in Osaka for a year. I enjoyed it very much. I loved the food. And, yes, I have worked for a big company. I worked for Nissan, the car company, that's why I was in Japan. That was three years ago, then I got a job back in London.
Have I stayed in an expensive hotel? No, never – only cheap hotels for me, I'm afraid, but I have flown in a jumbo jet – lots of times, actually. Oh, I've never cooked a meal for a lot of people. I love food but I don't like cooking much. Sometimes I cook for me and my girlfriend Tara, but she likes it better if we go out for a meal! And I've never met a famous person – oh, just a minute, well not met, but I've seen … er… I saw a famous politician at the airport once – oh, who was it? I can't remember his name, um … I've only seen one Shakespeare play, when I was at school, we saw *Romeo and Juliet*. It was OK. I've ridden a motorbike though. My brother's got one. It's very fast. Fortunately, I've never been to hospital. My brother has – he fell off his motorbike! Unfortunately, I've never won a competition. I do the lottery every week, but I've never, ever won a thing!

T 14.5

A honeymoon in Venice
T = Tara, A = Amy

T We're having a great time!
A Tell me about it! What have you done so far?
T Well, we've been to St Mark's Square. That was the first thing we did. It's right in the centre of Venice. We sat outside in the sun and had a coffee. We've seen the paintings in the Doge's Palace. It was wonderful. But we haven't climbed up St Mark's Bell Tower yet. It was too busy. We're going early tomorrow morning.
A Have you been in a gondola yet?
T Oh yes, we have! We had a gondola trip yesterday evening. It was so romantic! And we've just had a fantastic boat ride along the Grand Canal and we went under the Rialto Bridge! But we haven't walked across it yet. I wanna do that.
A Wow! You're busy! Have you visited the Murano glass factories yet? Don't forget – I want a glass horse!
T I haven't forgotten. In fact, we took a boat to Murano island yesterday, and I got your horse. OK?
A Oh, thank you, thank you! So what else are you going to do?
T Well, I'd like to go to the beach, you know – at the Lido. It's so hot here! But we haven't really decided what else to do yet. There's so much to see.
A Oh, you're so lucky! Have a lovely time. Give my love to Ryan!
T Yeah. Bye, Amy. See you next week at the airport!

T 14.6

All around the world
Chorus

I've been around the world and I
I can't find my baby
I don't know when, I don't know why
Why he's gone away
And I don't know where he can be, my baby
But I'm gonna find him

We had a quarrel and I let myself go
I said so many things, things he didn't know
And I was oh so bad
And I don't think he's coming back

He gave the reason, the reasons he should go
And he said so many things he's never said before
And he was oh so mad
And I don't think he's coming, coming back
I did too much lying, wasted too much time
Now I'm here crying.

Chorus

So open-hearted, he never did me wrong
I was the one, the weakest one of all
And now I'm oh so sad
And I don't think he's coming back, coming back
I did too much lying, wasted too much time
Now I'm here crying.

Chorus

I've been around the world looking for my baby
Been around the world and I'm gonna
I'm gonna find him

T 14.7

British Airways flight BA516 to Geneva boarding at gate 4, last call. Flight BA516 to Geneva, last call.

Scandinavian Airlines flight SK 832 to Frankfurt is delayed one hour. Flight SK 832 to Frankfurt, delayed one hour.

Air France flight 472 to Amsterdam is now boarding at gate 17. Flight AF 472 to Amsterdam, now boarding, gate 17.

Lufthansa flight 309 to Miami is now boarding at gate 32. Flight LH 309 to Miami, now boarding, gate 32.

Virgin Airlines flight to New York, VS 876 to New York. Please wait in the departure lounge until a further announcement. Thank you.

Passengers are reminded to keep their hand luggage with them at all times.

T 14.8

1   A   Listen! … BA 516 to Geneva. That's our flight.
    B   Did the announcement say gate 4 or 14?
    A   I couldn't hear. I think it said 4.
    B   Look! There it is on the departure board It *is* gate 4.
    A   OK. Come on! Let's go.

2   A   Can I have your ticket, please?
    B   Yes, of course.
    A   Thank you. How many suitcases have you got?
    B   Just one.
    A   And have you got much hand luggage?
    B   Just this bag.
    A   That's fine.
    B   Oh … can I have a seat next to the window?
    A   Yes, that's OK. Here's your boarding pass. Have a nice flight!

3   A   Ryan! Tara! Over here!
    B   Hi! Amy! Great to see you!
    A   It's great to see you too. You look terrific! Did you have a good honeymoon?
    B   Fantastic. Everything was fantastic.
    A   Well, you haven't missed anything here. Nothing much has happened at all!

4   A   There's my flight. It's time to go.
    B   Oh no! It's been a wonderful two weeks. I can't believe it's over.
    A   I know. When can we see each other again?
    B   Soon, I hope. I'll email every day.
    A   I'll phone too. Goodbye, my darling. Give my love to your family.
    B   Goodbye, Lukas.

Song: Teacher's Book p153

Grammar Reference

 UNIT 1

1.1 Verb *to be*

Positive

I	am		
He She It	is	from the USA.	
We You They	are		

I'm = I am

He's = He is
She's = She is
It's = It is

We're = We are
You're = You are
They're = They are

Question

	am	I	
Where	is	he she it	from?
	are	we you they	

I'm 20

I'm 20.
I'm 20 years old.   NOT   ~~I'm 20 years.~~
                            ~~I have 20 years.~~

1.2 Possessive adjectives

What's	my your his her	name?
This is	its our your their	house.

What's = What is

1.3 Question words

What is your phone number?
Where are you from?
How are you?

1.4 *a/an*

It's a	ticket. newspaper. magazine.

It's an	apple. envelope. English dictionary.

We use *an* before a vowel.

I'm a doctor.
I'm a student.   NOT   ~~I'm doctor.~~
                         ~~I'm student.~~

1.5 Plural nouns

1 Most nouns add -*s* in the plural.
   stamp**s**   key**s**   camera**s**

2 If the noun ends in -*s*, -*ss*, -*sh*, or -*ch*, add -*es*.
   bus → bus**es**   class → class**es**   wish → wish**es**
   match → match**es**

3 If the noun ends in a consonant + -*y*, the -*y* changes to -*ies*.
   country countr**ies**   party part**ies**
   But if the noun ends in a vowel + -*y*, the -*y* doesn't change.
   key ke**ys**   day da**ys**

4 Some nouns are irregular. Dictionaries show this.
   child children   person people
   woman women   man men

1.6 Numbers 1–20

1	one	6	six	11	eleven	16	sixteen
2	two	7	seven	12	twelve	17	seventeen
3	three	8	eight	13	thirteen	18	eighteen
4	four	9	nine	14	fourteen	19	nineteen
5	five	10	ten	15	fifteen	20	twenty

1.7 Prepositions

Where are you **from**?
I live **in** a house **in** Fortaleza.
What's this **in** English?

EXERCISES

1 Complete the sentences. Use *am, is,* or *are*.
   1 How _____ you?
   2 I _____ fine, thanks.
   3 Patrick _____ my brother.
   4 We _____ both 23 years old.
   5 Katy and Paul _____ married.

2 Complete the conversation. Use *my, your, her,* or *his*.
   Ann Hi, (1) _____ name's Ann. What's (2) _____
   name?
   Nick Hi! (3) _____ name's Nick. This is my sister. (4)
   _____ name's Maria.
   Ann Hi. This is my brother. (5) _____ name is Tom.

3 Choose the correct question word.
   1 How / What is your name?
   2 What / How are you?
   3 What / Where are you from?

4 Complete the sentences. Use *a* or *an*.
   1 It's _____ stamp.   4 I'm _____ student.
   2 He's _____ teacher.   5 It's _____ orange.
   3 It's _____ apple.

5 Write the plural form.
   1 dictionary _____   4 child _____
   2 student _____   5 day _____
   3 orange _____

UNIT 2

2.1 Verb *to be*

Questions with question words

What	is her surname?		Answers
What	is her surname? is his job? is her address?		Jefferson. He's a policeman. 34, Church Street.
Where	is she are you are they	from?	Mexico.
Who	is Lara? is she?		She's Patrick's daughter.
How old	is he? are you?		Twenty-two.
How much	is an ice-cream?		One pound 50p.

Yes/No questions

Is	he she it	young?
Are	you they	married?

Short answers

Yes, he is.
No, she isn't.
Yes, it is.

No, I'm not./No, we aren't.
Yes, they are./No, they aren't.

Negative

I	'm not	
He She It	isn't	from the States.
We You They	aren't	

I'm not = I am not (~~I amn't~~)

He isn't = He is not
She isn't = She is not
It isn't = It is not

We aren't = We are not
You aren't = You are not
They aren't = They are not

2.2 Possessive *'s*

My wife**'s** name is Judy.   That's Andrea**'s** dictionary.

2.3 Numbers 21–100

21	twenty-one	30	thirty
22	twenty-two	31	thirty-one
23	twenty-three	40	forty
24	twenty-four	50	fifty
25	twenty-five	60	sixty
26	twenty-six	70	seventy
27	twenty-seven	80	eighty
28	twenty-eight	90	ninety
29	twenty-nine	100	one hundred

2.4 Prepositions

This is a photo **of** my family.
It's good practice **for** you.
I'm **at** home. My mother and father are **at** work.
I'm **at** The Embassy Language School.
I'm **in** Brighton. I'm **in** a class **with** eight students.
I live **with** an English family **in** an old house.

EXERCISES

1 Complete the questions. Use *What, Where, Who, How much,* or *How old.*

1 _____ are you?   I'm 22.
2 _____ is Nick?   He's at home.
3 _____ is this?   It's £40.
4 _____ is your job?   I'm a teacher.
5 _____ is that?   It's Alex.

2 Make questions and negative sentences.

1 you / are / cold / ? _____
2 we / speak / English / don't _____
3 cafés / they / do / like / ? _____
4 I'm / from / Italy / not _____
5 does / play / she / tennis / ? _____

3 Rewrite the sentences. Use the possessive *'s.*

1 Jane + book   <u>Jane's book</u>
2 my friend + bag   _____
3 my family + house   _____
4 John + son   _____
5 Andrea + brother   _____
6 his wife + name   _____

4 Match the numbers.

1	fifteen	a	11
2	twenty	b	12
3	thirteen	c	20
4	eleven	d	13
5	twelve	e	15

UNIT 3

3.1 Present Simple *he, she, it*

1 The Present Simple expresses a fact which is always true, or true for a long time.
     He **comes** from Switzerland.   She **works** in a bank.

2 It also expresses a habit.
     She **goes** skiing in winter.   He never **has** a holiday.

Positive

He She It	lives	in Australia.

Have is irregular.
She **has** a dog.
NOT she ~~haves~~

Negative

He She It	doesn't live	in France.

doesn't = does not

Question

Where does	he she it	live?

Yes/No questions

Does	he she it	live	in Australia? in France?

Short answers

Yes, he does.
No, she doesn't.
Yes, it does.

3.2 Spelling of the third person singular

1 Most verbs add *-s* in the third person singular.
　wear → wears　　speak → speaks　　live → lives
　But *go* and *do* are different. They add *-es*.
　　go → goes　　do → does

2 If the verb ends in *-s*, *-sh*, or *-ch*, add *-es*.
　finish → finishes　　watch → watches

3 If the verb ends in a consonant + *-y*, the *-y* changes to *-ies*.
　fly → flies　　study → studies
　But if the verb ends in a vowel + *-y* the *-y* does not change.
　play → plays

4 *Have* is irregular.
　have → has

3.3 Prepositions

She lives **in** Kenya.
He plays tennis **in** his free time.
A nurse looks **after** people **in** hospital.
He lives **on** an island **in** the west **of** Scotland.
He collects the post **from** the boat.
He drives the children **to** school.
Tourists come **by** boat.
It's **about** 6.30.

EXERCISES

1 Write the third person singular form of the verbs.

1 do	_____	4 speak	_____
2 watch	_____	5 have	_____
3 listen	_____	6 walk	_____

2 Change the sentences from positive to negative.
1 Olivier comes from Belgium. _____
2 Sandra works in a school. _____
3 Bill speaks Japanese. _____
4 My sister has two children. _____
5 Lucy goes to Greece every year. _____
6 Peter studies art at college. _____

3 Make questions.
1 study / Harry / German / at school / does / ?
_____
2 does / she / live / where / ?
_____
3 does / come / this stamp / where / from / ?
_____
4 sports / does / enjoy / she / what / ?
_____
5 Guy / got / has / dog / a / ?
_____

4 Complete the sentences. Use the Present Simple.
1 _____ he _____ in Greece? (live)
2 You _____ in a bank. (not work)
3 I _____ TV in the evenings. (watch)
4 Marta _____ a new boyfriend. (have)
5 I _____ Spanish. (not speak)
6 _____ Carlo _____ English? (study)

UNIT 4

4.1 Present Simple

Positive

I You We They	start	at 6.30.
He She It	starts	

Negative

I You We They	don't	start	at 6.30.
He She It	doesn't		

Question

When	do	I you we they	start?
	does	he she it	

***Yes/No* questions**

Do	you they	have	a camera?
Does	he she it	like	Chinese food?

Short answers

No, I don't./No, we don't.
Yes, they do.

Yes, he does.
No, she doesn't.
Yes, it does.

4.2 Adverbs of frequency

0%		50%		100%
never	sometimes	often	usually	always

1 These adverbs usually come before the main verb.
　She **never** eats meat.
　I **sometimes** play tennis on Saturdays.
　I don't **often** go swimming.
　I **usually** go to bed at about 11.00.
　We **always** have wine in the evenings.

2 *Sometimes* and *usually* can also come at the beginning or the end of a sentence.
　Sometimes we play cards.　　We play cards **sometimes**.
　Usually I walk to school.　　I walk to school **usually**.

3 *Never* and *always* can't come at the beginning or the end of a sentence.
　NOT　~~Never I go to the theatre.~~
　　　　~~Always I have tea in the morning.~~

4.3 *like/love* + verb + *-ing*

When *like* and *love* are followed by a verb, it is usually verb + *-ing*.
　I **like** cook**ing**.　　She **loves** listen**ing** to music.

4.4 Prepositions

She gets up early **on** weekdays.
She goes to the gym **on** Friday mornings.
They never go out **on** Saturday evenings.
Do you relax **at** weekends?
She gets up **at** six o'clock.
She gets up early **in** the morning.
We go out **in** the evening.
She goes surfing **in** summer.

EXERCISES

1 Complete the sentences. Use the positive form of the verbs in the box.

play	go	live	work	speak

1 My best friend _____ in Italy.
2 John and Kate _____ French and German.
3 Nadia often _____ running before breakfast.
4 I _____ six days a week.
5 My brother _____ the piano.

2 Make questions and short answers. Use the Present Simple.

1 he / like / swimming?

_____

No, _____ .

2 you / have / a computer?

_____

Yes, _____ .

3 they / live / in Paris?

_____

Yes, _____ .

4 she / start / at 9.00?

_____

No, _____ .

5 we / speak / English?

_____

Yes, _____ .

3 Put the adverb in the correct place.

1 George walks to work. (always) _____
2 Sandra watches TV. (never) _____
3 You don't go running. (often) _____

4 Find and correct two incorrect sentences.

1 Vicky loves listen to the radio. _____
2 My sister likes going shopping. _____
3 They love reading. _____
4 David likes to cooking. _____

UNIT 5

5.1 *There is/are*

Positive

There	is	a sofa.	(singular)
	are	two books.	(plural)

Negative

There	isn't	an armchair.	(singular)
	aren't	any flowers.	(plural)

Yes/No questions

Is	there	a table?
Are		any photos?

Short answers

Yes, there is.
No, there isn't.

Yes, there are.
No, there aren't.

5.2 *How many . . . ?*

How many books do you have?

5.3 *some/any*

Positive
There are **some** flowers.   *some* + plural noun
Negative
There aren't **any** cups.   *any* + plural noun
Question
Are there **any** books?   *any* + plural noun

5.4 *this, that, these, those*

We use *this/these* to talk about people/things that are near to us.
    I like **this** ice-cream.
    I want **these** shoes.

We use *that/those* to talk about people/things that aren't near to us.
    Do you like **that** picture on the wall?
    Who are **those** children outside?

5.5 Prepositions

He lives **in** the south **of** France.
There is a photo **on** the television.
There are two pictures **on** the wall.
The cinema is **on** the left, **opposite** the flower shop.
The bank is **next to** the supermarket.
The bus stop is **near** the park.
There is a post box **in front of** the post office.
There are magazines **under** the table.

EXERCISES

1 Match the two halves of the sentences.

1 Is there	a any boys?
2 There are	b a computer.
3 Are there	c a letter?
4 There isn't	d two girls.

2 Make sentences. Use the verb *be* (+, −, or ?) .

1 (?) _____ there any books?
2 (−) There _____ any champagne.
3 (+) There _____ five glasses.
4 (?) _____ there a dictionary?
5 (−) There _____ any magazines.
6 (+) There _____ a black dog.

3 Complete the sentences. Use *some*, *any*, or *many*.

1 How _____ apples are there?
2 There are _____ photos.
3 Are there _____ glasses?
4 There are _____ biscuits.
5 How _____ sandwiches do you want?

4 Choose the correct word.

1 I like this / these clock.
2 Do you want those / that books?
3 These / this flowers are beautiful!
4 Where is that / those café?

UNIT 6

6.1 *can/can't*

Can and *can't* have the same form in all persons.
There is no *do* or *does*.
Can is followed by the infinitive (without *to*).

could/couldn't

Could is the past of *can*.
Could and *couldn't* have the same form in all persons.
Could is followed by the infinitive (without *to*).

Positive

I He/She/It We You They	can could	swim.

Negative

I He/She/It We You They	can't couldn't	dance.	NOT He doesn't can dance.

Question

What	can could	I you he/she/it we they	do?

Yes/No questions

Can Could	you she they	drive? cook?

Short answers

No, I can't./No, we couldn't.
Yes, she can/could.
Yes, they can/could.

NOT Do you can drive?

6.2 *was/were*

Was/were is the past of *am/is/are*.

Positive

I He/She/It	was	in Paris yesterday. in England last year.
We You They	were	

Negative

I He/She/It	wasn't	at school yesterday. at the party last night.
We You They	weren't	

Question

Where	was	I? he/she/it?
	were	we/you/they?

Yes/No questions

Was	he she	at work? at home?
Were	you they	

Short answers

No, he wasn't.
Yes, she was.

Yes, I was./Yes, we were.
No, they weren't.

was born

Where	was	she he	born?
	were	you they	

I **was born** in Manchester in 1980.

NOT I am born in 1980.

6.3 Prepositions

I was **at** a party.
Yesterday there was a party **at** my house.
Can I speak **to** you?
He sits **at** his computer **for** hours.

EXERCISES

1 Correct the sentences.

1 Tanya can sing, but she couldn't dance.
   _____

2 Mark could to swim two years ago, but he couldn't ride a bicycle.
   _____

3 Do you can play tennis?
   _____

4 What I can do today?
   _____

2 Write sentences that are true for you. Use *can/can't* or *could/couldn't*.

1 I _____ play an instrument.
2 I _____ use a computer.
3 I _____ fly a plane.
4 I _____ cook.
5 I _____ ride a bike when I was six.
6 I _____ swim when I was two.
7 I _____ speak two languages when I was eight.
8 I _____ speak my language when I was four.

3 Rewrite the sentences in the past. Use *was* or *were*.

1 I'm in London. _____
2 They are at a party. _____
3 Where are you? _____
4 You aren't at school. _____
5 She's at home. _____
6 Are they in the restaurant? _____
7 Where's David? _____
8 We aren't at work. _____

UNIT 7

7.1 Past Simple – spelling of regular verbs

1 The normal rule is to add -ed.
   work**ed**   start**ed**
   If the verb ends in -e, add -d.
   live**d**   love**d**

2 If the verb has only one syllable and one vowel and one consonant, double the consonant.
   sto**pp**ed   pla**nn**ed

3 Verbs that end in a consonant + -y change to -ied.
   stud**ied**   carr**ied**

7.2 Past Simple

The Past Simple expresses a past action that is finished.
   I **lived** in Rome when I was six.
   She **started** work when she was eight.
The form of the Past Simple is the same in all persons.

Positive

I He/She/It We You They	moved went	to London in 1985.

Negative

We use *didn't* + infinitive (without *to*) in all persons.

I He/She/It We You They	didn't	move go	to London.

Question

We use *did* + infinitive (without *to*) in all persons.

When Where	did	I you he/she/it we/they	go?

Yes/No questions

Did	you she they etc.	like enjoy	the film? the party?

Short answers

No, I didn't.
No, we didn't.
Yes, she did.
No, they didn't.

There is list of irregular verbs on the inside back cover.

7.3 Time expressions

last	night week Saturday	month year

yesterday	morning afternoon evening

7.4 Prepositions

She travelled **around** the world.
She acted **in** over 50 films.
She worked **for** 20th Century Fox.
She went **to** school when she was 12.
She flew **across** the Atlantic.
Are you interested **in** modern art?

EXERCISES

1 Complete the sentences. Use the Past Simple.

1 I _____ playing football at 5 p.m. (stop)
2 She _____ in a café last summer. (work)
3 You _____ John last week. (not see)
4 _____ they _____ to university? (go)
5 Sarah _____ in New York in 2002. (live)
6 When _____ he _____ ? (arrive)
7 Peter _____ to travel round Europe. (decide)
8 Luke _____ two dogs and a cat. (have)
9 When _____ the film _____ ? (finish)
10 They _____ a holiday in India. (want)

2 Put the time expressions in the correct column.

morning	night	afternoon	year	evening	week

last	_____	yesterday	_____
	_____		_____
	_____		_____

3 Write the Past Simple of the verbs.

1 walk	_____	6 write	_____
2 go	_____	7 study	_____
3 see	_____	8 run	_____
4 eat	_____	9 sing	_____
5 become	_____	10 hear	_____

4 Write short answers that are true for you.

1 Did you watch TV last week? _____
2 Did you and your friends go out last weekend? _____
3 Did your father teach you to ride a bike? _____
4 Did your parents travel abroad when you were a child? _____

UNIT 8

8.1 Past Simple

Negative

Negatives in the Past Simple are the same in all persons.

I/He/She We/You/They	didn't	go out see Tom	last night.

ago

I went to the USA	ten years / two weeks / a month	ago.

8.2 Time expressions

in	the twentieth century / 1924 / the 1990s winter / summer / the evening / morning / September
on	10 October / Christmas Day / Saturday / Sunday evening
at	seven o'clock / weekends / night

8.3 Prepositions

He started **in** the 1820s.
Only US cars had windscreen wipers **by** 1916.
I tried to forget **about** him.
People didn't hear **about** his invention.

People laughed **at** her idea.
I fell **in** love **with** him.
They lived **by** the lake.

EXERCISES

1 Make sentences.

1 Sue / yesterday / to the cinema / went

_____

2 ago / I / met / Nick / two years

_____

3 last night / go / they / out / didn't

_____

4 three weeks / Jack / ago / was born

_____

5 Friday / we / last / met

_____

2 Rewrite the sentences. Use the negative form of the Past Simple.

1 I watched TV last night. _____
2 They travelled by train. _____
3 Mary sang in the concert last week. _____
4 Pete saw three men outside the bank. _____
5 We went to New York in 2002. _____

3 Complete the sentences. Use the Past Simple.

1 Nick _____ off his bike. (fall)
2 I _____ them an email. (send)
3 You _____ my glasses! (find)
4 She _____ a cup of coffee. (drink)
5 We _____ a new DVD. (buy)

4 Choose the correct preposition.

1 They met on / at / in 11 June.
2 Kate was born in / at / on the 1980s.
3 We play tennis on / in / at weekends.
4 She bought the flat at / on / in May.
5 What did you do in / at / on Monday?

 UNIT 9

9.1 Count and uncount nouns

Some nouns are countable.
   a book → **two books**   **an egg** → **six eggs**
Some nouns are uncountable.
   bread   rice
Some nouns are both!
   Do you like **ice-cream**?   We'd like three **ice-creams**, please.

9.2 *would like*

Would is the same in all persons.
We use *would like* in offers and requests.

Positive

I You He/She/It We They	'd like	a drink.	'd = would

Yes/No questions

Would	you he/she/it they	like a biscuit?

Short answers

Yes, please.
No, thank you.

9.3 *some* and *any*

We use *some* in positive sentences with uncount nouns and plural nouns.

There is	some	bread	on the table.
There are		oranges	

We use *some* in questions when we ask for things and offer things.

Can I have	some	coffee, please?
Would you like		grapes?

We use *any* in questions and negative sentences with uncount nouns and plural nouns.

Is there	any	water?
Does she have		children?
I can't see		rice.
There aren't		people.

(I don't know if there is any water / if she has any children.)

9.4 *How much . . . ?* and *How many . . . ?*

We use *How much … ?* with uncount nouns.
   How much rice is there?   There isn't much rice.
We use *How many … ?* with count nouns.
   How many apples are there?   There aren't many apples.

9.5 Prepositions

I've got a book **by** John Grisham.
What do you have **for** breakfast?
Germany has many kinds **of** sausages.

EXERCISES

1 Write C (countable) or U (uncountable).

1 milk	_____	5 apple	_____
2 money	_____	6 bread	_____
3 homework	_____	7 fruit	_____
4 CD	_____	8 tea	_____

2 Complete the sentences. Use *Would … like* or *'d like*.

1 I _____ a cup of coffee, please.
2 _____ they _____ some food?
3 _____ you _____ to go out tonight?
4 _____ she _____ a drink?

3 Choose the correct word.

1 Can I have any / some milk, please?
2 Do they have some / any sandwiches?
3 There are some / any oranges.
4 Would you like any / some coffee?
5 Are there any / some biscuits?

4 Complete the sentences. Use *is, are, some, any, much*, or *many*.

1 How _____ sugar is there?
2 I'd like _____ water, please.
3 _____ there any bread?
4 How _____ people did you see?
5 There _____ some letters for you.
6 Have you got _____ money?

UNIT 10

10.1 Comparative and superlative adjectives

	Adjective	Comparative	Superlative
One-syllable adjectives	old safe big hot	old**er** saf**er** big**ger*** hot**ter***	the old**est** the saf**est** the big**gest*** the hot**test***
Adjectives ending in -*y*	noisy dirty	nois**ier** dirt**ier**	the nois**iest** the dirt**iest**
Two or more syllable adjectives	boring beautiful	**more** boring **more** beautiful	the **most** boring the **most** beautiful
Irregular adjectives	good bad far	**better** **worse** **further**	the **best** the **worst** the **furthest**

* Adjectives which end in one vowel and one consonant double the consonant.

> You're **older than** me.
> New York is **dirtier than** Paris.
> Prague is one of **the most beautiful** cities in Europe.

10.2 *have got* and *have*

Have got means the same as *have* to talk about possession, but the form is very different. We often use *have got* in spoken English.

have got

Positive

I You We They	have	got	a cat. a garden.
He She It	has		

Negative

I You We They	haven't	got	a dog. a garage.
He She It	hasn't		

Questions

Have	I you we they	got	any money? a sister?
Has	he she it		

How many children **have they got**?

Short answers
Yes, I have./No, I haven't.
Yes, she has./No, she hasn't.

The past of both *have* and *have got* is *had*.

have

Positive

I You We They	have	a cat. a garden.
He She It	has	

Negative

I You We They	don't	have	a dog. a garage.
He She It	doesn't		

Questions

Do	I you we they	have	any money? a sister?
Does	he she it		

How many children **do they have**?

Short answers
Yes, I do./No, I don't.
Yes, she does./No, she doesn't.

10.3 Prepositions

The country is quieter **than** the city.
The house is 50 metres **from** the sea.
Everest is the highest mountain **in** the world.
He spends his time **on** the banks of the river.
He drove **along** the road.
He drove **round** the corner.
They ran **over** the bridge.
I walked **past** the pub.
He walked **up** the hill.
He ran **down** the hill.
The cat ran **through** the house.
He jumped **into** the lake.

EXERCISES

1 Write the comparative and superlative form.

1 easy   _____ ➔ _____
2 boring _____ ➔ _____
3 far   _____ ➔ _____
4 noisy   _____ ➔ _____
5 nice   _____ ➔ _____

2 Tick the correct sentence in each pair.

1 ☐ My computer's bigger than yours.
  ☐ My computer is more big than yours.

2 ☐ This is the noisyest city I know!
  ☐ This is the noisiest city I know!

3 ☐ It's the worse film in the world.
  ☐ It's the worst film in the world.

4 ☐ Seville is hotter than London.
  ☐ Seville is hoter than London.

5 ☐ Museums are boringer than parks.
  ☐ Museums are more boring than parks.

3 Make sentences. Use *have got* (+, –, or ?).

1 (+) I / a brother
_____

2 (?) you / a pet
_____

3 (–) they / a car
_____

4 (?) we / any money
_____

5 (–) he / a computer
_____

6 (+) it / a cinema
_____

UNIT 11

11.1 Present Continuous

1 The Present Continuous describes an activity that is happening now.
   She's **wearing** jeans.
   I'm **studying** English.

2 It also describes an activity in the near future.
   I'm **playing** tennis this afternoon.
   Jane's **seeing** her boyfriend tonight.

Positive and negative

I	am		
He She It	is	(not) going	outside.
We You They	are		

Question

	am	I	
Where	is	he she it	going?
	are	we you they	

Yes/No questions

Are you having a good time?
Is my English getting better?
Are they having a party?

Short answers

Yes, we are.
Yes, it is.
No, they aren't.

Spelling of verb + -ing

1 Most verbs just add -ing.
   wear → wear**ing**   go → go**ing**   cook → cook**ing**

2 If the infinitive ends in -e, drop the -e.
   write → writ**ing**   smile → smil**ing**

3 When a one-syllable verb has one vowel and ends in a consonant, double the consonant.
   sit → si**tt**ing   get → ge**tt**ing   run → ru**nn**ing

11.2 Present Simple and Present Continuous

1 The Present Simple describes things that are always true, or true for a long time.
   I **come** from Switzerland.
   He **works** in a bank.

2 The Present Continuous describes activities happening now, and temporary activities.
   Why **are you wearing** a suit? You usually wear jeans.

11.3 *Whose* + possessive pronouns

Whose … ? asks about possession.

Subject	Object	Adjective	Pronoun
I	me	my	mine
You	you	your	yours
He	him	his	his
She	her	her	hers
We	us	our	ours
They	them	their	theirs

Whose is this book? Whose book is this? Whose is it?	It's	mine. yours. hers. his. ours. theirs.

11.4 Prepositions

We've got this jumper **in** red.
He's talking **to** Mandy.
There's a girl **with** fair hair.
I'm looking **for** a jumper.
I always pay **by** credit card.

EXERCISES

1 Complete the sentences. Use the Present Continuous.

1 He _____ maths at university. (study)
2 I _____ away this weekend. (not go)
3 _____ they _____ ? (work)
4 She _____ the party. (not enjoy)
5 _____ you _____ Sam tonight? (see)

2 Write the -ing form.

1 write   _____
2 stop   _____
3 travel   _____
4 go   _____
5 dance   _____

3 Complete the sentences. Use *Whose* or *Who's*.

1 _____ books are these?
2 _____ standing at the door?
3 _____ going to pass the exam?
4 _____ is this pen?
5 _____ dog is that?

4 Complete the sentences. Use the Present Simple or Continuous.

1 Juan _____ from Barcelona. (come)
2 I _____ Jo at 6 p.m. tonight. (meet)
3 Why _____ you _____ now? (laugh)
4 She always _____ nice clothes. (wear)
5 We're late! _____ you _____ ? (come)

UNIT 12

12.1 *going to*

1 *Going to* expresses a person's plans and intentions.

> She's **going to** be a ballet dancer when she grows up.
> We're **going to** stay in a villa in France this summer.

2 Often there is no difference between *going to* and the Present Continuous to refer to a future intention.

> I'm **seeing** Peter tonight.
> I'm **going to see** Peter tonight.

3 We also use *going to* when we can see now that something is sure to happen in the future.

> Careful! That glass is **going to** fall!

Positive and negative

I	am		
He/She/It	is	(not) going to	have a break. stay at home.
We/You/They	are		

Questions

When	am	I	going to	have a break? stay at home?
	is	he/she/it		
	are	we/you/they		

With the verbs *to go* and *to come*, we usually use the Present Continuous for future plans.

> We'**re going** to Paris next week.
> Joe and Tim **are coming** for lunch tomorrow.

12.2 Infinitive of purpose

The infinitive can express why a person does something.

> I'm saving my money **to buy** a CD player.
> (= I want to buy a CD player)

> We're going to Paris **to have** a holiday.
> (= we want to have a holiday)

NOT
I'm saving my money ~~for to buy~~ a CD player.
I'm saving my money ~~for buy~~ a CD player.

12.3 Prepositions

What did he do **as** a child?   What's **on** TV tonight?
He grew up **in** the city.   What's **on at** the cinema?
I'm going **to** Florida **in** a year's time.

EXERCISES

1 Complete the sentences. Use *going to* (+, –, or ?).

1 (+) Look! It _____ be a lovely day!
2 (?) _____ Bill _____ see Dan tonight?
3 (–) I _____ study this weekend.
4 (+) Be careful! You _____ fall.
5 (–) We _____ play football today.
6 (?) _____ you _____ cook dinner tonight?
7 (+) He _____ pass the exam.
8 (–) I _____ work tomorrow.
9 (?) _____ they _____ stay with us?

2 Rewrite the sentences. Use an infinitive of purpose.

1 I'm going out because I want to walk the dog.
   _____

2 They're saving money because they want to buy a flat.
   _____

3 She's going to the bank because she wants to get some cash.
   _____

4 Nick is running because he wants to get fit.
   _____

5 You are studying because you want to learn English.
   _____

6 I'm going to the chemist's because I want to buy aspirin.
   _____

UNIT 13

13.1 Question forms

When did Shakespeare live?
Where did Hans Christian Andersen come from?
Who did she marry?
Who created Mickey Mouse?
How do you get to school?
What do you have for breakfast?
What happens at the end of the story?
Why do you want to learn English?
How many people are there in the class?
How much does she earn?
How far is it to the centre?
What sort of car do you have?
Which newspaper do you read?

13.2 Adjectives and adverbs

Adjectives describe nouns.
> a **big** dog   a **careful** driver

Adverbs describe verbs.
> She ran **quickly**.   He drives too **fast**.

To form regular adverbs, add *-ly* to the adjective.
Words ending in *-y* change to *-ily*.

Adjective	Adverb
quick	quickly
bad	badly
careful	carefully
immediate	immediately
easy	easily

Some adverbs are irregular.

Adjective	Adverb
good	well
hard	hard
early	early
fast	fast

13.3 Prepositions

What's the story **about**?
What happens **at** the end of the story?

EXERCISES

1 Complete the sentences. Use a suitable question word.
1 _____ many children have you got?
2 _____ does Gianni come from?
3 _____ are you doing?
4 _____ does the class start?
5 _____ much time have we got?

2 Correct the sentences.
1 Who Sally married? _____
2 What does happen at the start of the film? _____
3 Which town you live in? _____
4 How far it is to the town hall? _____
5 Why you want to buy that CD? _____

3 Change the adjectives into adverbs.
1 good _____ 4 fast _____
2 hard _____ 5 careful _____
3 immediate _____

4 Choose the correct adjective.
1 This film is very bored / boring.
2 I was amazed / amazing when I saw it.
3 Pete was boring / bored, so he went home.
4 This article is very interesting / interested.
5 She's frightening / frightened of dogs.

UNIT 14

14.1 Present Perfect

1 The Present Perfect refers to an action that happened some time before now.
> She's **travelled** to most parts of the world.
> **Have you** ever **been** in a car accident?

2 If we want to say *when* these actions happened, we must use the Past Simple.
> She **went** to Russia two years ago.
> I **was** in a crash when I was 10.

3 Notice the time expressions used with the Past Simple.

| I left | last night/yesterday/in 1990/at three o'clock/on Monday. |

Positive and negative

I You We They	have		
		(not) been	to the States.
He She It	has		

I've been = I have been
You've been = You have been
We've been = We have been
They've been = They have been

He's been = He has been
She's been = She has been
It's been = It has been

been and *gone*

She's **gone** to Portugal. (= she's there now)
She's **been** to Portugal. (= now she has returned)

Question

Where	have	I you we they	been?
	has	she he it	

Yes/No questions
Have you been to Russia?

Short answers
Yes, I have./No, I haven't.

ever and *never*

We use *ever* in questions and *never* in negative sentences.
> Have you **ever** been to Russia?   I've **never** been to Russia.

14.2 *yet* and *just*

We use *just* in positive sentences. We use *yet* in negative sentences and questions.
> Have you done your homework **yet**?
> I haven't done it **yet** (but I'm going to).
> I have **just** done it (a short time before now).

14.3 Prepositions

She works **for** a big company.
Ryan and Tara are **on** honeymoon.
Hamlet is a play **by** Shakespeare.

EXERCISES

1 Tick the correct sentence in each pair.
1 ☐ I went to Finland last year.
   ☐ I have been to Finland last year.
2 ☐ Have you ever met a famous person?
   ☐ Did you ever meet a famous person?
3 ☐ Kate's not here. She went to Paris.
   ☐ Kate's not here. She's gone to Paris.
4 ☐ You have met him when you were six.
   ☐ You met him when you were six.

2 Complete the sentences. Use the Present Perfect (+, –, or ?).
1 (+) He _____ all over the world. (travel)
2 (?) _____ you ever _____ this film? (see)
3 (–) We _____ on holiday this year. (be)
4 (+) They _____ your letter. (read)
5 (?) _____ Bill _____ the shopping? (do)
6 (–) We _____ the card yet. (send)

3 Put the adverb in the correct place.
1 Have you finished the report? (yet) _____
2 I've been to Australia. (never) _____
3 Tom has called. (just) _____
4 Has Tony lived in London? (ever) _____

4 Write short answers that are true for you.
1 Have you ever been to Manchester? _____
2 Have you taken any exams this year? _____
3 Have any of your friends ever played in a rock band? _____
4 Has your best friend ever lied to you? _____
5 Has the lesson finished yet? _____

Pairwork activities Student A

This picture of a living room is not complete.
Ask Student B questions to find out where the things in
the box go. Draw them in the correct place.

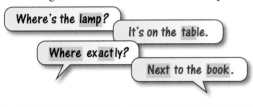

| lamp | magazines | photos | plants | clock | rug |

1 You are the operator. Ask questions to find out who
your partner wants to phone. Start: *International
Directory Enquiries. Which country, please?*

Country	
Town	
Last name	
Initial	
Address	

Finish: *The number you require is 75 842 2209*

2 You want to call Fernando. Answer Student B's
questions to get Fernando's telephone number.

UNIT 8 *p60* **Famous inventions**

When were things invented? With a partner, ask and answer questions.

When was Coca-Cola invented?

In 1886.

That's . . . years ago.

1 Coca-Cola was invented in _____.
2 The camera was invented in __1826__.
3 The record player was invented in _____.
4 The first plane was invented in __1903__.
5 Jeans were invented in _____.
6 Hamburgers were invented in __1895__.
7 Cars were invented in _____.
8 The telephone was invented in __1876__.
9 The television was invented in _____.
10 Bicycles were invented in about __1840__.

 UNIT 8 *p62* **Did you know that?**

With a partner, make similar conversations.

A Did you know that Marco Polo brought spaghetti back from China?
B Really? He didn't! That's incredible!
A Well, it's true.
B Did you know that Napoleon was afraid of cats?
A He wasn't! I don't believe it!
B Well, it's true!

Did you know that ...

... Vincent van Gogh sold only two of his paintings while he was alive?
... the actress Shirley Temple was a millionaire before she was ten?
... Shakespeare spelled his name in eleven different ways?
... in 1979 it snowed in the Sahara desert?
... King Louis XIV of France had a bath only three times in his life?

 UNIT 10 *p76* **I've got more than you!**

Work with a partner. You are both famous film stars. Ask and answer questions to find out who is richer!

I've got five boats. How many have you got?

Twelve. I've got this one, four in the Mediterranean, two in the South Pacific, two in the Caribbean, and three in Asia.

Well, I've got thirty cars!

That's nothing! I've got ...

5 boats	8 gold watches	4 houses
50 cars	80 gold and diamond rings	150 million dollars
100 Arab horses	25 servants	

 **UNIT 11** *p84* **Who's at the party?**

Work with a partner. You each have a picture of a party. Talk about the pictures to find ten differences. Do not show your picture to your partner!

In my picture three people are dancing.

In my picture four people are dancing.

There's a girl with fair hair.

Is she wearing a black dress?

Pairwork activities Student B

 UNIT 2 *p13* **Who is he?**

Surname	
First name	Patrick
Country	
Job	Accountant
Address	
Phone number	(21) 434 1075
Age	
Married	Yes

 UNIT 5 *p37* **What's in your picture?**

This picture of a living room is complete. Student A's picture is incomplete. Answer Student A's questions about the things in the box to help him/her complete the picture.

Where's the lamp?
It's on the table.
Where exactly?
Next to the book.

lamp	magazines	photos	plants	clock	rug

 UNIT 6 *p50* **On the phone**

1 You want to call Yoshi. Answer Student A's questions to get Yoshi's telephone number.

Yoshi Ishigawa
BUSINESSMAN

659 Tearaimizu-cho
KYOTO 604-8152
JAPAN

Tel: _____
email: **ishigawa@nkg.or.jp**

2 You are the operator. Ask questions to find out who your partner wants to phone. Start: *International Directory Enquiries. Which country, please?*

Country	
Town	
Last name	
Initial	
Address	

Finish: *The number you require is 998 764 9832*

 UNIT 8 *p60* **Famous inventions**

When were things invented? With a partner, ask and answer questions.

When was the camera invented?
In 1826.
That's . . . years ago.

1 Coca-Cola was invented in __1886__ .
2 The camera was invented in _____ .
3 The record player was invented in __1878__ .
4 The first plane was invented in _____ .
5 Jeans were invented in __1873__ .
6 Hamburgers were invented in _____ .
7 Cars were invented in __1893__ .
8 The telephone was invented in _____ .
9 The television was invented in __1926__ .
10 Bicycles were invented in about _____ .

UNIT 8 *p62* Did you know that?

With a partner, make similar conversations.

> **A** Did you know that Marco Polo brought spaghetti back from China?
> **B** Really? He didn't! That's incredible!
> **A** Well, it's true.
> **B** Did you know that Napoleon was afraid of cats?
> **A** He wasn't! I don't believe it!
> **B** Well, it's true!

Did you know that ...

… it took 1,700 years to build the Great Wall of China?

… Walt Disney used his own voice for the character of Mickey Mouse?

… Shakespeare and Cervantes both died on 23 April 1616?

… King Francis I of France bought the painting *Mona Lisa* to put in his bathroom?

… when Shakespeare was alive, there were no actresses, only male actors?

UNIT 10 *p76* I've got more than you!

Work with a partner. You are both famous film stars. Ask and answer questions to find out who is richer!

> I've got five boats. How many have you got?

> Twelve. I've got this one, four in the Mediterranean, two in the South Pacific, two in the Caribbean, and three in Asia.

> Well, I've got thirty cars!

> That's nothing! I've got …

12 boats	18 gold watches	5 houses
30 cars	50 gold and diamond rings	50 million dollars
275 Arab horses	10 servants	

UNIT 11 *p84* Who's at the party?

Work with a partner. You each have a picture of a party. Talk about the pictures to find ten differences. Do not show your picture to your partner!

> In my picture three people are dancing.

> In my picture four people are dancing.

> There's a girl with fair hair.

> Is she wearing a black dress?

UNIT 12 *p96* The weather

Work with a partner. Find out about the weather round the world yesterday. Look at the information on this page. Ask and answer questions to complete the information.

> What was the weather like in Athens?

> It was sunny and warm. 18 degrees.

WORLD WEATHER NOON YESTERDAY

		°C			°C
Athens	S	18	London		
Berlin			Los Angeles	Fg	21
Bombay	R	31	Luxor		
Edinburgh			Milan	Fg	19
Geneva	C	12	Moscow		
Hong Kong			Oslo	Sn	2
Lisbon	C	19			

S = sunny
C = cloudy
Fg = foggy
R = rainy
Sn = snowy

Word list

Here is a list of most of the new words in the units of *New Headway Elementary* Student's Book.

adj = adjective
adv = adverb
conj = conjunction
opp = opposite
pl = plural
prep = preposition
pron = pronoun
pp = past participle
n = noun
v = verb
infml = informal
US = American English

UNIT 1

apple *n* /'æpl/
Australia *n* /ɒ'streɪliːə/
bag *n* /bæg/
because *conj* /bɪ'kɒz/
Brazil *n* /brə'zɪl/
brother *n* /'brʌðə/
camera *n* /'kæmərə/
children *n pl* /'tʃɪldrən/
cinema *n* /'sɪnəmə/
country *n* /'kʌntri/
day *n* /deɪ/
dictionary *n* /'dɪkʃənri/
England *n* /'ɪŋglənd/
fine *adj* /faɪn/
flat *n* /flæt/
France *n* /frɑːns/
from *prep* /frɒm/
Germany *n* /'dʒɜːməni/
goodbye /gʊd'baɪ/
have *v* /hæv/
hello /hə'ləʊ/
her *pron* /hɜː/
his *pron* /hɪz/
Hungary *n* /'hʌŋgəri/
international *adj* /ˌɪntə'næʃnəl/
Italy *n* /'ɪtəli/
Japan *n* /dʒə'pæn/
job *n* /dʒɒb/
key *n* /kiː/
language *n* /'læŋgwɪdʒ/
learn *v* /lɜːn/
letter *n* /'letə/
live *v* /lɪv/
magazine *n* /mægə'ziːn/
married *adj* /'mærɪd/
me *pron* /miː/
Mexico *n* /'meksɪkəʊ/
mobile *n* / 'məʊbaɪl/
my *pron* /maɪ/
name *n* /neɪm/
newspaper *n* /'njuːspeɪpə/
nice *adj* /naɪs/
not bad *adj infml* /ˌnɒt 'bæd/
orange *n* /'ɒrɪndʒ/
Poland *n* /'pəʊlənd/
postcard *n* /'pəʊskɑːd/
Russia *n* /'rʌʃə/
See you *v infml* /'siː juː/
sister *n* /'sɪstə/
Spain *n* /speɪn/
spell *v* /spel/
stamp *n* /stæmp/
student *n* /'stjuːdənt/
teacher *n* /'tiːtʃə/
telephone number *n*
　　/'teləfəʊn ˌnʌmbə/
music *n* /'mjuːzɪk/
thank you /'θæŋk juː/
thanks /θæŋks/
the USA *n* /ðə ˌjuː es' eɪ/
this (book) /ðɪs/
ticket *n* /'tɪkɪt/

very well *adj* /veri 'wel/
want *v* /wɒnt/
what *adv* /wɒt/
where *adv* /weə/
your *pron* /jɔː/

UNIT 2

accountant *n* /ə'kaʊntənt/
actor *n* /'æktə/
address *n* /ə'dres/
age *n* /eɪdʒ/
American *adj* /ə'merɪkən/
anything else /ˌeniθɪŋ 'els/
apple pie *n* /ˌæpl 'paɪ/
at home *adv* /ət 'həʊm/
at work *adv* /ət 'wɜːk/
aunt *n* /ɑːnt/
bar *n* /bɑː/
big *adj* /bɪg/
boyfriend *n* /'bɔɪfrend/
café *n* /'kæfeɪ/
cake *n* /keɪk/
Can I have … ? /ˌkæn aɪ 'hæv/
Can I help? /ˌkæn aɪ 'help/
centre *n* /'sentə/
cheap *adj* /tʃiːp/
chicken *n* /'tʃɪkɪn/
chips *n pl* /tʃɪps/
chocolate *n* /'tʃɒklət/
classroom *n* /'klɑːsrʊm/
coffee *n* /'kɒfi/
cold *adj* /kəʊld/
daughter *n* /'dɔːtə/
different *adj* /'dɪfrənt/
difficult *adj* /'dɪfɪkəlt/
drink *v* /drɪŋk/
easy *adj* /'iːzi/
egg *n* /eg/
email *n* /'iːmeɪl/
exciting *adj* /ɪk'saɪtɪŋ/
expensive *adj* /ɪk'spensɪv/
family *n* /'fæməli/
fast *adj* /fɑːst/
father *n* /'fɑːðə/
first name *n* /'fɜːst neɪm/
fish *n* /fɪʃ/
friendly *adj* /'frendli/
funny *adj* /'fʌni/
girlfriend *n* /'gɜːlfrend/
good *adj* /gʊd/
grandfather *n* /'grænfɑːðə/
grandmother *n* /'grænmʌðə/
hamburger *n* /'hæmbɜːgə/
happy *adj* /'hæpi/
here *adv* /hɪə/
Here you are /'hɪə juː ˌɑː/
hi /haɪ/
holiday *n* /'hɒlɪdeɪ/
horrible *adj* /'hɒrəbl/
hot *adj* /hɒt/
how are you? *adv* /ˌhaʊ 'ɑː juː/
how much? *adv* /ˌhaʊ 'mʌtʃ/

how old? *adv* /ˌhaʊ 'əʊld/
husband *n* /'hʌzbənd/
ice-cream *n* /aɪs 'kriːm/
Ireland *n* /'aɪələnd/
journalist *n* /'dʒɜːnəlɪst/
love *n* /lʌv/
lovely *adj* /'lʌvli/
menu *n* /'menjuː/
mineral water *n* /'mɪnərəl ˌwɔːtə/
Monday *n* /'mʌndeɪ/
morning *n* /'mɔːnɪŋ/
mother *n* /'mʌðə/
near *adj* /nɪə/
new *adj* /njuː/
nightclub *n* /'naɪtklʌb/
now *adv* /naʊ/
nurse *n* /nɜːs/
old *adj* /əʊld/
orange juice *n* /'ɒrɪndʒ dʒuːs/
photo *n* /'fəʊtəʊ/
pizza *n* /'piːtsə/
please /pliːz/
Poland *n* /'pəʊlənd/
pound *n* /paʊnd/
practice *n* /'præktɪs/
price *n* /praɪs/
restaurant *n* /'restrɒnt/
salad *n* /'sæləd/
sea *n* /siː/
slow *adj* /sləʊ/
small *adj* /smɔːl/
software designer *n* /'sɒftweə
　　dɪˌzaɪnə/
son *n* /sʌn/
soon *adv* /suːn/
speak *v* /spiːk/
surname *n* /'sɜːneɪm/
Switzerland *n* /'swɪtsələnd/
tea *n* /tiː/
town *n* /taʊn/
tuna *n* /'tjuːnə/
uncle *n* /'ʌŋkl/
understand *v* /ʌndə'stænd/
university *n* /ˌjuːnɪ'vɜːsəti/
who? *pron* /huː/
wife *n* /waɪf/
write *v* /raɪt/
young *adj* /jʌŋ/

UNIT 3

a little *adj* /ə ˈlɪtl/
afternoon *n* /ˌɑːftəˈnuːn/
ambulance *n* /ˈæmbjələns/
Arabic *adj* /ˈærəbɪk/
architect *n* /ˈɑːkɪtekt/
barman *n* /ˈbɑːmən/
be quiet *v* /bi ˈkwaɪət/
beautiful *adj* /ˈbjuːtɪfl/
beer *n* /bɪə/
before *prep* /bɪˈfɔː/
boat *n* /bəʊt/
boring *adj* /ˈbɔːrɪŋ/
boy *n* /bɔɪ/
breakfast *n* /ˈbrekfəst/
building *n* /ˈbɪldɪŋ/
businesswoman *n*
　/ˈbɪznəsˌwʊmən/
busy *adj* /ˈbɪzi/
but *conj* /bʌt/
Canada *n* /ˈkænədə/
Canadian *adj* /kəˈneɪdɪən/
chef *n* /ʃef/
city *n* /ˈsɪti/
clock *n* /klɒk/
clothes *n* /kləʊðz/
collect *v* /kəˈlekt/
come *v* /kʌm/
concert *n* /ˈkɒnsət/
cook *v* /kʊk/
court *n* /kɔːt/
deliver *v* /dɪˈlɪvə/
design *v* /dɪˈzaɪn/
do the accounts *v* /ˌduː ði:
　əˈkaʊnts/
dog *n* /dɒg/
drive *n* /draɪv/
end *n* /end/
every day *adv* /ˌevri ˈdeɪ/
Excuse me /ɪkˈskjuːz ˌmiː/
film *n* /fɪlm/
fireman *n* /ˈfaɪəmən/
fly *v* /flaɪ/
flying doctor *n* /ˌflaɪɪŋ ˈdɒktə/
football *n* /ˈfʊtbɔːl/
free time *n* /ˌfriː ˈtaɪm/
French *adj* /frentʃ/
German *adj* /ˈdʒɜːmən/
get up *v* /ˌget ˈʌp/
girl *n* /gɜːl/
glass *n* /glɑːs/
go *v* /gəʊ/
go to bed *v* /ˌgəʊ tə ˈbed/
guest *n* /gest/
help *v* /help/
hospital *n* /ˈhɒspɪtl/
hotel *n* /həʊˈtel/
hour *n* /ˈaʊə/
house *n* /haʊs/
Hungarian *adj* /hʌŋˈgeərɪən/
hurry up *v* /ˌhʌri ˈʌp/
island *n* /ˈaɪlənd/
just after *adv* /dʒʌst ˈɑːftə/
just before *adv* /dʒʌst bɪˈfɔː/
Kenya *n* /ˈkenjə/
late *adj* /leɪt/
lawyer *n* /ˈlɔɪjə/

like *v* /laɪk/
listen *v* /ˈlɪsən/
live *v* /lɪv/
look after *v* /ˌlʊk ˈɑːftə/
make *v* /meɪk/
man *n* /mæn/
Mexico *n* /ˈmeksɪkəʊ/
model *n* /ˈmɒdl/
music *n* /ˈmjuːzɪk/
never *adv* /ˈnevə/
never mind /ˈnevə maɪnd/
non-stop *adv* /ˌnɒn ˈstɒp/
of course /əv ˈkɔːs/
office *n* /ˈɒfɪs/
only *adj* /ˈəʊnli/
ordinary *adj* /ˈɔːdənri/
people *n pl* /ˈpiːpl/
perhaps *adv* /pəˈhæps/
petrol *n* /ˈpetrəl/
pianist *n* /ˈpɪənɪst/
pilot *n* /ˈpaɪlət/
plane *n* /pleɪn/
play *v* /pleɪ/
policeman *n* /pəˈliːsmən/
post *n* /pəʊst/
postman *n* /ˈpəʊsmən/
professor *n* /prəˈfesə/
pub *n* /pʌb/
radio *n* /ˈreɪdɪəʊ/
relax *v* /rɪˈlæks/
riding *v* /ˈraɪdɪŋ/
school *n* /skuːl/
Scotland *n* /ˈskɒtlənd/
sell *v* /sel/
serve *v* /sɜːv/
shop *n* /ʃɒp/
shop assistant *n* /ˈʃɒp əˌsɪstənt/
sick *adj* /sɪk/
singer *n* /ˈsɪŋə/
sit down *v* /ˌsɪt ˈdaʊn/
small *adj* /smɔːl/
Somali *adj* /səˈmɑːli/
Somalia *n* /səˈmɑːlɪə/
Spanish *adj* /ˈspænɪʃ/
summer *n* /ˈsʌmə/
supper *n* /ˈsʌpə/
taxi driver *n* /ˈtæksi ˌdraɪvə/
television *n* /ˈteləvɪʒn/
tennis *n* /ˈtenɪs/
That's right! /ˌðæts ˈraɪt/
then *adv* /ðen/
there *adv* /ðeə/
thing *n* /θɪŋ/
tired *adj* /ˈtaɪəd/
too *adv* /tuː/
tourist *n* /ˈtʊərɪst/
tourist guide *n* /ˈtʊərɪst gaɪd/
tourist office *n* /ˈtʊərɪst ˌɒfɪs/
undertaker *n* /ˈʌndəteɪkə/
vanilla *adj* /vəˈnɪlə/
vegetarian food *n* /vedʒəˈteərɪən
　fuːd/
walk *n, v* /wɔːk/
watch *n, v* /wɒtʃ/
wear *v* /weə/
week *n* /wiːk/
weekday *n* /ˈwiːkdeɪ/
west *n* /west/

wine *n* /waɪn/
work *v* /wɜːk/
world *n* /ˈwɜːld/

UNIT 4

a lot *pron* /ə ˈlɒt/
after *adv* /ˈɑːftə/
alcohol *n* /ˈælkəhɒl/
always *adv* /ˈɔːlweɪz/
autumn *n* /ˈɔːtəm/
bad *adj* /bæd/
beach *n* /biːtʃ/
best *adj* /best/
boyfriend *n* /ˈbɔɪfrend/
bus *n* /bʌs/
car *n* /kɑː/
Christmas *n* /ˈkrɪsməs/
club *n* /klʌb/
coach trip *n* /ˈkəʊtʃ ˌtrɪp/
colour *n* /ˈkʌlə/
computer *n* /kəmˈpjuːtə/
computer game *n* /kəmˈpjuːtə
　geɪm/
cool *adj* /kuːl/
cooking *n* /ˈkʊkɪŋ/
cousin *n* /ˈkʌzn/
dance *n* /dɑːns/
dancing *n* /ˈdɑːnsɪŋ/
daytime *n* /ˈdeɪtaɪm/
deposit *n* /dɪˈpɒzɪt/
dinner *n* /ˈdɪnə/
do *v* /duː/
don't worry *v* /ˌdəʊnt ˈwʌri/
drink *n* /drɪŋk/
DVD *n* /ˌdiː viː ˈdiː/
early *adj* /ˈɜːli/
eat *v* /iːt/
England *n* /ˈɪŋglənd/
family *n* /ˈfæməli/
fast *adj* /fɑːst/
fast food *n* /fɑːst ˈfuːd/
favourite *adj* /ˈfeɪvrɪt/
festival *n* /ˈfestɪvl/
flower *n* /ˈflaʊə/
garden *n* /ˈgɑːdn/
go out *v* /ˌgəʊ ˈaʊt/
go running *v* /gəʊ ˈrʌnɪŋ/
gym *n* /dʒɪm/
hard *adv* /hɑːd/
here *adv* /hɪə/
hot *adj* /hɒt/
how? *adv* /haʊ/
I'm sorry /ˌaɪm ˈsɒri/
interesting *adj* /ˈɪntrəstɪŋ/
It doesn't matter /ɪt ˌdʌznt
　ˈmætə/
joke *n* /ˈdʒəʊk/
leisure activity *n* /ˈleʒə(r)
　ækˌtɪvəti/
long *adj* /lɒŋ/
lunchtime *n* /ˈlʌntʃtaɪm/
match *n* /mætʃ/
mountain *n* /ˈmaʊntɪn/
near *adv* /nɪə/
never *adv* /ˈnevə/

next *adj* /nekst/
nice *adj* /naɪs/
north *n* /nɔːθ/
Norway *n* /ˈnɔːweɪ/
often *adv* /ˈɒfən/, /ˈɒftən/
oh dear /ˌəʊ ˈdɪə/
open *v* /ˈəʊpən/
orange *n* /ˈɒrɪndʒ/
pardon? /ˈpɑːdn/
park *n* /pɑːk/
parents *n pl* /ˈpeərənts/
pink *adj* /pɪŋk/
Portuguese *adj* /ˌpɔːtʃuˈgiz/
rainy *adj* /ˈreɪni/
reading *n* /ˈriːdɪŋ/
really? /ˈrɪəli/
red *adj* /red/
rugby *n* /ˈrʌgbi/
running *n* /ˈrʌnɪŋ/
sailing *n* /ˈseɪlɪŋ/
season *n* /ˈsiːzn/
skiing *n* /ˈskiːɪŋ/
smoke *v* /sməʊk/
sometimes *adv* /ˈsʌmtaɪmz/
south *n* /saʊθ/
special *adj* /ˈspeʃl/
spend *v* /spend/
sport *n* /spɔːt/
spring *n* /sprɪŋ/
start *v* /stɑːt/
still *adv* /stɪl/
sunbathing *n* /ˈsʌnbeɪðɪŋ/
sunny *adj* /ˈsʌni/
surfing *n* /ˈsɜːfɪŋ/
swimming pool *n* /ˈswɪmɪŋ puːl/
take *v* /teɪk/
take photos *v* /ˌteɪk ˈfəʊtəʊz/
team *n* /tiːm/
Thailand *n* /ˈtaɪlænd/
ticket *n* /ˈtɪkɪt/
That's OK /ˈðæts əʊˌkeɪ/
trip *n* /trɪp/
traffic *n* /ˈtræfɪk/
train *v* /treɪn/
travel *v* /ˈtrævl/
tropical *adj* /ˈtrɒpɪkl/
usually *adv* /ˈjuːʒəli/
visit *v* /ˈvɪzɪt/
warm *adj* /wɔːm/
waterskiing *n* /ˈwɔːtəˌskiːɪŋ/
water sports *n* /ˈwɔːtə ˌspɔːts/
weekday *n* /ˈwiːkdeɪ/
What does ... mean? /wɒt dəz
　ˈ... miːn/
what time? /wɒt ˈtaɪm/
what? /wɒt/
when? /wen/
where? /weə/
white *adj* /waɪt/
why? /waɪ/
win *v* /wɪn/
window *n* /ˈwɪndəʊ/
windsurfing *n* /ˈwɪndˌsɜːfɪŋ/
winter *n* /ˈwɪntə/
work *n* /wɜːk/
year *n* /jɪə/

UNIT 5

address book n /ə'dres ˌbʊk/
agree v /ə'griː/
all the time /ˌɔːl ðə 'taɪm/
any /'eni/
armchair n /'ɑːmtʃeə/
bank n /bæŋk/
baker's n /'beɪkəz/
bathroom n /'bɑːθrʊm/
bedroom n /'bedrʊm/
best adj /best/
block n /blɒk/
book n /bʊk/
bookshelf n /'bʊkʃelf/
bookshop n /'bʊkʃɒp/
both pron /bəʊθ/
bread n /bred/
briefcase n /'briːfkeɪs/
bubble n /'bʌbl/
bus stop n /'bʌs ˌstɒp/
bus ticket n /'bʌs ˌtɪkɪt/
car park n /'kɑː ˌpɑːk/
cat n /kæt/
champagne n /ʃæm'peɪn/
Cheers! /tʃɪəz/
chemist's n /'kemɪsts/
Chinese adj /ˌtʃaɪ'niːz/
church n /tʃɜːtʃ/
cinema n /'sɪnəmɑː/
clock n /klɒk/
collect v /kə'lekt/
comfortable adj /'kʌmftəbl/
completely adv /kəm'pliːtli/
computer n /kəm'pjuːtə/
cooker n /'kʊkə/
corner n /'kɔːnə/
cup n /kʌp/
cupboard n /'kʌbəd/
curtains n /'kɜːtnz/
designer n /dɪ'zaɪnə/
dining room n /'daɪnɪŋ ˌrʊm/
dirty adj /'dɜːti/
dog n /dɒg/
DVD player n /ˌdiːviː'diː ˌpleɪə/
especially adv /ɪ'speʃəli/
everything pron /'evriθɪŋ/
exactly adv /ɪg'zæktli/
eyes n /aɪz/
far adv /fɑː/
fireplace n /'faɪəpleɪs/
flat n /flæt/
floor n /flɔː/
fork n /fɔːk/
fridge n /frɪdʒ/
front door n /ˌfrʌnt 'dɔː/
furniture n /'fɜːnɪtʃə/
future n /'fjuːtʃə/
garden n /'gɑːdn/
glass n /glɑːs/
home n /həʊm/
how many? /ˌhaʊ 'meni/

idea n /aɪ'dɪə/
in front of prep /ɪn 'frʌnt əv/
Internet café n /ˌɪntənet 'kæfeɪ/
just (= only) adv /dʒʌst/
kitchen n /'kɪtʃɪn/
knife n /naɪf/
lamp n /læmp/
left adv (opp right) /left/
living room n /'lɪvɪŋ ˌrʊm/
lots (of books) /lɒts/
mirror n /'mɪrə/
mobile n /ˌməʊbaɪl/
modern adj /'mɒdən/
most of the time /'məʊst əv ðə
     ˌtaɪm/
music shop n /'mjuːzɪk ˌʃɒp/
natural adj /'nætʃrəl/
next to prep /'nekst ˌtuː/
not a lot adj /nɒt ə 'lɒt/
notebook n /'nəʊtbʊk/
on prep /ɒn/
over there /ˌəʊvə 'ðeə/
park n /pɑːk/
pen n /pen/
perfect adj /'pɜːfɪkt/
picture n /'pɪktʃə/
plant n /plɑːnt/
plate n /pleɪt/
post box n /'pəʊst bɒks/
radio n /'reɪdiəʊ/
railway station n /'reɪlweɪ ˌsteɪʃn/
reasons n pl /'riːznz/
record n /'rekɔːd/
room n /rʊm/, /ruːm/
round adj /raʊnd/
route n /ruːt/
rug n /rʌg/
sandwich n /'sænwɪdʒ/
shelf n /ʃelf/
sleep v /sliːp/
sofa n /'səʊfə/
some /sʌm/
spoon n /spuːn/
stamps n pl /stæmps/
stop (bus) n /stɒp/
stereo n /'steriəʊ/
sunny adj /'sʌni/
supermarket n /'suːpəˌmɑːkɪt/
table n /teɪbl/
tall adj /tɔːl/
Thanks a lot! /ˌθæŋks ə 'lɒt/
telephone n /'telɪfəʊn/
television n /'telɪvɪʒn/
think v /θɪŋk/
under prep /'ʌndə/
upstairs adv /ʌp'steəz/
verandah n /və'rændə/
visitors n pl /'vɪzɪtəz/
wall n /wɔːl/
washing machine n /'wɒʃɪŋ
     məˌʃiːn/
window n /'wɪndəʊ/

UNIT 6

advertisement n /əd'vɜːtɪsmənt/
all right /ˌɔːl 'raɪt/
at the moment /ət ðə 'məʊmənt/
believe v /bɪ'liːv/
bestseller n /best'selə/
(the) blues n /(ðə) 'bluːz/
brilliant adj /'brɪliənt/
can't stop v /ˌkɑːnt 'stɒp/
character n /'kærəktə/
check v /tʃek/
conversation n /kɒnvə'seɪʃn/
countryside n /'kʌntrisaɪd/
do homework v /ˌduː
     'həʊmwɜːk/
draw v /drɔː/
drive v /draɪv/
drums n /drʌmz/
eye n /aɪ/
fall in love v /ˌfɔːl ɪn 'lʌv/
fantastic adj /fæn'tæstɪk/
fantasy n /'fæntəsi/
fax number n /'fæks ˌnʌmbə/
feel v /fiːl/
flamenco n /flə'meŋkəʊ/
foreign adj /'fɒrən/
genius n /'dʒiːniəs/
golf n /gɒlf/
hear v /hɪə/
head n /hed/
hour n /'aʊə/
ill adj /ɪl/
I'm afraid /ˌaɪm ə'freɪd/
initial n /ɪ'nɪʃl/
interview n /'ɪntəvjuː/
Japanese adj /dʒæpə'niːz/
job n /dʒɒb/
know v /nəʊ/
last month adv /ˌlɑːst 'mʌnθ/
later adv /'leɪtə/
laugh v /lɑːf/
little adj /'lɪtl/
look forward to v /ˌlʊk 'fɔːwəd tʊ/
magic n /'mædʒɪk/
manager n /'mænɪdʒə/
message n /'mesɪdʒ/
no-one n /'nəʊwʌn/
note n /nəʊt/
now adv /naʊ/
number one n /ˌnʌmbə 'wʌn/
paint v /peɪnt/
party n /'pɑːti/
play n /pleɪ/
poetry n /'pəʊətri/
pop music n /'pɒp ˌmjuːzik/
prefer v /prɪ'fɜː/
read v /riːd/
really adv /'riːəli/
receptionist n /rɪ'sepʃənɪst/
river n /'rɪvə/
sea n /siː/

see v /siː/
sell v /sel/
shy adj /ʃaɪ/
sing v /sɪŋ/
sit v /sɪt/
so adj /səʊ/
soul singer n /'səʊl ˌsɪŋə/
spelling n /'spelɪŋ/
spend v /spend/
stop v /stɒp/
story n /'stɔːri/
suddenly adv /'sʌdnli/
surprised adj /sə'praɪzd/
surprising adj /sə'praɪzɪŋ/
swim v /swɪm/
talented adj /'tæləntɪd/
teenager n /'tiːneɪdʒə/
theatre n /'θɪətə/
today adv /tə'deɪ/
travel v /'trævl/
translate v /trænz'leɪt/
until conj /ʌn'tɪl/
use v /juːz/
very adv /'veri/
very well adv /ˌveri 'wel/
village n /'vɪlɪdʒ/
voice n /vɔɪs/
was born v /wəz 'bɔːn/
wear v /weə/
wedding n /'wedɪŋ/
well adv /wel/
worried adj /'wʌrɪd/
yesterday adv /'jestədeɪ/
yesterday evening adv /jestədeɪ
     'iːvnɪŋ/

UNIT 7

act *v* /ækt/
activity *n* /æk'tɪvəti/
aeroplane *n* /'eərəpleɪn/
after that *adv* /ˌɑ:ftə 'ðæt/
agree *v* /ə'gri:/
air show *n* /'eə ʃəʊ/
another *pron* /ə'nʌðə/
April *n* /'eɪprəl/
astronaut *n* /'æstrənɔ:t/
at that moment /ət 'ðæt
  məʊmənt/
athlete *n* /'æθli:t/
Atlantic *n* /ət'læntɪk/
become *v* /bɪ'kʌm/
begin *v* /bɪ'gɪn/
birthday *n* /'bɜ:θdeɪ/
break a record /breɪk ə
  'rekɔ:d/
car crash *n* /'kɑ: kræʃ/
career *n* /kə'rɪə/
car park *n* /'kɑ: pɑ:k/
century *n* /'sentʃəri/
champion *n* /'tʃæmpiən/
change *v* /tʃeɪndʒ/
Christmas Day *n* /ˌkrɪsməs 'deɪ/
Congratulations!
  /kənˌgrætʃʊ'leɪʃnz/
countryside *n* /'kʌntrisaɪd/
dangerous *adj* /'deɪndʒərəs/
decide *v* /dɪ'saɪd/
die *v* /daɪ/
disappear *v* /dɪsə'pɪə/
earn *v* /ɜ:n/
email *n* /'i:meɪl/
end *n v* /end/
Europe *n* /'jʊərəp/
everybody *pron* /'evrɪbɒdi/
excellent *adj* /'eksələnt/
experience *n* /ɪk'spɪəriəns/
famous *adj* /'feɪməs/
farm *n* /fɑ:m/
fighter jet *n* /'faɪtə ˌdʒet/
film star *n* /'fɪlm stɑ:/
film studio *n* /'fɪlm ˌstju:diəʊ/
finally *adv* /'faɪnəli/
first (... next) *adv* /fɜ:st/
flight *n* /flaɪt/
foreign minister *n* /'fɒrən
  ˌmɪnɪstə/
fortunately *adv* /'fɔ:tʃənətli/
guitar *n* /gɪ'tɑ:/
handbag *n* /'hændbæg/
have a holiday *v* /ˌhæv ə
  'hɒlədeɪ/
immediately *adv* /ɪ'mi:diətli/
important *adj* /ɪm'pɔ:tənt/
Independence Day *n*
  /ˌɪndɪ'pendəns ˌdeɪ/
join *v* /dʒɔɪn/
June *n* /dʒu:n/

later *adv* /'leɪtə/
leader *n* /'li:də/
leave *v* /li:v/
life *n* /laɪf/
march *n* /mɑ:tʃ/
marry *v* /'mæri/
meal *n* /mi:l/
medal *n* /'medl/
million *n* /'mɪljən/
money *n* /'mʌni/
Mother's Day *n* /'mʌðəz ˌdeɪ/
nearly *adv* /'nɪəli/
news *n* /nju:z/
November *n* /nəʊ'vembə/
olympics *n* /ə'lɪmpɪks/
over *prep* /'əʊvə/
orange juice *n* /'ɒrɪndʒ dʒu:s/
own *n* /əʊn/
Pacific Ocean *n* /pəˌsɪfɪk 'əʊʃən/
personal computer *n* /ˌpɜ:sənəl
  kəm'pju:tə/
pilot *n* /'paɪlət/
politician *n* /ˌpɒlə'tɪʃn/
politics *n* /'pɒlətɪks/
popular *adj* /'pɒpjələ/
present (= birthday) *n* /'preznt/
president *n* /'prezɪdənt/
prime minister *n* /ˌpraɪm
  'mɪnɪstə/
public *n* /'pʌblɪk/
remember *v* /rɪ'membə/
retire *v* /rɪ'taɪə/
rich *adj* /rɪtʃ/
satellite *n* /'sætəlaɪt/
secret *adj* /'si:krət/
sell *v* /sel/
September *n* /sep'tembə/
shoes *n* /ʃu:z/
short *adj* /ʃɔ:t/
sleep *v* /sli:p/
soon *adv* /su:n/
space *n* /speɪs/
star *n* /stɑ:/
start *v* /stɑ:t/
study *v* /'stʌdi/
subject (school) *n* /'sʌbdʒekt/
sure *adj* /ʃʊə/, /ʃɔ:/
survive *v* /sə'vaɪv/
temple *n* /'templ/
test flight *n* /'test flaɪt/
test pilot *n* /'test paɪlət/
thank goodness /ˌθæŋk 'gʊdnəs/
think *v* /θɪŋk/
tomorrow *adv* /tə'mɒrəʊ/
travel *v* /'trævəl/
war *n* /wɔ:/
win *v* /wɪn/

UNIT 8

advice *v* /əd'vaɪs/
afraid *adj* /ə'freɪd/
(3 years) ago *adv* /ə'gəʊ/
all the time *adv* /ˌɔ:l ðə 'taɪm/
arrive *v* /ə'raɪv/
(coffee) break *n* /breɪk/
bicycle *n* (bike) /'baɪsɪkl/
birthday *n* /'bɜ:θdeɪ/
call *v* /kɔ:l/
Christmas Day *n* /ˌkrɪsməs 'deɪ/
clean *v* /kli:n/
couple *n pl* /'kʌpl/
cry *v* /kraɪ/
date *n* /deɪt/
design *n* /dɪ'zaɪn/
driver *n* /'draɪvə/
easy *adj* /'i:zi/
Easter Day *n* /'i:stə 'deɪ/
everyone *n* /'evriwʌn/
experiment *n* /ɪk'sperɪmənt/
fall *n* US (autumn) /fɔ:l/
fall in love /fɔ:l ɪn lʌv/
feelings *n pl* /'fi:lɪŋz/
forget *v* /fə'get/
get engaged *v* /ˌget ɪn'geɪdʒd/
get married *v* /ˌget 'mærɪd/
give *v* /gɪv/
Good luck! /ˌgʊd 'lʌk/
government *n* /'gʌvənmənt/
green *adj* /gri:n/
Halloween *n* /ˌhæləʊ'i:n/
horse *n* /hɔ:s/
idea *n* /aɪ'dɪə/
in a hurry /ˌɪn ə 'hʌri/
incredible *adj* /ɪn'kredəbl/
inside *prep* /'ɪnsaɪd/
invent *v* /ɪn'vent/
invention *n* /ɪn'venʃn/
invitation *n* /ˌɪnvɪ'teɪʃn/
jeans *n pl* /dʒi:nz/
laugh *v* /lɑ:f/
long ago *adv* /lɒŋ ə'gəʊ/
midnight *n* /'mɪdnaɪt/
mistake *n* /mɪs'teɪk/
Mother's Day *n* /'mʌðəz deɪ/
New Year's Eve *n* /nju: jɪəz 'i:v/
notice *v* /'nəʊtɪs/
nowadays *adv* /'naʊədeɪz/
opera *n* /'ɒprə/
painter *n* /'peɪntə/
phone call *n* /'fəʊn ˌkɔ:l/
same to you /seɪm tə 'ju:/
send *v* /send/
snow *n* /snəʊ/
spaghetti *n* /spə'geti/
studio *n* /'stju:diəʊ/
sweet *n* /'swɪ:t/
term *n* /tɜ:m/
Thanksgiving *n* /θæŋks'gɪvɪŋ/
tomorrow *n* /tə'mɒrəʊ/

type *n* /taɪp/
unhappy *adj* /ʌn'hæpi/
Valentine's Day *n* /'væləntaɪnz
  deɪ/
wedding day *n* /'wedɪŋ deɪ/
windscreen wiper *n* /'wɪndskri:n
  ˌwaɪpə/

UNIT 9

a bit n /ə ˈbɪt/
all sorts n pl /ˈɔːl ˈsɔːts/
anybody pron /ˈenibɒdi/
anything else? /eniθɪŋ ˈels/
anyway adv /ˈeniweɪ/
apple juice n /ˈæpl dʒuːs/
away from adv /əˈweɪ frəm/
bacon n /ˈbeɪkən/
banana n /bəˈnɑːnə/
beef n /biːf/
beer n /bɪə/
biscuit n /ˈbɪskɪt/
book v /bʊk/
borrow v /ˈbɒrəʊ/
bottle n /ˈbɒtl/
box n /bɒks/
bread n /bred/
Caribbean n /kærɪˈbiːən/
carrot n /ˈkærət/
central adj /ˈsentrəl/
check in/out v /ˌtʃek ˈɪn/ˈaʊt/
cheese n /tʃiːz/
Chile n /ˈtʃɪli/
chilli n /ˈtʃɪli/
China n /ˈtʃaɪnə/
Chinese adj /tʃaɪˈniːz/
chocolate n /ˈtʃɒklət/
chopsticks n pl /ˈtʃɒpstɪks/
close v /kləʊz/
coffee n /ˈkɒfi/
control v /kənˈtrəʊl/
course (of a meal) n /kɔːs/
cream n /kriːm/
delicious adj /dɪˈlɪʃəs/
depend v /dɪˈpend/
dessert n /dɪˈzɜːt/
disgusting adj /dɪsˈɡʌstɪŋ/
dollar n /ˈdɒlə/
double room n /ˌdʌbl ˈrʊm/
egg n /eɡ/
either adv /ˈaɪðə/
environment n /ɪnˈvaɪrənmənt/
especially adv /ɪˈspeʃəli/
farm v /fɑːm/
finger n /ˈfɪŋɡə/
fish n /fɪʃ/
for example /ˌfər ɪɡˈzɑːmpl/
foreign adj /ˈfɒrən/
fruit n /fruːt/
full adj /fʊl/
garlic n /ˈɡɑːlɪk/
glad adj /ɡlæd/
ham n /hæm/
herring n /ˈherɪŋ/
history n /ˈhɪstri/
homework n /ˈhəʊmwɜːk/
horrible adj /ˈhɒrəbl/
human adj /ˈhjuːmən/
hungry adj /ˈhʌŋɡri/
ice-cream n /aɪs ˈkriːm/
India n /ˈɪndiə/
kilo n /ˈkiːləʊ/
land n /lænd/
lend v /lend/
lunch n /lʌntʃ/
main (meal) adj /meɪn/

meat n /miːt/
menu n /ˈmenjuː/
(the) Middle East n /(ðə) ˌmɪdl ˈiːst/
milk n /mɪlk/
move on v /muːv ˈɒn/
mushroom n /ˈmʌʃrʊm/
noodles n pl /ˈnuːdlz/
north n /nɔːθ/
orange n /ˈɒrɪndʒ/
part (of the world) n /pɑːt/
pass (= give) v /pɑːs/
pasta n /ˈpæstə/
pea n /piː/
petrol n /ˈpetrəl/
poor adj /pɔː/
possible adj /ˈpɒsəbl/
potatoes n pl /pəˈteɪtəʊz/
recipe n /ˈresəpi/
rice n /raɪs/
right now adv /ˌraɪt ˈnaʊ/
salt n /sɔːlt/, /sɒlt/
sardine n /sɑːˈdiːn/
sausages n pl /ˈsɒsɪdʒɪz/
Scandinavian adj /skændɪˈneɪviən/
shopping list n /ˈʃɒpɪŋ ˌlɪst/
single room n /ˌsɪŋɡl ˈrʊm/
south n /saʊθ/
sparkling water n /spɑːklɪŋ ˈwɔːtə/
still water n /stɪl ˈwɔːtə/
strawberry n /ˈstrɔːbəri/
sugar n /ˈʃʊɡə/
table n /ˈteɪbl/
tea n /tiː/
toast n /təʊst/
together adv /təˈɡeðə/
tomato n /təˈmɑːtəʊ/
trainers n pl /ˈtreɪnəz/
transport v /trænsˈpɔːt/
typical adj /ˈtɪpɪkl/
vegetable n /ˈvedʒtəbl/
washing-up n /ˌwɒʃɪŋ ˈʌp/
yoghurt n /ˈjɒɡət/
yours faithfully /ˌjɔːz ˈfeɪθfəli/

UNIT 10

air n /eə/
Arab n /ˈærəb/
bank (of the river) n /bæŋk/
birthplace n /ˈbɜːθpleɪs/
bridge n /brɪdʒ/
building n /ˈbɪldɪŋ/
busy adj /ˈbɪzi/
capital city n /ˌkæpɪtl ˈsɪti/
car park n /ˈkɑː ˌpɑːk/
cathedral n /kəˈθiːdrəl/
church n /tʃɜːtʃ/
clean adj /kliːn/
coast n /kəʊst/
commercial adj /kəˈmɜːʃl/
composer n /kəmˈpəʊzə/
concert n /ˈkɒnsət/
cosmopolitan adj /ˌkɒzməˈpɒlɪtən/
cottage n /ˈkɒtɪdʒ/
country (not the city) n /ˈkʌntri/
corner n /ˈkɔːnə/
cultural centre n /ˈkʌltʃərəl ˌsentə/
dirty adj /ˈdɜːti/
district n /ˈdɪstrɪkt/
exhibition n /ˌeksɪˈbɪʃn/
expensive adj /ɪkˈspensɪv/
factory n /ˈfæktri/
field n /fiːld/
fiesta n /fiˈestə/
group n /ɡruːp/
gypsy n /ˈdʒɪpsi/
hand clapping n /ˈhænd ˌklæpɪŋ/
hill n /hɪl/
historical adj /hɪsˈtɒrɪkl/
immigrant n /ˈɪmɪɡrənt/
independent adj /ˌɪndɪˈpendənt/
influence n /ˈɪnfluːəns/
intelligent adj /ɪnˈtelɪdʒənt/
lake n /leɪk/
Latin adj /ˈlætɪn/
library n /ˈlaɪbrəri/
mixture n /ˈmɪkstʃə/
mountain n /ˈmaʊntɪn/
mud n /mʌd/
museum n /mjuːˈzɪəm/
noisy adj /ˈnɔɪzi/
off prep /ɒf/
open v /ˈəʊpən/
park n /pɑːk/
past prep /pɑːst/
population n /pɒpjəˈleɪʃn/
port n /pɔːt/
practise v /ˈpræktɪs/
pretty adj /ˈprɪti/
quiet adj /ˈkwaɪət/
resort n /rɪˈzɔːt/
river n /ˈrɪvə/
rule v /ruːl/
safe adj /seɪf/
sail v /seɪl/
salsa n /ˈsælsə/
second adj /ˈsekənd/
ship n /ʃɪp/
slave n /sleɪv/

socialist revolution /ˌsəʊʃəlɪst revəˈluːʃn/
song n /sɒŋ/
spice n /ˈspaɪs/
stand v /stænd/
street n /striːt/
surfboard n /ˈsɜːfbɔːd/
tall adj /tɔːl/
tango n /ˈtæŋɡəʊ/
tobacco n /təˈbækəʊ/
village n /ˈvɪlɪdʒ/
wide adj /waɪd/
wood n /wʊd/

UNIT 11

baby *n* /'beɪbi/
ballet shoe *n* /'bæleɪ ʃu:/
baseball cap *n* /'beɪsbɔ:l ˌkæp/
boot *n* /bu:t/
changing rooms *n pl* /'tʃeɪndʒɪŋ ˌru:mz/
cherish *v* /'tʃerɪʃ/
chewing gum *n* /'tʃu:ɪŋ ˌgʌm/
choose *v* /tʃu:z/
coat *n* /kəʊt/
credit card *n* /'kredɪt ˌka:d/
dark *adj* /da:k/
deny *v* /dɪ'naɪ/
dress *n* /dres/
fair (hair) *adj* /feə/
fresh *adj* /freʃ/
good-looking *adj* /ˌgʊd'lʊkɪŋ/
grey *adj* /greɪ/
hair *n* /heə/
handsome *adj* /'hænsəm/
happiness *n* /'hæpinəs/
hat *n* /hæt/
jacket *n* /'dʒækɪt/
joy *n* /dʒɔɪ/
jumper *n* /'dʒʌmpə/
kiss *v* /kɪs/
long *adj* /lɒŋ/
pay *v* /peɪ/
shirt *n* /ʃɜ:t/
shoe *n* /ʃu:/
shorts *n pl* /ʃɔ:ts/
size *n* /saɪz/
skirt *n* /skɜ:t/
smile *v* /smaɪl/
solitary *adj* /'sɒlətri/, /'sɒlətəri/
something *n* /'sʌmθɪŋ/
suit *n* /su:t/
suitcase *n* /'su:tkeɪs/
sunglasses *n pl* /'sʌngla:sɪz/
sunrise *n* /'sʌnraɪz/
T-shirt *n* /'ti:ʃɜ:t/
talk *v* /tɔ:k/
tie *n* /taɪ/
tennis racket *n* /'tenɪs ˌrækɪt/
trainers *n pl* /'treɪnəz/
trousers *n pl* /'traʊzəz/
try on *v* /ˌtraɪ 'ɒn/
umbrella *n* /ʌm'brelə/
whose? *pron* /hu:z/
wing *n* /wɪŋ/

UNIT 12

adventure *n* /əd'ventʃə/
art *n* /a:t/
bottom *n* /'bɒtəm/
breath *n* /'breθ/
breathe *v* /bri:ð/
calm *adj* /ka:m/
catch (a bus) *v* /kætʃ/
climb *v* /klaɪm/
cloudy *adj* /'klaʊdi/
continue *v* /kən'tɪnju:/
cool *adj* /ku:l/
conservation *n* /kɒnsə'veɪʃn/
(18) degrees *n pl* /dɪ'gri:z/
deep *adj* /di:p/
discover *v* /dɪ'skʌvə/
drive *v* /draɪv/
due (a baby) *adj* /dju:/
fall *v* /fɔ:l/
foggy *adj* /'fɒgi/
free-diving *n* /'fri: daɪvɪŋ/
free-running *n* /'fri: rʌnɪŋ/
freedom *n* /'fri:dəm/
grow up *v* /ˌgrəʊ 'ʌp/
gymnastics *n* /dʒɪm'næstɪks/
join *v* /dʒɔɪn/
jump *v* /dʒʌmp/
lion *n* /'laɪən/
meeting *n* /'mi:tɪŋ/
metre *n* /'mi:tə/
move *n* /mu:v/
Oh my goodness! /əʊ maɪ 'gʊdnəs/
outside *prep* /'aʊtsaɪd/
oxygen *n* /'ɒksɪdʒən/
pain *n* /peɪn/
peace *n* /pi:s/
philosophy *n* /fɪ'lɒsəfi/
plan *n, v* /plæn/
quiet *adj* /'kwaɪət/
rainforest *n* /'reɪnfɒrɪst/
retire *v* /rɪ'taɪə/
roof *n* /ru:f/
safe *adj* /seɪf/
scuba-dive *v* /'sku:bədaɪv/
sneeze *v* /sni:z/
snowy *adj* /'snəʊi/
stay *v* /steɪ/
suggestion *n* /sə'dʒestʃən/
sunbathe *v* /'sʌnbeɪð/
swimming costume *n* /'swɪmɪŋ ˌkɒstju:m/
try *v* /traɪ/
umbrella *n* /ʌm'brelə/
underwater *adj, adv* /ʌndə'wɔ:tə/
view *n* /vju:/
weather *n* /'weðə/
windy *adj* /'wɪndi/

UNIT 13

annoyed *adj* /ə'nɔɪd/
annoying *adj* /ə'nɔɪɪŋ/
asleep *adj* /ə'sli:p/
badly *adv* /'bædli/
belong *v* /bɪ'lɒŋ/
burglar *n* /'bɜ:glə/
careful *adj* /'keəfl/
carefully *adv* /'keəfəli/
cent *n* /sent/
chain *n* /tʃeɪn/
comb *n* /kəʊm/
count *v* /kaʊnt/
create *v* /kri:'eɪt/
cry *v* /kraɪ/
cut *v* /kʌt/
deodorant *n* /di:'əʊdərənt/
dwarf *n* /dwɔ:f/
explain *v* /ɪk'spleɪn/
fast *adv* /fa:st/
fluently *adv* /'flu:əntli/
fortunately *adv* /'fɔ:tʃənətli/
gun *n* /gʌn/
habit *n* /'hæbɪt/
immediately *adv* /ɪ'mi:diətli/
it doesn't matter /ɪt ˌdʌznt 'mætə/
marathon *n* /'mærəθən/
mirror *v* /'mɪrə/
nationality *n* /næʃə'næləti/
plaster *n* /'pla:stə/
please *v* /pli:z/
quietly *adv* /'kwaɪətli/
quiz *n* /kwɪz/
rose *n* /rəʊz/
scream *v* /skri:m/
shampoo *n* /ʃæm'pu:/
slowly *adv* /'sləʊli/
special *adj* /'speʃl/
suddenly *adv* /'sʌdnli/
suncream *n* /'sʌnkri:m/
support (a team) *v* /sə'pɔ:t/
tiring *adj* /'taɪərɪŋ/
toothbrush *n* /'tu:θbrʌʃ/
toothpaste *n* /'tu:θpeɪst/
typical *adj* /'tɪpɪkl/
unhappiness *n* /ʌn'hæpinəs/
worried *adj* /'wʌrɪd/
worrying *adj* /'wʌriɪŋ/

UNIT 14

abroad *adv* /ə'brɔ:d/
airport *n* /'eəpɔ:t/
attack *v* /ə'tæk/
announcement *n* /ə'naʊnsmənt/
arrival hall *n* /ə'raɪvl ˌhɔ:l/
Belgium *n* /'beldʒəm/
board *v* /bɔ:d/
boarding pass *n* /'bɔ:dɪŋ ˌpa:s/
boat ride *n* /'bəʊt ˌraɪd/
business class *n* /'bɪznəs ˌkla:s/
check in *v* /ˌtʃek 'ɪn/
check-in desk *n* /'tʃek ɪn ˌdesk/
comfort *n* /'kʌmfət/
competition *n* /kɒmpə'tɪʃn/
cycle *v* /'saɪkl/
deliver *v* /dɪ'lɪvə/
departures board *n* /dɪ'pa:tʃəz ˌbɔ:d/
departure gate *n* /dɪ'pa:tʃə ˌgeɪt/
departure lounge *n* /dɪ'pa:tʃə ˌlaʊndʒ/
excellent *adj* /'eksələnt/
execute *v* /eksɪkjʊt/
flag *n* /flæg/
flight *n* /flaɪt/
fly *v* /flaɪ/
gate (in an airport) *n* /geɪt/
(the) Government *n* /'gʌvənmənt/
hand luggage *n* /'hænd ˌlʌgɪdʒ/
hearse *n* /hɜ:s/
hitch-hike *v* /'hɪtʃ,haɪk/
honeymoon *n* /'hʌnimu:n/
horse and cart *n* /ˌhɔ:s ən 'ka:t/
hurt *v* /hɜ:t/
jumbo jet *n* /ˌdʒʌmbəʊ 'dʒet/
kill *v* /kɪl/
knee *n* /ni:/
last call *n* /ˌla:st 'kɔ:l/
lie *v* /laɪ/
lift *n* /lɪft/
locust *n* /'ləʊkəst/
loud *adj* /laʊd/
luggage *n* /'lʌgɪdʒ/
mad *adj* /mæd/
miss *v* /mɪs/
motorbike *n* /'məʊtəbaɪk/
now boarding /ˌnaʊ 'bɔ:dɪŋ/
pack (a bag) *v* /pæk/
passenger *n* /'pæsɪndʒə/
passport control *n* /ˌpa:spɔ:t kən'trəʊl/
primary school *n* /'praɪməri sku:l/
(the) Pyramids *n pl* /ðə 'pɪrəmɪdz/
quarrel *n* /'kwɒrəl/
reason *n* /'ri:zən/
retired *adj* /rɪ'taɪəd/
seat *n* /si:t/
secondary school *n* /'sekəndri sku:l/
stay *v* /steɪ/
three-course (meal) *n* /ˌθri: kɔ:s 'mi:l/
tornado *n* /tɔ:'neɪdəʊ/
trolley *n* /'trɒli/
washing-up *n* /ˌwɒʃɪŋ 'ʌp/
waste (of time) *v* /'weɪst/

Irregular verbs

Base form	Past Simple	Past participle
be	was/were	been
become	became	become
begin	began	begun
break	broke	broken
bring	brought	brought
build	built	built
buy	bought	bought
can	could	been able
catch	caught	caught
choose	chose	chosen
come	came	come
cost	cost	cost
cut	cut	cut
do	did	done
drink	drank	drunk
drive	drove	driven
eat	ate	eaten
fall	fell	fallen
feel	felt	felt
fight	fought	fought
find	found	found
fly	flew	flown
forget	forgot	forgotten
get	got	got
give	gave	given
go	went	gone/been
grow	grew	grown
have	had	had
hear	heard	heard
hit	hit	hit
keep	kept	kept
know	knew	known
learn	learnt/learned	learnt/learned
leave	left	left
lose	lost	lost
make	made	made
meet	met	met
pay	paid	paid
put	put	put
read /riːd/	read /red/	read /red/
ride	rode	ridden
run	ran	run
say	said	said
see	saw	seen
sell	sold	sold
send	sent	sent
shut	shut	shut
sing	sang	sung
sit	sat	sat
sleep	slept	slept
speak	spoke	spoken
spend	spent	spent
stand	stood	stood
steal	stole	stolen
swim	swam	swum
take	took	taken
tell	told	told
think	thought	thought
understand	understood	understood
wake	woke	woken
wear	wore	worn
win	won	won
write	wrote	written

Verb patterns

Verb + -ing

like love enjoy hate finish stop	swimming cooking

Verb + to + infinitive

choose decide forget promise need help hope try want would like would love	to go to work

Verb + -ing or to + infinitive

begin start	raining/to rain

Modal auxiliary verbs

can could shall will would	go arrive

Phonetic symbols

Consonants

1	/p/	as in	**pen**	/pen/
2	/b/	as in	**big**	/bɪg/
3	/t/	as in	**tea**	/ti:/
4	/d/	as in	**do**	/du:/
5	/k/	as in	**cat**	/kæt/
6	/g/	as in	**go**	/gəʊ/
7	/f/	as in	**four**	/fɔ:/
8	/v/	as in	**very**	/'veri/
9	/s/	as in	**son**	/sʌn/
10	/z/	as in	**zoo**	/zu:/
11	/l/	as in	**live**	/lɪv/
12	/m/	as in	**my**	/maɪ/
13	/n/	as in	**near**	/nɪə/
14	/h/	as in	**happy**	/'hæpi/
15	/r/	as in	**red**	/red/
16	/j/	as in	**yes**	/jes/
17	/w/	as in	**want**	/wɒnt/
18	/θ/	as in	**thanks**	/θæŋks/
19	/ð/	as in	**the**	/ðə/
20	/ʃ/	as in	**she**	/ʃi:/
21	/ʒ/	as in	**television**	/'telɪvɪʒn/
22	/tʃ/	as in	**child**	/tʃaɪld/
23	/dʒ/	as in	**German**	/'dʒɜ:mən/
24	/ŋ/	as in	**English**	/'ɪŋglɪʃ/

Vowels

25	/i:/	as in	**see**	/si:/
26	/ɪ/	as in	**his**	/hɪz/
27	/i/	as in	**twenty**	/'twenti/
28	/e/	as in	**ten**	/ten/
29	/æ/	as in	**stamp**	/stæmp/
30	/ɑ:/	as in	**father**	/'fɑ:ðə/ car /kɑ:/
31	/ɒ/	as in	**hot**	/hɒt/
32	/ɔ:/	as in	**morning**	/'mɔ:nɪŋ/
33	/ʊ/	as in	**football**	/'fʊtbɔ:l/
34	/u:/	as in	**you**	/ju:/
35	/ʌ/	as in	**sun**	/sʌn/
36	/ɜ:/	as in	**learn**	/lɜ:n/
37	/ə/	as in	**letter**	/'letə/

Diphthongs (two vowels together)

38	/eɪ/	as in	**name**	/neɪm/
39	/əʊ/	as in	**no**	/nəʊ/
40	/aɪ/	as in	**my**	/maɪ/
41	/aʊ/	as in	**how**	/haʊ/
42	/ɔɪ/	as in	**boy**	/bɔɪ/
43	/ɪə/	as in	**hear**	/hɪə/
44	/eə/	as in	**where**	/weə/
45	/ʊə/	as in	**tour**	/tʊə/

OXFORD
UNIVERSITY PRESS

Great Clarendon Street, Oxford OX2 6DP

Oxford University Press is a department of the University of Oxford.
It furthers the University's objective of excellence in research, scholarship,
and education by publishing worldwide in

Oxford New York

Auckland Cape Town Dar es Salaam Hong Kong Karachi
Kuala Lumpur Madrid Melbourne Mexico City Nairobi
New Delhi Shanghai Taipei Toronto

With offices in

Argentina Austria Brazil Chile Czech Republic France Greece
Guatemala Hungary Italy Japan Poland Portugal Singapore
South Korea Switzerland Thailand Turkey Ukraine Vietnam

OXFORD and OXFORD ENGLISH are registered trade marks of
Oxford University Press in the UK and in certain other countries

© Oxford University Press 2006

The moral rights of the author have been asserted
Database right Oxford University Press (maker)

First published 2006
2010 2009 2008 2007 2006
10 9 8 7 6 5 4 3 2

ISBN-13: 978 0 19 471509 6
ISBN-10: 0 19 471509 4

Printed in China

ACKNOWLEDGEMENTS

Grammar Reference written by: Kenna Bourke

The authors and publisher are grateful to those who have given permission to reproduce the following extracts and adaptations of copyright material: p24–25 'It's a job for nine men, but someone's got to do it' by Rebecca Fowler, 3 May 1998, *The Mail Night and Day Magazine*. Reproduced by permission of *The Mail on Sunday*. p40–41 'Wellrounded' by Muriel Zagha, 4 April 2004, *The Sunday Telegraph Magazine*. Reproduced by permission of the Telegraph Group Limited. p48–49 Taken from 'Joss Stone Feels Bad For Britney' by ChartAttack.com Staff, 22 October 2003, www.chartattack.com. Reproduced by permission. p86 'Flying Without Wings' Words & Music by Steve Mac & Wayne Hector © Copyright 1999 Rokstone Music (50%)/Rondor Music (London) Limited (50%). All Rights Reserved. International Copyright Secured. p95–96 Taken from 'The art of Le Parkour' by Hugh Schofield, 19 April 2002, BBC News Online. Reproduced by permission of JP BOSSON Management and the BBC. p95–96 'Into the deep' by Libby Brooks, 23 July 2003, *The Guardian* © The Guardian. Reproduced by permission. p102–104 'The Christmas Presents.' Reproduced by permission of Oxford University Press from New Yorkers Short Stories by O. Henry, Oxford Bookworms Library 2 © Oxford University Press 2000. p110–111 Taken from Josie Dew's web site www.josiedew.co.uk, 2 April 2004. Reproduced by permission. p110–111 Taken from 'Hitch-hiker takes to road – at 90' by Steve Duffy, 23 April 2004, BBC News Online. Reproduced by permission of http://www.bbc.co.uk/wales/news and Mr Bowen-Jones. p112 'All Around The World' Words & Music by Lisa Stansfield, Ian Devaney & Andrew Morris © Copyright 1989 Block And Gilber Music Limited. BMG Music Publishing Limited. All Rights Reserved. International Copyright Secured.

Illustrations by: Kathy Baxendale p 96; Emma Dodd pp 146, 147, 148, 149; Mark Duffin pp 76–77 (globes), 84("The House is a Mess!"); Andy Hammond pp 16, 76 (cartoon "I've got more than you!"), 92; Paul Fisher-Johnson pp 102–103, 104; Ned Jolliffe pp 43, 58, 88; Dettmer Otto p 81; Gavin Reece p 84 (party scene); Debbie Ryder p 80; Tom Sperling p48 (Dragon in sky)

Commissioned Photography by: Gareth Boden pp 6–7, 8 (Danka), 11 (Lisa, Marco & Emma), 12 (Lisa), 16 (Danka), 17 (Danka's host family), 19 (James & Danka), 27 (time conversation 1), 28–29 (Ceri), 35, 36, 37, 38 (Suzie & Matt), 39 (Suzie & Matt), 44 (Lucia, Dominic), 45 (Ben & Ana, Philip & Elena), 47 (Emma & Marco), 54 (James), 64 (Valentine), 89, 106–107, 108 (Ryan), 115, 116 (Suzie & livingroom), 118 (Robert), 122, 125; Maggie Milner p 13 (Patrick), 14 (family), 148 (Patrick); MM Studios pp 10, 38 (cups & cutlery), 48–49 (CD and book), 68–69 (market stall), 103–104 (hair clips, ribbon etc), 105 (Chemist's products)

We are grateful to the following for providing locations: Cibo Café and Restaurant, Oxford pp 17, 19; Quarks Internet Café and Games Zone, Richmond pp 6, 7; Caroline Reading, Oxford pp 36–39; Roberto Gerrards, Hertford & the owner Rob Farrell p 89; The Vine, Ware p 106; The Swan Language School, Oxford pp 17, 35, 125; Mr Tudor Bowen-Jones p 110

We would also like to thank the following for permission to reproduce the following photographs: Action Images p 28 (rugby match/R.Heathcote); Action Plus p 47 (Woods/G.Kirk); Alamy pp12 (Massachusetts/Neil Setchfield), pp 13 (Cork/D.A.Barnes), 25 (Isle of Vatersay/David Robertson), 26 (pilot/A.Hess), 31 (dancing/ J.Wiedel), 32 (Sumalee/A.Ryman), 42 (Seoul/J.Bower), 56 (Gagarin/Popperfoto), 57 (Earhart standing/Popperfoto), 63 (Eric & Lori/J.Frank), 71 (rice harvest/Pictor International), 77 (Barbados/S.Grandadam), 79 (Havana/D.Noton), 80 (Hyde Park/Alan Copson City Pictures), 80 (health centre/VIEW Pictures Ltd), 80 (Art museum/Robert Harding Picture Library), 80 (West End/Alan Copson City Pictures), 80 (Portsmouth/Boating Images Photo Library), 80 (thatched cottage/Rod Edwards), 82 (Simon/ Creatas), 92 (Great Wall/View Stock China), 92 (Grand Canyon/T.Gervis),

92 (rainforest/ Robert Harding World Imagery), 92 (lions/T.Manley), 93 (scuba/ G.Bell), 93 (surfing/D.Peebles), 96 (foggy/Imagina/ A.Tsunoda), 101 (annoyed/ Goodshoot), 118 (Wales/The Photolibrary Wales), 119 (girls/ L.Beddoe), 120 (Elmtree Images), 121 (P.Barritt); AMREF p 21 (flying doctor); The Anthony Blake Photo Library pp18 (apple pie/Joff Lee), 18 (salad Nicoise/Eaglemoss Consumer Publications), 18 (chicken salad/Tim Hill), 18 (pizza/Roger Stowell), 18 (chocolate cake/Sam Stowell), 18 (tea/Howard Shooter), 18 (cod and chips/Sue Atkinson), 18 (sparkling water/Maximilian Stock), 18 (burger/Robert Lawson), 18 (coffee/James Murphy), 18 (ice cream/Tim Hill), 18 (orange juice/Sue Atkinson), 66 (pizza/J.Lee Studios), 69 (market/ D.Marsden), 72 (Sachertorte/M.Brigdale), 72 (Bife/J.Lee Studios), Art Directors & Trip Photo Library pp 42 (Samoa), 76 (Maldives), Associated Press pp 94 (Streeter portrait/ H.Cabluck), 95 (Streeter diving/P.Shearer); Axiom pp 15 (umbrella/ J.Holmes), 14 (family outside home/J.Sparshatt), 18 (Brighton Pier/C.Parker), 79 (Seville/P.Quayle); Corbis pp 9 (daughters/R.Ressmeyer), 9 (hammock/S.Maze), 15 (family/Ronnie Kaufman), 15 (grandfather & grandchildren/Randy Faris), 32 (beach/D.G.Houser), 33 (festival/M.S.Lewis), 42 (Lisbon/N.Wheeler), 42 (New England/P.Schermeister), 42 (Alise/T.A.Gipstein), 47 (Einstein/ Bettmann), 47 (Brontë/Bettmann), 47 (Dali/Bettmann), 52 (with Gary Cooper/J.Springer), 53 (swearing in/Bettmann), 53 (young adult/Bettmann), 55 (Reagan & Thatcher/ W.McNamee), 55 (Olympics/M.King), 56 (Earhart cockpit/Bettmann), 59 (S.Kennedy), 60 (Coca-cola/G.Naylor), 60 (photographs/H.A.Roberts), 60 (television/Hulton-Deutsch Collection), 61 (records/Hulton-Deutsch Collection), 62 (Macmillan/Hulton-Deutsch Collection), 64 (New Year/ Reuters), 64 (Halloween/A.Skelley), 64 (birthday/N.Schaefer), 66 (apple juice), 71 (salamis/O.Franken), 71 (sardines/J.Van Hasselt), 77 (Fiji/J.Butchofsky-Houser), 92 (whale watching/ N.Fobes), 93 (Everest/R.Holmes), 99 (Aladdin/C.Collins), 99 (Pinocchio/Bettmann), 101 (bored/J.L.Pelaez), 101 (tired/ R.Bruderer), 101 (interested/H.Bradley); courtesy of Josie Dew p 111; Eyevine p 48 (Christopher Paolini/Polaris/ D.Loneman); Fabfoodpix.com pp 67 (tea), 67 (chocolate), 67 (chips); Getty Images pp 8 (Akiko & Miho/R.McVay), 8 (Rosa/D.Bosler), 8 (Tiago/M.Powell), 8 (Henning/M.Goldman), 8 (Luc & Dominique/D.Roth), 9 (Tiago/M.Powell), 14 (Ireland/Terry Donnelly/The Image Bank), 15 (in car/Photodisc Red/P.Mason), 27 (time conversation 2/A.Danaher), 31 (television/D.Day), 31 (gym/ S.Bottomley), 31 (photography/Daly & Newton), 31 (computer game/Holos), 31 (cinema/GDT), 32 (mountains/P.Eriksson), 39 (Yoshi/J.Riley), 42 (Candy & Bert/R.Chapple), 44 (Eva/ S.W.Jones), 46 (swimmers past/Hulton Archive), 46 (swimmers present/C.Cole), 51 (woman on phone/Anthony Masterson/Botanica), 51 (Asian woman on phone/Marc Romanelli/The Image Bank), 51 (Jo/C.Renee), 51 (call centre/D.Lees), 52 (finger up/Hulton Archive), 54 (Apple Mac/Liaison/D.Walker), 60 (cars/Topical Press Agency), 61 (bikes/Topical Press Agency), 62 (Daguerre/Hulton Archive), 64 (Easter eggs/ G.Gay), 65 (wedding/C.Havens), 66 (Daisy/S.Biver), 66 (Piers/ D.Roth), 70 (Arabs/W.Eastep), 70 (children eating/D.Sundberg), 72 (Sergio/B.Lang), 72 (Madalena/K.Steele), 72 (Graham/ S.Joel), 72 (Anke/M.Krasowitz), 74 (J.Lamb), 75 (teen boy/Barry Rosenthal/The Image Bank), 77 (hammock/M.McQueen), 78 (Buenos Aires/C.Ehlers), 83 (Dan, John, Clifford & Albert/ T.Raymond), 85 (girl with boots/S.Rausser), 85 (footballers/J.Cummins), 85 (couple and baby/ Brand X Pictures), 85 (woman with bags/J.L.Morales), 86–87 (woman and gulls/M.Barraud), 90 (young footballer/Jean Louis Batt/Photographer's Choice), 96 (buttercups/Photonica), 97 (umbrellas/Bald Headed Picture/Taxi), 97 (couple in rain/Andreas Pollok/Taxi), 101 (worried/J.Pumfrey), 105 (B.Ayres), 108 (S.Rothfeld), 112 (man walking/Tim Ridley/The Image Bank), 113 (AFP/F.J.Brown), 119 (women/ G.&M.D.de Lossy); Independent on Sunday p 73 (D.Brown); Insight-Visual.com p 24–25 (Seumas McSporran); Katz pp 79 (Flamenco/Laif/N.Hilger), 79 (Salsa/Laif/F.Tophoven), 78 (Tango/Laif/M.Gonzalez); The Kobal Collection pp 65 (hamburgers/The Advertising Archive Ltd), 61 (jeans/The Advertising Archive Ltd); Lonely Planet Images pp 21 (Mexican guide/C.Beall), 71 (noodles/ P.Dymond), 71 (truck/D.McKinlay); Mary Evans Picture Library pp 98 (Cinderella), 98 (Hansel & Gretel), 98 (Romeo & Juliet), 98 (Sleeping Beauty/Tom Gillmor Collection), 98 (Snow White), 99 (Don Quixote), 99 (Sherlock Holmes), 124; National Motor Museum p 62 (Anderson); PA Photos p 52 (waving/EPA); Photostage/Donald Cooper p 26 (actor); Pictures Colour Library pp80 (Cadre Idris/George Chetland), 80 (The Duomo, Milan/Brian Lawrence Images Ltd)p 123 (Corsica); Popperfoto pp 60 (phone calls), 61 (planes); Punchstock pp8 (friends/ Image Source), 8 (Jason/ Photodisc), 8 (Svetlana/Photodisc), 9 (Svetlana/Photodisc), 11 (Alice/Photodisc), 13 (Jefferson/ Photodisc), 15 (family eating/Digital Vision/C.Edwards), 26 (nurse/Photodisc), 26 (shop assistant/Photodisc), 31 (girl reading/Brand X Pictures), 33 (Daniella/Goodshoot), 33 (Axel/Thinkstock), 34 (RubberBall), 42 (Manola/Photodisc), 42 (Kwan/Image Source), 51 (woman on mobile/Digital Vision), 63 (Carly/Bananastock), 65 (Mother's Day/ Bananastock), 72 (breakfast/Dynamic Graphics Group/IT Stock Free), 72 (Bruschetta/Foodcollection.com), 80 (canoeing/Design Pics), 80 (factory at night/ imageshop), 82 (Alison, Ella & Alfie/Photodisc), 96 (snowy/Brand X Pictures), 100 (Brand X Pictures), 101 (excited/RubberBall), 112 (globe/MediIomages), 118 (Daniella/Goodshoot); Retna Pictures p 26 (model/Graylock.com/G.James); Rex Features pp 22 (Iman/DMI/D.Herrick), 23 (Giorgio Locatelli/T.Buckingham), 49 (Joss Stone/B.Rasic), 53 (sailor suit/SNAP/ SYP), 55 (Michael Jackson/Skyline), 55 (Tina Turner & Mick Jagger/Sipa Press), 57 (rocket/ITD), 86 (Westlife/J.Craine), 95 (Belle portrait/P.Cooper), 95 (free running/A.Paradise), 99 (Mickey Mouse/N.Jorgensen) 112 (Lisa Stansfield/Brian Rasic), Robert Harding World Imagery p 65 (Christmas/Digital Vision); Royalty-free Images pp 8 (flags/Photodisc), 11 (Charles/Imagesource), 26 (chef/Photodisc), 26 (lawyer/Photodisc), 26 (journalist/Photodisc), 26 (architect/Photodisc), 30 (cooking/Photodisc), 30 (running/Photodisc), 30 (skiing/ Photodisc), 31 (football/Photodisc), 31 (sailing/Photodisc), 31 (listening to music/Corbis/Digital Stock), 31 (swimming/ Photodisc), 31 (eating/Photodisc), 31 (sunbathing/Photodisc), 45 (sunbathing/Photodisc), 65 (Thanksgiving/Photodisc), 66 (pasta/ Photodisc), 66 (cheese/Stockbyte), 66 (bananas/Photodisc), 66 (strawberries/Photodisc), 66 (carrots/Ingram), 66 (biscuits/ Ingram), 67 (coffee/ Stockbyte), 66 (milk/Stockbyte), 67 (beer/ Stockbyte), 67 (fish/Stockbyte), 67 (apples/ Stockbyte), 67 (orange juice/Photoshoot), 67 (peas/Stockbyte), 67 (tomatoes/ Photodisc), 67 (hamburger/Photodisc), 67 (strawberries/ Photodisc), 83 (Naomi/Photodisc), 82 (Andy/Photodisc), 82 (Poppy/Photodisc), 83 (Colin/Photodisc), 83 (Kate & Sofia/Corbis/Digital Stock), 85 (sitting boy/ Photodisc), 85 (man in coat/Photodisc), 91 (Punchstock), 114 (piano/Photodisc), 114 (mother & daughter/Photodisc), 117 (Corbis), 118 (temple/Photodisc); Marco Tassinari pp 40, 41; The Photolibrary Wales p 110 (S.Benbow)